Reversing Ageing

The Natural Way

*Adding life to years, not just years
to life, is the goal of ageing research.*

DR EDWARD SCHNEIDER
DEAN OF GERONTOLOGY
UNIVERSITY OF SOUTHERN CALIFORNIA

Reversing Ageing

The Natural Way

Paul Galbraith

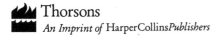
Thorsons
An Imprint of HarperCollins*Publishers*

Thorsons
An Imprint of HarperCollins*Publishers*
77–85 Fulham Palace Road,
Hammersmith, London W6 8JB

First published by Thomas C. Lothian Pty Ltd, Melbourne, Australia 1993
This UK edition published by Thorsons 1998
10 9 8 7 6 5 4 3 2 1

Paul Galbraith asserts the moral right to
be identified as the author of this work

A catalogue record for this book
is available from the British Library

ISBN 0 7225 3673 9

Printed and bound in Great Britain by Scotprint Ltd, Musselburgh, Scotland.

Contents

Introduction

This book covers all the most effective rejuvenation techniques, incorporating proven ancient yoga rejuvenation exercises with the latest scientific discoveries. The aim is to achieve the maximum age reversal for the minimum time and effort expenditure, just what busy people need. The techniques represent an excellent time and effort investment, since you will not only become younger but also live longer and dramatically increase your vitality level.

Let's face it, we all want to look and feel younger – but what most of us don't realize is that the knowledge is now available for us to achieve this.

There is every reason why we should want to become younger, apart from the vanity consideration. Our self-image and confidence improve when we look and feel younger, especially when our friends comment on this. Looking and feeling younger also gives us more scope in jobs, sports and socially. It means more energy and fewer aches and pains.

As you can see, there is plenty of incentive to become younger and it's not difficult to achieve. Just apply the principles in this book and you can turn the clock back ten to twenty years.

The human body has an inbuilt ability to rejuvenate and heal itself – it just needs the right conditions. This book presents those conditions.

The 3 basic ways to reverse ageing are discussed in detail. These are:

1   The Correct Lifestyle Factors.
2   Specific Rejuvenation Techniques.
3   The Look Younger Exercises.

A faulty lifestyle interferes with the body's innate ability to rejuvenate itself. The following lifestyle factors are discussed in detail from the view points both of ancient yoga and modern scientific research:

Optimum nutrition, including rejuvenation foods/supplements/herbs.
Optimum fitness, including a technique to use after exercise to take years off your face.
Deep rejuvenating sleep every night.

The specific rejuvenation techniques include:
– The most potent yoga rejuvenation exercises.
– The three rejuvenation breathing exercises.
– The most effective relaxation exercise.
– How to achieve super brain power (memory and intelligence).
– How to use your shower for rejuvenation.
– Rejuvenating your sex glands including the three herbs for sexual vigour.
– Hair and skin rejuvenation including a cream which really removes wrinkles.

The look younger exercises result in:
– A slim, firm stomach.
– Lifting sagging breasts in females and a powerful chest in men.
– A natural face lift.
– Increased height.

These are the most effective techniques from both ancient yoga and modern science, the fruits of East and West. The contribution of yoga to age reversal has been immense and modern science is only just beginning to confirm what advanced yogis discovered thousands of years ago.

To achieve basic age reversal of about 10 years, it's sufficient to carry out just the correct lifestyle factors in Part 2. But if you are after super rejuvenation and wish to turn the clock back 15 years or so, you will need to do some of the specific rejuvenation techniques in Part 3 of the book – in particular yoga postures, breathing exercises and the deep relaxation exercise.

Human beings are strange creatures. If we buy an item such as a video recorder we carefully read the instructions about how to get optimum results from it and make it last as long as possible. We are far more important than video recorders yet few of us bother to consider how we can operate at our optimum level and prevent ourselves from deteriorating. That's the aim of this book – to show you how to reverse ageing, so that you look and feel younger, and thereafter how to slow down the ageing process.

Much of the ageing process is due to disease and minor repeated ailments. This gradually wears down the body, as well as lowering resistance. We no longer suffer from many of the diseases of old, such as polio and diphtheria, because improved hygiene and medical science have overcome them. Today we suffer from lifestyle diseases, such as heart disease, strokes, cancer, arthritis and chronic tiredness instead. These diseases are in epidemic proportions in western countries and are starting to emerge in developing countries. If we can prevent and cure them, we can reverse the ageing process.

I suggest that you work through one chapter at a time, and then apply the principles of the chapter before starting a new one. This also allows your body and mind to gradually adapt to your new lifestyle. I also suggest that you skim the book every six months or so to check and improve your rejuvenation techniques. Each review will provide additional insight.

PART ONE

Becoming Younger
– The Principles

How to Become Younger

Why Reversing Ageing is Possible

The reason why reversing ageing is possible, is due to the fact that ageing really consists of 2 parts. One part is what we call natural ageing. This is programmed into our genes and therefore we can't do anything about it at this stage.

The other part of ageing is called unnatural premature ageing and is due to faulty lifestyle factors. This is the part of ageing we can reverse and the reason why most of us age prematurely and suffer from degenerative diseases.

To take an example, let's say you have aged 20 years. Only about 10 years of that ageing is natural ageing which we can do nothing about. But the other 10 years of ageing is unnatural premature ageing and this can be reversed.

Once you have got rid of this 10 years or so of premature ageing, from then on you can slow down the ageing process by keeping up the correct lifestyle factors. So instead of looking 10 years older every 10 years, you will only look about 5 years older.

Ageing is a gradual degeneration of the whole body. The rate of degeneration is mainly determined by lifestyle and not by chronological age. This degeneration can be slowed down and, in most cases, reversed by following the rejuvenation principles in this book.

What we regard as normal as we age, such as increasing blood pressure and hardening of the arteries, is not necessarily natural. It is normal for our society since our society as a whole has adopted faulty lifestyle habits, but for other more primitive societies, it is not. As their population ages, there is no increase in blood pressure or hardening of the arteries. It may be normal in one society for blood pressure to increase as you get older, but it is certainly not natural, since it doesn't happen in all societies.

So the yardstick should be not what is normal, which is a variable factor dependent on a society's lifestyle habits, but instead what is natural. If we follow Nature's laws to live a healthy lifestyle, then it is natural not to get increased blood pressure and blocking of the arteries as we get older.

> The rate of ageing is determined by lifestyle.

> You can reverse ageing by following the rejuvenation principles in this book.

A lot of what we call ageing is really the outcome of repeated, self-inflicted abuse of the body; for example, lack of exercise, poor sleep and worry.

Other major factors in ageing and reduced lifespan are the chronic degenerative diseases such as heart disease and cancer. Again the main cause of these diseases is faulty lifestyle.

As you can see, the major factor in ageing is faulty lifestyle. Correct your lifestyle and you can reverse the ageing process considerably.

The Causes of Ageing

Faulty Lifestyle
The main factors causing a faulty lifestyle are poor nutrition, lack of proper exercise, poor sleep, stress, cigarette smoking, drinking excess alcohol and overexposure to sunshine.

Nowadays old people die from disease, not from growing old, and disease, whether it be cancer or heart disease, is mainly due to faulty lifestyle.

Heredity
The genes people inherit from their parents also have an effect on ageing. Genes are situated in every cell and determine our inherited characteristics.

This is a fixed factor and there is nothing we can do, at the present time, to influence the genes. This is why lifestyle is so important to reversing ageing, since it is the factor we can do something about.

The Mother's Health During Pregnancy
It is very important to lead a healthy lifestyle during pregnancy. For example, smoking cigarettes and drinking excess alcohol definitely affect the health of the new-born baby and reduce the baby's chance of a long life.

The Mechanism of Ageing

Ageing of the body occurs at a cellular level. Most of the body's cells continually renew themselves as they wear out. Exact replicas of the old cells are made by a process in which cells simply divide into two. The exceptions to this rule are brain cells, which cannot reproduce themselves. Once a brain cell dies, you have one fewer brain cell for the rest of your life. Since the brain is the most important organ for reversing ageing, you will appreciate why I have devoted one whole chapter to it.

Unlike other cells, brain cells cannot be replaced when they die.

Each living cell can reproduce about fifty times before it dies, a death that is generally programmed into normal cells and probably a result of the evolutionary pressure or old organisims to give way to new, more vigorous ones.

As the body ages, the cells begin to deteriorate and function less efficiently. The tissues break down, skin loses elasticity, muscles weaken, hair thins, eyesight and hearing fail, teeth decay, immunity decreases and degenerative diseases increase. Part of this breakdown results from the faulty replication of cells, especially as they reach their fifty-cycle reproductive limit. Each subsequent replication of a cell is a little different from its parent, because of lifestyle factors such as stress, toxins and disease. This imperfect replication of every cell, multiplied over time, results in changes in our appearance and health which we call ageing.

Each replication of a cell is a little different from its parent because of faulty lifestyle factors such as stress, toxins and disease. This is the basis of ageing.

The Effect of Free Radicals on Ageing

Cells replicate according to a plan called the genetic code. The genetic code is controlled by DNA (deoxyribonucleic acid) and DNA's 'messenger', RNA (ribonucleic acid), which establishes the genetic pattern throughout the cell biochemically.

So what keeps the DNA genetic code from copying itself exactly? Increasingly scientists are finding that our bodies degenerate because they are constantly under attack by a class of highly corrosive oxidising molecules called free radicals.

Free radicals are a major cause of ageing.

Free radicals are fragment molecules with unattached electrons. Because they have these unattached electrons, such molecules have unbound sites which react with essential chemicals in the cells and render them useless for normal living processes. Moreover, each time a free radical succeeds in completing itself by stripping another molecule, it knocks more fragments – more free radicals – from the previously whole molecule. In other words, free radicals initiate a dangerous chemical chain reaction which prevents cells from acting out their normal functions, and this also damages the RNA and DNA needed for cell duplication.

Free radicals can be prevented or neutralised by certain vitamins.

The main precipitating causes of free radicals are strong sunlight, air pollution, cigarette smoking and poor nutrition. You can't do much in the short term about air pollution, but you can at least avoid strong sunlight, stop smoking cigarettes and improve your nutrition.

Many of the effects of ageing can be prevented and even reversed by changing your lifestyle.

Another way of tackling this problem is to take antioxidants, which break down and neutralise free radicals. The most effective antioxidants are the vitamins A, C and E and the mineral selenium. These are treated in detail in the chapter on supplements.

I strongly suggest that you supplement your diet with antioxidants, since it's currently believed by many scientists that free radicals are the greatest cause of ageing, and probably of cancer as well.

The Effects of Ageing

The following are typical effects of ageing. By following a healthy lifestyle, as outlined in this book and specifically this chapter, many of these effects can be prevented.

1 Chronic tiredness and irritability.
2 Poor sleep.
3 Conversion of muscle to fat.
4 The skin loses its elasticity, causing wrinkling.
5 Hair turns grey and becomes more sparse.
6 A loss of calcium makes the bones brittle and liable to fracture.
7 The spinal discs become thinner, resulting in height loss, stooping and back pain.
8 The eyesight deteriorates and the eyes become more prone to cataracts and glaucoma.
9 Hearing becomes impaired.
10 Loss of teeth, often caused by gum disease.
11 The joints become stiffer, resulting in more difficult movement. Arthritis often occurs.
12 Resistance to infection is reduced.
13 Reduced efficiency of the heart and lungs, hardening of the arteries and high blood pressure.
14 Digestive problems are common, as are ulcers and constipation.
15 Degenerative diseases develop. The chance of getting cancer doubles every eight years after forty-five years of age. The rate of heart attacks and strokes increase. Arthritis becomes common.
16 The brain reduces in size by 10 percent between thirty and seventy years of age. There is a reduction in short-term memory and learning ability. Depression is common and senile dementia, which can start as young as forty years, is common after sixty years of age.

As you can see, ageing is not pleasant, so it is imperative that you start making changes to your lifestyle now, to prevent or delay the symptoms. Many ageing effects can even be reversed by radically changing your lifestyle. Keep in mind that this takes time, since the body cannot reverse the effects of twenty or thirty years of faulty lifestyle overnight.

Ageing and Your Skin

The Effects of Ageing on Your Skin
The following is what happens to your skin as it ages.

1 It loses elasticity.
2 It gets rougher.
3 It changes from a rosy colour to a yellowish colour.

You lose 10–20 percent of your skin's pigment cells each decade. You therefore have less natural protection from the sun and are more prone to cancer. Your skin also becomes less evenly pigmented, causing the formation of 'age spots'.

You lose 50 percent of your immune cells (Langerhams' cells) which protect your skin from cancer.

The Sun and Skin Ageing

The two major causes of facial-skin ageing are the sun and lack of vitamin C.

The most effective way of keeping your skin young is to keep out of the sun. When sunlight strikes the skin cells it reacts with oxygen, creating free radicals. These free radicals damage the skin cells, causing premature ageing.

If you want proof that the sun is the major cause of skin ageing, compare the skin of your buttocks, which have never been exposed to the sun, with facial skin.

Vitamin C and Skin Ageing
Scientists have shown that ageing, including facial wrinkles, is largely caused by the destruction of collagen, the intercellular 'cement' which binds the body's cells together.

After sun damage, lack of vitamin C is the next major cause of the destruction of collagen. Adequate vitamin C preserves collagen integrity and elasticity, which results in tight, unwrinkled skin and a smooth healthy complexion.

How to Get Rid of Wrinkles

Wrinkles can be reduced by a new cream.

There is a cream called Tretinoin or 'Retin A', which has been shown to reverse some of the ageing effects on the skin. Tretinoin is a cream derived from vitamin A which can be obtained from your local pharmacy.

You can boost your immune system to help reverse ageing by taking the correct vitamins.

A couple of years ago the *Journal of the American Medical Association* published a study which showed that Retin A stimulates new skin cell growth, filling in small creases and wrinkles. The new skin growth is smoother and healthier than your normal skin. In short, it produces skin rejuvenation.

It is important that you apply the Retin A cream correctly to get maximum results:

1 Apply before you go to bed; washing your face before application. Wash the cream off in the morning.
2 Protect your new, younger, sensitive skin by avoiding direct sunlight. If you go out into direct sunlight between 10 a.m. and 4 p.m. use a sunblock cream for maximum protection (SPF 15). If you go to the beach, sit under an umbrella.

When you first use the cream it is normal to get a skin reaction: irritation or peeling. This is just the cream working by getting rid of your old skin cells.

Be patient. It takes about six months to work, and you'll achieve maximum results after about a further year.

Don't use Retin A cream if you are pregnant or nursing.

Your Immune System and Ageing

The integrity of your immune system is essential for reversing ageing. The immune system fights disease, which would otherwise cause premature ageing and a shorter life. Without the immune system, infections or cancer would soon overwhelm the body.

Unless you radically change your lifestyle, your immune system will gradually lose its effectiveness until, by seventy years of age or even well before, it will have lost up to 90 percent of its strength.

Normally the immune system produces antibodies which attack foreign cells which may invade the body as a result of infection. As we get older, the body fails to distinguish foreign cells and it reacts by attacking some of its own cells.

Nutrients to Boost Your Immune System

Vitamin A strengthens the immune system and helps the body to fight cancer. It is best taken in the form of beta carotene, since it is found in nutritious, low-fat foods such as carrots, spinach, cabbage and tomatoes.

Vitamin C is the most important immune-boosting vitamin. It causes an increase in the production of interferon, the body's own defence chemical.

Vitamin E, like vitamin C, is an important immune-boosting vitamin. It also protects you against infection, and prevents cancer by neutralising cancer-causing chemicals.

You can boost your immune system to help reverse ageing by taking the correct vitamins.

Selenium and **zinc** are the most important minerals for strengthening the immune system and preventing cancer.

Brain Rejuvenation

As well as general lifestyle conditions such as good nutrition, exercise and good sleep, there are a few specific factors which are very important for brain rejuvenation.

For details on brain rejuvenation, see 'Super Brain Power' pages 171–179.

LOW FAT DIET

Excess dietary fat, especially saturated fat, clogs the arteries in the brain. This reduces the blood flow to the brain and causes it to age prematurely. Conversely, if you lower the saturated fat level in your diet sufficiently, the body will eventually flush out the fat from the walls of your arteries. This will restore the normal blood supply to the brain, resulting in brain rejuvenation.

LECITHIN

Studies have shown that lecithin can improve both intelligence and memory.

ZINC

Zinc is essential for normal brain function.

ANTIOXIDANTS

The brain has many cells which contain fat and are particularly prone to oxidation damage by free radicals. Antioxidants such as betacarotene, vitamins C and E, selenium and zinc destroy the destructive free radicals, making your brain younger.

VITAMIN B COMPLEX

B_3, B_5, B_6, B_{12} and thiamine are vital for normal brain functioning. Deficiencies of the B vitamins have been shown to cause mental sluggishness, poor memory, and mood disorders.

Why We Now Live Longer

The vast increase in our life expectancy in the last 100 years is due to one main factor: *improved hygiene*. This prevents a lot of the diseases, such as typhoid or tuberculosis, which used to cause mass epidemics and devastate whole population groups. If this improvement of just one aspect of lifestyle has produced such a big effect on the average life expectancy, imagine the effect if we were to adopt all the other lifestyle aspects, such as good nutrition and exercise programmes, as well.

It is true that new medical treatments such as antibiotics and transplants help to save lives and will increase life expectancy, but this is only a minor factor compared to the improvement in hygiene. It also must be remembered that some of the more powerful drugs have powerful side effects, and will actually damage some of the organs of the body. Even less powerful drugs which are used over a long period, such as tranquillisers, will in time adversely affect the brain and nervous system. This will lead to a reduced life expectancy for the population and tend to counteract the positive effects of medical science.

What is the Natural Lifespan of Humans?

The normal lifespan of western people today is between sixty and seventy years. This does not imply that this is our *natural* lifespan.

The 'normal' lifespan is a life lived at variance to nature's laws. We overeat, eat too much of the wrong foods, under-exercise, live stressful lives, sleep badly, breathe polluted air, and so on. This is how the average 'normal' person lives. This, of course, produces a lifespan far short of our true potential.

'Natural lifespan' is how long we would live if we lived how nature intended us to.

Even though improved sanitation has enabled us to live longer, extending our average lifespan from forty-seven to around seventy years in this century, it has had no effect on our maximum lifespan. Official records 100 years ago showed that around 110 years was the *maximum* age ever reached. Today's records show the same figure. It seems that about 100 years is our genetic lifespan potential.

There are two ways of assessing our natural lifespan:

1 Study people who live in more natural conditions, such as the Hunza people of northern Pakistan. The average lifespan of these people is around 100 years.
2 Study the ratio of lifespan to maturity age in animals who live in their natural, wild state. It has been found that in this state most animals live seven times their puberty age. Relating this to humans, again we arrive at around ninety years.

This means that we are dying about twenty years before we should. Not only that, but the last decade of life is often spent in a poor state of health, with some diseases such as cancer or heart disease developing. This prevents us from fully enjoying our hard-earned retirement years.

By following the principles outlined below, you will not only live a lot longer, but also enjoy good health in the later years.

Our true natural lifespan is ninety to 100 years, so most of us are dying twenty or thirty years before we should.

How to Become Younger and Live Longer

Certain common factors were found in people who lived to over 100 years.

There have been many studies done of people who have lived over 100 years, to try to determine if there are any common factors involved. Most of the research has been done in peasant communities, such as still exist in Russia, Turkey and Bulgaria, simply because that is where most of the world's centenarians live.

Certain common factors were found. The most common was that the vast majority of them did not eat very much, and they ate only when hungry.

Most of them were also vegetarians or ate very little meat, were slim, lived simple lives, were physically active and didn't worry. All were married and when their spouses had died many had remarried.

To reverse the ageing effects of twenty or more years of faulty lifestyle, we must get the nervous system and glands working at peak efficiency.

To become younger, physically and mentally, we must reverse the ageing effects of twenty years or more of faulty lifestyle. This can only be done by getting the body, especially the nervous system and glands, working at peak efficiency. The most important part of the nervous system, the brain, must be given special attention, since it affects the rest of the body. Any improvements to the brain will cause an improvement to the rest of the body, via the pituitary gland and the spine.

Optimum Nutrition

What's Wrong with Our Diet?

The typical western diet is a recipe for premature ageing and disease. We eat far too much of the wrong foods – excessive fat and the wrong kind (saturated); too much protein and the wrong kind (animal protein); and excessive refined grains, sugar and salt.

The typical western diet is a recipe for premature ageing and disease.

We need to eat more raw food (fruits, salad, bean sprouts and raw nuts), replace most of our saturated fats with unsaturated fats (vegetable oils) and replace some of our animal protein with vegetable protein (soya bean products, nuts, lentils, etc.)

The effects of our poor diet are:

1 **Premature ageing**. Excess fat clogs up our arteries, causing reduced blood flow and therefore reduced nourishment to all the body's tissues. Excess fat also causes heart disease. Refined carbohydrates are low in nutrient value and therefore we have to eat a lot of them to get sufficient nutrients. This causes obesity. Excess animal protein overloads our tissues with toxins, causing accelerated ageing of the tissues.

2 **Chronic fatigue**. This is due to two main factors. Firstly, excessive fat clogs up the arteries in the neck and brain, causing a reduced blood flow to the brain. Secondly, many of us are undernourished because we eat too many processed foods, cooked foods and refined carbohydrates (white bread, cakes, etc) at the expense of raw foods.

3 **Degenerative diseases**. Poor diet is a major factor in the cause of cancer, heart disease, stroke, diabetes and other degenerative diseases which drastically reduce our lifespan and cause premature ageing.

4 **Reduced immunity to diseases**. Reduced immunity results in increased infections and diseases which again reduce our lifespan and cause premature ageing.

5 **Obesity**. This is due to excess refined carbohydrate, particularly sugar, as well as excess fat. Obesity is a major factor in reducing lifespan and looking older.

Optimum nutrition for reversing ageing is discussed in detail on pages 58–98.

Don't Overeat

Overeating is a major cause of premature ageing. Food which is in excess of the body's requirements is not broken down properly and acts like a poison in the body. In addition, overeating wastes up to 60 percent of your body's vital energy on digestion, resulting in chronic fatigue and reduced mental clarity. Overeating is also a major cause of obesity and heart disease. The extra food is actually causing malnutrition, since there is reduced assimilation of all the food you eat.

An analysis of the longest lived populations was carried out by the *National Geographic* in 1971. The study included the Hunza people of northern Pakistan, Vilcabamba in Ecuador and Georgia in Russia. It was found that the traditional diets of these people contained only half to two-thirds of the calories of the average American diet. Their fat intake was a quarter and their protein intake a half of the Americans'. The carbohydrate intake was about the same, but consisted of unprocessed carbohydrate, unlike the American carbohydrate intake.

Experiments with animals fed on a low-calorie diet showed improved health and life extension of 30 to 100 percent over that of the unrestricted control animals. They also had reduced rates of cancers heart disease, kidney disease, dryness of skin and discolouration of hair.

Overeating can be prevented if you do the following:

1 **Eat more nourishing food – such as fruit and salad**. This satisfies the appetite centre of the brain much more quickly and you will eat less.

2 **Reduce your sugar and fat intake**. Since one of the main factors in premature ageing is excess calories, we should cut down on calorie-rich foods containing sugar and fat.

3 **Eat slowly**. This leads to more efficient digestion, improved nourishment and hence reduced appetite.

4 **Spread your food intake over several small meals**, rather than two or three big meals. For example, have small snacks of fruit in between your main meals. This also leads to better nourishment.

5 **Aerobic exercise**. This type of exercise has been scientifically shown to reduce appetite.

Overeating wastes up to 60 percent of your body's vital energy on digestion.

Other Anti-Ageing Factors

Deep Sleep

Deep sleep
rejuvenates the body
more than any other
factor.

Deep sleep has the greatest *immediate* effect on the rejuvenation of the body. Correct nutrition is more important in longer term rejuvenation, since the benefits take longer to manifest themselves. If you sleep badly for just one night, you know about it immediately the next day from the way you feel and look.

During deep sleep, nature restores and heals the body. The nervous system, including the brain, is given a rest and the body is recharged with energy.

The elements which contribute to deep sleep are: good nutrition, reduced coffee and alcohol, a light evening meal with the emphasis on vegetables, aerobic exercise, specific deep sleep exercises, not retiring too late, keeping the bedroom windows open, a firm bed and a hot bath before bed. If, having satisfied all these requirements, you still can't get a good night's sleep, you should try changing the position of your bed to face north, take sleep herbs and practise autosuggestion before sleep.

For details of the factors contributing to deep sleep, see pages 47–57.

Aerobic Exercise

Aerobic exercise is essential for maximum rejuvenation, since it increases the supply of oxygen and nutrients to every part of the body, including the rejuvenation centre itself, the brain. This makes you stay younger and live longer.

Aerobic exercise is even more effective than dieting in reducing body fat and statistics clearly show that less fat means a longer life.It also causes you to look and feel younger.

All these benefits come from doing aerobic exercise for about twenty minutes three times a week, which makes it an excellent time investment.

Research shows
that exercise by the
middle-aged and
elderly can turn back
the clock by ten to
twenty-five years.

Researchers have found that even moderate exercise can retard or actually reverse the effects of ageing. Recent studies in physiology show that exercise by the middle-aged and elderly can turn back the clock ten to twenty-five years. Furthermore, the findings show that no matter when in life a person starts to exercise, improvements can occur.

Among the demonstrated benefits are improved heart and respiratory function, increased muscle strength, denser bones, quicker reaction times and reduced susceptibility to depression.

Exercise works because it is *disuse* which accounts for about half of the functional decline that usually occurs between the ages of thirty and seventy. Research over the last two decades has contradicted the widespread belief that the elderly cannot improve physiologically and, at best, can only slow their decline. One early study was by Herbert de Vries, a pioneer in the use of exercise physiology in gerontology. In his study more than 200 men and women in a Californian retirement community, aged between fifty-six and eighty-seven, participated in a fitness programme which included a walk-jog routine, callisthenics and stretching. After only six weeks their blood pressure dropped, body fat decreased, maximum oxygen transport increased and neuromuscular signs of nervous tension diminished.

'Men and women of sixty and seventy became as fit and energetic as people twenty or thirty years younger,' de Vries noted. 'The ones who improved most were those who had been the least active and the most out of shape.'

These recent studies have shown that the functional decline of advancing age can be delayed by exercise. The best types of aerobic exercise are jogging, brisk walking, swimming, cycling, rowing and aerobics.

Yoga

Yoga is a natural system of physical and mental culture designed to increase your vitality level and produce rejuvenation. It is the most effective exercise system ever designed for reversing the ageing process and promoting a long life.

Yoga works on the whole system, the body and mind; specifically on the body's rejuvenation centres; the brain, spine and glands. This means that you look and feel younger and you will also sleep better, which further promotes rejuvenation.

The yoga 'Asanas' (postures) presented in this book are those which yogis consider essential for rejuvenation. This streamlined routine will take only around twenty minutes to do.

Yoga breathing results in an increase in oxygen and 'prana' (the life principle) to all tissues of the body, including the brain and glands. This oxygenation of the tissues causes them to become healthier and improves their function.

Yoga breathing results in an increase in oxygen and 'prana' (the vital energy) to all tissues of the body, including the brain and glands. This oxygenation of the tissues causes them to become healthier and improves their function.

The three yoga breathing exercises presented in this book are the yogis' favourites for rejuvenation and vitality. They are also completely safe.

For details on the yoga asanas and the yoga breathing exercises, see pages 115–153.

Mental Stimulation

As ageing progresses the brain gets smaller, and this process is accelerated if you overindulge in alcohol. But it has also been shown that the brain can grow as we age, if it is frequently stimulated and if we lead a healthy lifestye. It is the old principle of 'use it or lose it'. Mental exercise is as important to the brain as physical exercise is to the body, and further studies have shown that frequent mental stimulation can reverse brain ageing. Older animals living in enriched environments where they can keep learning actually show organic changes in the brain. The nerve connections grow more complex, more like the brains of younger animals.

Yoga is the most effective exercise system for reversing the ageing process ever devised.

Yoga works on the body's 'rejuvenation centres': the brain, spine and glands.

Studies show that frequent mental stimulation can reverse brain ageing.

There are many things you can do to stimulate your brain. Of course, if your job provides a lot of mental stimulation, there is no need to do anything extra. If your work is routine, try playing games such as bridge or scrabble or doing crossword puzzles. If you enjoy learning, do a part-time evening course in a subject you are interested in, or a subject which will enhance your career or even start you on a new one.

Smoking and Premature Ageing

For smokers, smoking is the number one cause of premature ageing.

Even if you don't smoke, keep on reading, since passive smoking (inhaling smoke from other people smoking near you) is just as harmful as smoking yourself.

For smokers, smoking is the number one cause of premature ageing and reduced life span, so giving up smoking is the most important single action you can take to prevent premature ageing and live longer.

The common expression, 'I'm dying for a cigarette', is very appropriate. Fatal smoking-related diseases are now epidemic and yet they are self-inflicted and easily preventable.

The Effects of Smoking
1   If you smoke two packets of cigarettes a day, you have 70 percent more chance of dying of disease than non-smokers, and can expect to shorten your life by nine years.
2   Smoking increases your chance of getting lung cancer between ten and twenty-five times.
3   Smoking has severe ageing effects on your heart and blood vessels and is a major factor in causing heart disease.
4   Smoking reduces fitness.
5   Smoking causes you to have more colds, infections and coughing.
6   Smoking causes chronic tiredness.
7   Smoking causes premature ageing of the skin.
8   Smoking causes reduced fertility in men and women and can cause impotence in men.

Only about one in five non-smokers will fail to reach retirement age. Of smokers of over twenty-five cigarettes a day, two in five will not reach this age. In other words the risk is doubled.

If you give up smoking now, you can reverse most of its ageing effects and live longer.

To give you an idea of the risk of smoking, consider the following facts. Of 1,000 young male adults who smoke cigarettes, on average one will be murdered, six will be killed on the roads and 250 will die prematurely of tobacco-related disease.

The good news is that if you give up smoking now, you can reverse most of the bad effects of smoking and live longer. The longer you delay giving up, the worse the damage to your body is and the less reversal of the damage is possible.

How to Stop Smoking

It is not easy. There are no miracle cures, and no foolproof methods. Think of the man telling his friend he has no trouble giving it up, since he has given it up twenty times today already. Yet there are millions giving it up every year, so it can be done.

Firstly, you have to really want to give it up. The incentive should be the harm you are inflicting upon your own body and the resulting reduction in the quality and length of your life.

Secondly, you have to realise that, whatever method you use to help break the habit, you still need to exercise some will power. Smoking is a physical and mental addiction, which means that there will be withdrawal symptoms. Look upon giving it up as a challenge, and think of the satisfaction and sense of achievement once you break the habit, not to mention the health benefits.

You must also realise that half-hearted attempts won't work. You must be determined to break the habit totally once and for all. The idea of cutting down gradually doesn't work – it means that you are not really serious about giving up and you are still hanging on to the nicotine habit.

Until you break the habit avoid friends who smoke and places where you would normally be expected to smoke. Try to avoid stressful situations too.

To help with the withdrawal symptoms, eat nourishing food, do some aerobic exercise such as brisk walking or jogging and do the yoga breathing exercises on pages 144–152. These will make you feel better and therefore you'll be less inclined to want a cigarette.

Think of the immediate rewards of stopping smoking:

1 You'll look and smell better.
2 Food will taste better.
3 The stains on your fingers and teeth will begin to go.
4 You'll be less easily out of breath and your stamina will improve.
5 Your morning cough will disappear.
6 You will immediately have more money. Buy yourself a treat with the extra money, then you'll feel one of the benefits immediately and be rewarding yourself for your success. This encourages you to keep the effort up.

The two best methods to help you give up smoking are hypnosis (group or individual) and nicotine chewing gum.

If you want to try hypnosis, make sure the practitioner is a registered hypnotist. Look in the yellow pages of your telephone directory or ask your doctor.

Scientific trials have shown that nicotine chewing gum does reduce the craving for a cigarette, which is a common cause of failure in the first two weeks of giving up smoking.

How to Make Smoking Safer, Until You're Ready to Give Up

1 Use a low tar cigarette.
2 Use filter tipped cigarettes.
3 Try not to inhale.
4 Increase the intervals between each puff and between cigarettes.
5 Leave long stubs. The tar concentration in the bottom half of the cigarette, and particularly in the stub, is very much greater than in the top half. This also means that you smoke less overall.

Passive Smoking

There is now conclusive evidence that exposure to cigarette smoke in the air can harm non-smokers. In 1986 an authoritative report was published by the USA Surgeon-General which supported this conclusion, and a year later a similar report was issued by the British Government.

One of the most conclusive findings was that the spouse of a smoker runs two or three times the non-smoker's risk of developing lung cancer.

It has also been found that the children of parents who smoke are much more likely to develop bronchitis or pneumonia, especially in the first year of life. Other forms of throat, ear and lung diseases are also more common among the children of smokers.

Certain people are more prone to the effects of smoke in the atmosphere than others. Asthmatics may develop acute attacks as a result of exposure to smoke, and other people may develop conjunctivitis or a dry irritation of the throat.

Chemical analysis of 'side-stream smoke', which is the smoke given off at the tip of the cigarette directly into the atmosphere, shows that it is more toxic than the smoke inhaled by the smoker.

Cigarette smoke in the air is more toxic than the smoke inhaled by the smoker.

Because of the above facts, many public authorities are now trying to establish smoke-free environments in restaurants, theatres, public transport and at work.

Non-smokers who object to cigarette smoke can all play a part in the move towards smoke-free environments by protesting whenever they are exposed to a smoke-filled atmosphere.

Conclusion

It is worth repeating that staying young depends to a large extent on the principle of *use it or lose it*. If you exercise your heart and lungs by doing aerobic exercise, studies show that your heart and lungs will last longer. Studies also show that if you maintain an active sex life you will maintain your youthful level of sex hormones, and if you do some mentally stimulating activities, you will keep your mind young. At seventy-two years of age, Einstein started work on a new theory of the universe. Nature doesn't like inactivity; we are designed to be physically and mentally active, so adopt the healthful activities outlined in this chapter.

If you carry out the vitality and rejuvenation principles in this book you will stay young much longer as well as live longer. There's no point in living to old age and displaying the typical characteristics of old age, such as senility and sickness. If you seriously follow this programme, you will acquire an ageless appearance as you grow older in years.

Highlights

1 Ageing is mainly caused by our faulty lifestyle and can be slowed down by the rejuvenation principles in this book.

2 Ageing occurs at a cellular level and is influenced by heredity and free radicals.

3 We now live longer compared to 100 years ago, due mainly to improved hygiene. Around 100 years is our genetic life span potential.

4 Studies of people who have lived beyond 100 years found that they did not overeat, they were mostly vegetarians or ate little meat, they were slim, lived simple lives, were physically active, didn't worry and were married.

5 The main nutritional faults causing premature ageing are excess fat and too much saturated fat, eating refined carbohydrates, excess protein and too much of the wrong type (from animal sources).

6 The effects of our poor diet are premature ageing, degenerative diseases, obesity and reduced immunity to diseases.

7 For optimum nutrition to stay young, you should not overeat.

8 The other anti-ageing factors are deep sleep, aerobic exercise, yoga, mental stimulation and positive thoughts.

9 Smoking, including passive smoking, is the number one cause of premature ageing and short life. To give up smoking you need to really want to give it up and to exert some will power. Hypnosis and nicotine chewing gum can help.

Looking Young and Vital

To look young and vital on the outside, you have to become young on the inside.

If you want to look younger on the outside, you have to become young on the inside. Science has found a relation between how young you look and physiological tests to measure ageing. The bodies of people who look younger than they are are *biologically* younger than their chronological age.

The most effective way to make your body biologically younger is to practise the vitality/rejuvenation factors presented in this book. This includes good nutrition, aerobic exercise, yoga and sufficient deep sleep.

This chapter discusses the other factors which make you look younger and more vital. You will be shown how to develop a slim firm stomach, expand your chest or lift and firm up sagging breasts, increase your height, have a face-lift naturally and grow healthy, thicker and shinier hair.

How to Develop a Slim, Firm Stomach

Good Nutrition

The major dietary cause of obesity is excess fat and sugar in the diet. To reduce your fat intake, reduce dairy products – especially cream, butter, cheese and eggs – as well as meat, and try to have less fried food. Sugar is in most supermarket foods, so try to eat more fresh foods such as fruits, vegetables and whole grains. Avoid ice cream and soft drinks which are loaded with sugar. Try to gradually reduce the sugar in your coffee or tea.

Aerobic Exercise

Exercise such as jogging and brisk walking will also increase the efficiency of your metabolism (see pages 32–46).

Yoga

The yoga postures will get your glands working at peak efficiency. Since the thyroid gland is responsible for your fat metabolism, yoga will result in the efficient burning up of your excess fat.

The Three Most Effective Stomach Exercises

These exercises will tone and firm up your stomach muscles but they won't cause a reduction in stomach fat. The only way to lose fat anywhere in the body is by reducing your calories (especially fats and sugars) and doing yoga and aerobic exercises. People doing even 100 sit-ups a day will not reduce their stomach fat, so the most important factors are diet, aerobic exercise and yoga.

Note: For the most effective way to lose fat and maintain the fat loss, see my book: 'The Double Fat Burning Exercise Programme'.

Exercise 1: Lie on your back with your knees bent, anchoring your feet under a ledge of some kind. Place your hands behind your head. Lift your body to about 45° (halfway between lying down and sitting up) using your stomach muscles. Hold for about two seconds and return to lying down. Do twelve times. This exercise will tone up your stomach muscles.

Exercise 2 (Isometric). This is the same as Exercise 1 except that you stop about halfway between sitting up and lying down and stay in that position for about eight seconds. Do this once, have a rest and then repeat. Make sure that you feel a strain on the stomach muscles.

Isometric exercises are the fastest way to build firm muscles.

If you find this too difficult to start with, do it without your hands behind your head. As your stomach muscles get stronger, place your hands behind your head and hold yourself in a position closer to the floor.

Isometric exercises are the fastest way to build firm muscles.

Exercise 3 (Isotonic). Lie on your back and lift both legs to about 45° then let the legs down to a count of about eight seconds. Repeat twice more.

While 'isometric' refers to building muscle while the body is in a stationary position, 'isotonic' refers to building muscle while the body is in movement. Both are extremely efficient methods for building firm muscle.

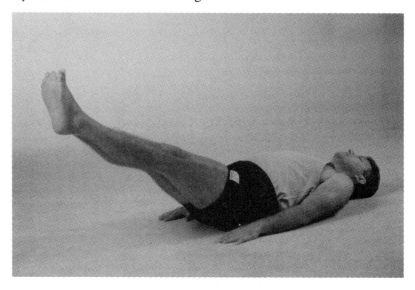

Chest Expansion and Lifting Sagging Breasts

There are several reasons why you should try to develop a large powerful chest:

- **Increased breathing capacity**. This will result in extra vitality and increased resistance to disease and add extra years to your life.
- **Increased strength and health of lungs and heart**. The chest exercises will also improve your lungs and heart.
- **Looking better and increased self-confidence**. A flat chest looks bad and indicates a low vitality level.

The following three exercises are the most effective exercises for chest expansion and for lifting sagging breasts. One has been chosen from each of Chinese Kung Fu/Tai Chi, Indian Yoga and Western body building.

Exercise 1: The Chinese Chest/Expansion/Breast-Lifting Exercise
All the movements for this exercise must be done with the fists, arms and chest muscles in tension (that is, contracted).

(a) Starting position: legs apart and knees bent, arms and fists tensed up. Begin inhaling.

(b) Inhaling, bring your fists up in two intersecting arcs that cross in front of your face. If the exercise is being performed properly your upper arms should be parallel to the floor. From this point, the exercise is essentially a circular movement performed simultaneously with both arms, which inscribe two intersecting circles in the air.

(c) Still inhaling, continue the arc your fists were making in the previous movement, until they are no longer intersecting and are above your head. Since your arms are moving in a circular fashion, your elbows must be bent. Also note that up to this point the back of each hand is facing away from you; this will continue through one more movement and then will change.

(d) Exhaling, bring your fists down to eye level, keeping them on the same plane as the rest of your torso. Stay in this position until you have exhaled completely.

(e) Inhaling, turn your fists outward so that the backs of your hands are now uppermost. Then bring both arms downwards in front of your body, forming two circles that will once again intersect.

This is the most effective exercise there is for chest expansion and lifting sagging breasts; you can feel it working as you are doing it! It was used by the ancient Kung Fu masters to develop a powerful chest.

This chest/breast exercise was used by the ancient Kung Fu masters to develop powerful chests. You can feel it working as you do it.

Exercise 2: The Yoga Chest-Expansion/Breast Lifting Exercise
Unlike Exercise 1, this exercise is done without tensing up any of the muscles.

(a) Stand easily and erect. Gracefully raise arms and bend elbows. Bring hands in to touch chest.

(b) Move arms out and straight back as far as possible. Clasp hands and straighten arms. Gently bend backwards from the waist as far as possible without strain and hold.

(c) Bring clasped arms up over your back and bend forward from the waist as far as possible. Relax your neck and hold.

(d) Slowly Straighten up. Unclasp hands and relax. Repeat.

Exercise 3: The Western Isometric Chest Expansion Exercise
While exercises 1 and 2 are the best isotonic exercises for chest expansion and sagging breasts, this is the most effective isometric exercise.

This exercise is very simple to perform and yet it's the most potent Western body-building exercise for developing the chest and bust. No weights or apparatus are required – it's purely natural.

Just make fists with both hands. Bring your fists together at the level of your chest. Both elbows should be out at the side, parallel with the floor, and the fists should be a few centimetres from the chest. The arms are in a straight line with each other. Now, push both fists together as hard as you can for about eight seconds. Repeat.

Sagging breasts can be helped even more by doing the inverted yoga postures: the headstand and the shoulder stand. These postures work by reversing the effects of the downward pull of gravity.

The yoga breath-retention exercise described on page 148 will also assist in chest expansion and lifting the breasts.

How to Increase Your Height

There are several reasons why you may wish to increase your height.

Firstly, you'll look slimmer and younger, since we associate getting old with reduced height and getting fatter.

Secondly, the increased height comes from increasing the height of your spinal discs, which means increased spinal flexibility and youthfulness. Ageing is, to some extent, due to reduced spinal disc size and reduced spinal flexibility, since this puts pressure on your spinal nerves and affects all the organs in your body.

Last but not least, when you are taller you feel more confident and better about yourself.

Between the ages of twenty-five and seventy years, the average man loses up to 7 centimeters in height. The greatest cause of this is the gradual reduction in size of the spinal discs in between your spinal vertebrae. Ageing causes these discs to gradually wear away until eventually you almost have bone against bone. This loss of height can easily be prevented and you can actually increase your height by up to 4 centimetres within one year by doing the yoga exercise routine described in this book.

The yoga exercises will stretch the spine and increase the height of your spinal discs as no other exercise system can. The yoga plough posture is the most potent spine-stretcher that exists. The headstand reverses the normal downward pull on the vertebrae, opening up the spinal disc spaces. If you don't wish to do the headstand, purchase a reverse-gravity apparatus from a sports or exercise equipment store (see illustration).

Proof of the effect of gravity on your height is the fact that you are just over 1 centimeter taller in the morning when you get out of bed than in the evening. Lying horizontally in bed all night has stopped the downward pull of gravity and allowed your spinal discs to regain some of their lost height.

A Do-It-Yourself Face Lift

As we get older, the face tends to drop, due to two main factors. The first is our old enemy, gravity, which continues to exert its downward pull on the whole body, including the face, throughout life. The effect is cumulative, so as we get older it is more pronounced. The other reason for the face dropping is the fact that as we get older, the muscles (including the facial muscles) gradually lose their tone and sag. As with all problems, the solution is to treat the cause. We need a technique to reverse the effects of gravity and also firm up the facial muscles. Fortunately, there are very simple ways of achieving this.

Reversing gravity is best done by doing the inverted yoga postures – the headstand, shoulder stand and reverse posture. Incidentally, the reverse posture will also reduce facial wrinkles if practised regularly. If you don't wish to do yoga, purchase a reverse-gravity apparatus.

There are two specific exercises for the face which will produce a natural face lift and tone up the facial muscles.

Face-Lifting Exercise 1
Raise your eyebrows and open eyes widely. Open your mouth as wide as possible and stick your tongue out. Hold for about 10 seconds.

Face-Lifting Exercise 2
Raise the muscles of the face and chin. Squeeze up the muscles of the cheeks towards the eyes. Squeeze up the muscles of the eyes until they appear as slits. Squeeze hard, but don't strain. Now, against this pressure, try to open the eyes very wide. Hold for about 10 seconds.

If you need a face lift, the above exercises will save you expensive and sometimes risky surgery. Even if you don't need a face-lift, these exercises will improve your appearance and make you look younger.

Younger Skin

As discussed in the first chapter, the two major causes of facial skin ageing are the sun and lack of vitamin C.

To prevent skin ageing from the sun, wear a hat and sunglasses if outside for long periods on sunny days. At the beach, sit under an umbrella and apply sun cream (maximum protection factor 15) to the face before you swim.

To ensure adequate vitamin C, eat citrus fruits, kiwi fruit, potatoes, cabbage, broccoli and tomatoes. As a supplement take 1000-mg of vitamin C daily, split into two tablets, each taken after a meal. Vitamin C will reduce facial wrinkles and promote a smoother, younger skin.

Use Tretinoin (Retin A) Cream to reverse some of the ageing effects on the skin.

On sunny days, wear a hat and sunglasses.

Healthy Hair

Healthy hair is largely the result of a healthy body. By adopting the vitality and rejuvenation principles in this book, you will not only achieve good health but, as a bonus, your hair will become healthier. In fact your hair very accurately mirrors the health of your body. When you are sick or have had low vitality for some time, you'll notice that your hair loses its shine and looks lifeless. When your health returns, your hair will recover its shine and become thicker.

Nutrients for Healthy Hair
Firstly, make sure you have a healthy nutritional programme, without excess fat in your diet. Fat clogs all the blood vessels in your body, including the blood vessels supplying the hair follicles.

Reduce or eliminate salt, white sugar, alcohol and tobacco. Research has shown excess salt to cause hair loss. Both white sugar and alcohol destroy vitamin B which is essential for healthy hair. Tobacco causes constriction of the blood vessels supplying the scalp, resulting in reduced nourishment to the scalp.

NIACIN

Research in Sweden has shown that niacin will cause hair to regrow on the scalp. Niacin works by causing dilation (widening) of the blood vessels, resulting in increased blood supply and hence nourishment to the hair follicles.

OTHER B VITAMINS

Especially B_6 (folic acid) and pantothenic acid. B_6 aids protein metabolism and, since hair is formed from protein, this vitamin helps to promote healthy hair.

B_5 helps to prevent premature ageing, including hair loss and going grey.

VITAMIN C

Essential for healthy hair.

VITAMIN E

Vitamin E produces an increased blood flow to the scalp. Japanese researchers have found that a topical application of vitamin E on rats made their hair grow 2.4 times faster than normal.

IODINE

Iodine is a mineral which is essential for normal thyroid gland function. Poor thyroid function causes loss of hair and also makes the hair become dry and thin.

The best source of iodine is kelp. You can buy kelp tablets from health shops. Take one 1000-mg tablet with your evening meal. Kelp is also rich in calcium, magnesium, potassium and phosphorous, which also promote healthy hair.

LECITHIN

Lecithin is rich in choline, inositol and phosphorous, all of which are hair growth stimulants. The best sources of lecithin are soya beans, such as in soya milk.

Do-It-Yourself Salon Treatments

You need go no further than your kitchen for soft, shiny, healthy hair.

1 **Egg Yolk**. Beat two egg yolks thoroughly into a cup of warm water. Massage into scalp and hair. Leave for 15–30 minutes before rinsing and shampooing.
2 **Olive Oil**. Massage warmed oil into your scalp. Leave for 15–30 minutes and then shampoo.

3   **Apple Cider Vinegar**. Add one part apple cider vinegar to about twenty parts water and rinse through your hair after shampooing.

Herbs for Hair Rejuvenation
Herbs play a vital role in making hair strong and shiny and in stimulating its growth.

- **Nettle**. Nettle stimulates blood circulation to the scalp to condition hair and is particularly good for oily hair.

- **Henna**. This gives hair a bright sheen and is good for damaged or brittle hair.

- **Chamomile**. This is a hair brightener.

- **Marshmallow**. Marshmallow adds lustre to hair and is particularly good for dry hair.

- **Horsetail**. This herb strengthens and adds sheen to hair.

- **To highlight blonde hair**, combine the herbs chamomile, calendula and yarrow.

- **To highlight dark hair**, combine the herbs sage, parsley and rosemary.

To make an infusion of mixed herbs, just pour boiling water over fresh or dried herbs, leave until lukewarm and then strain. You may rub it daily into the scalp or apply it as a rinse after shampooing. To use as a rinse, just fill the bathroom sink with the infusion and soak your hair in it, or use a bowl and pour the liquid several times over your wet hair.

Other Factors Producing Healthy Hair
Aerobic exercise. Exercises such as jogging cause an increase in blood circulation to the whole body, including the scalp.

Yoga headstand or reverse-gravity apparatus. This also causes an increase in blood supply to the scalp due to the effect of gravity.

Reduce stress. Stress or tension causes constriction of the tiny blood vessels in the scalp, which will result in reduced blood flow and hence less nourishment to the hair follicles. The best way to prevent stress is to think positively, exercise and avoid stressful situations.

Scalp massage. This relaxes the muscles of the scalp, resulting in increased blood flow to the hair follicles. Just place the finger tips of both hands firmly on your scalp. Massage firmly in a circular motion in one spot for a few seconds, then place your fingers in a new position. Continue this procedure until you have covered the whole scalp.

Vigorous hair brushing. This stimulates the oil glands and the hair roots in the scalp, which results in an increased blood supply to the area. Vigorous brushing also helps prevent grey hair and reverses existing greying. It's best to use a natural bristle brush rather than a synthetic nylon brush.

Shampoo. Use a natural, mild shampoo, such as those containing jojoba, aloe-vera and rosemary. The strong commercial shampoos remove too much natural oil from the glands in the scalp.

Although there is a hereditary factor in hair type and hair loss, the health of the hair depends to a large extent on good blood circulation to the scalp and relaxed scalp muscles. If you take the measures discussed above your hair will become thicker, shinier and darker.

Highlights

1 To develop a *slim, firm stomach*: have good nutrition, especially reduced fats and sugars; do specific stomach exercises, yoga and aerobic exercises.

2 For *chest expansion* or *sagging breasts*, do the three exercises described in this chapter.

3 If you wish to *increase your height*, the most effective way is to increase the height of your spinal discs by doing the yoga exercises.

4 You can have a *natural face lift*, without surgery, by doing the yoga headstand or using reverse-gravity apparatus and doing the two natural face lift exercises.

5 *Healthy hair* is largely the result of a healthy body, since the hair is a part of the body. Important nutrients for healthy hair are niacin, other B vitamins, vitamin C, vitamin E, iodine and lecithin.

   Other factors producing healthy hair are aerobic exercises, yoga headstand, reducing stress, scalp massage and vigorous hair brushing.

6 For younger skin, keep the face out of the sun and take adequate vitamin C.

PART TWO

The Lifestyle Factors

Aerobic Exercise for Reversing Ageing

He who cannot find time for exercise will have to find time for illness.

LORD DERBY

Aerobic exercise is the supreme exercise from the West. It has been researched thoroughly and is a credit to the modern scientific approach. We now know the safest and best way to do it, and its benefits have been substantiated by many scientific studies.

Aerobic exercise is important, since only this type of exercise can produce cardiovascular fitness. This fitness plays a very important part in vitality and youthfulness, as you will see later. In fact you will never reach your maximum rejuvenation potential or vitality level unless you become fit.

This type of exercise is not difficult to do and is not very time consuming. You will need to put in about a twenty-minute session four times a week. Once you experience the well-being of being fit, you'll never regret starting.

Aerobic Exercise and How it Works

Only aerobic exercise can produce fitness, which results in age reversal.

This is steady continuous exercise which raises the heart rate to 80 percent of the maximum heart rate for your age for at least twenty minutes. This creates a high demand for oxygen to supply the exercising muscles.

Aerobic exercise has two major effects on the body:

1 It produces a *stronger heart and healthier lungs*. This results in the cardiovascular system delivering oxygen more efficiently to every cell in the body (including the brain and glands).
2 The muscles become more efficient at absorbing oxygen from the blood and therefore at converting stored fat to muscle and energy.

Both these effects cause you to feel and look good, as well as reversing ageing.

The Benefits of Aerobic Exercise

1 Aerobic exercise makes the heart a more efficient pump, able to meet the demands of strenuous activity with fewer beats because it can pump out more blood with each contraction.
This type of exercise also helps to prevent heart attacks (a reduction of 39 percent according to one study).

2 The circulation is increased to all parts of the body, resulting in increased efficiency of all the internal organs and glands.

3 Blood pressure is reduced.

4 Total blood cholesterol levels are reduced. Perhaps more importantly, aerobic exercise causes a reduction in the bad low-density cholesterol which clogs the arteries and an increase in the high-density cholesterol which helps to clean the arteries out.

5 Excess weight is lost. Aerobic exercise causes the conversion of body fat to lean muscle tissue.

6 Exercising against gravity (such as walking or running as opposed to swimming) increases the calcium content of bones, helping to prevent osteoporosis and fractures in later life. One study found that a group of women aged sixty-nine to ninety-five who exercised thirty minutes a day, three days a week for three years, experienced a 2.3 percent *increase* in the mineral content of the radius bone in their arms, whereas a group of non-exercisers showed a 3.3 percent loss.

7 An American study of more than 5000 former university athletes has shown that women who exercise have lower rates of breast and reproductive system cancers.

8 The perspiration from exercise causes increased toxin elimination and healthier skin.

9 The nervous system is improved by exercise. According to studies at the University of Texas, sixty-year-old men who have jogged or played squash for twenty years or more have reaction times equal to, or better than, inactive men in their twenties.

10 Exercise causes a slowing down of the ageing process. One study found that for every one hour of exercise, you'll add two and a half hours to your life. This makes exercise a very good time investment.

11 Exercise results in fewer health problems and pains.

12 Exercise is a natural tranquilliser and antidepressant. It releases stress.

Exercise also results in an increase in confidence, optimism and creativity. In a 1985 survey of 1033 men and women, respondents who exercised regularly described themselves as more confident and creative than did their sedentary counterparts.

All the above benefits of aerobic exercise result in rejuvenation of the body and mind as well as increased vitality.

> Aerobic exercise causes the conversion of body fat to lean muscle tissue.

> One study found that for every hour of exercise, you add two and a half hours to your life – an excellent time investment!

If you consider that all these benefits come from exercising for only about twenty minutes a day, three or four days a week, you can see that it is an excellent time investment.

Any Age Limit to Starting?

You can start at any age and receive all the benefits.

No. Many people start aerobic exercise when they are over sixty years old and receive all its benefits. Of course the younger you start the more cumulative benefit you will receive.

Losing Weight:
Is Exercise Better Than Dieting?

The answer is *yes*! Most people who diet give it up. Not only do they regain the lost weight, but also the regained weight has more fat and less muscle than before. If you exercise, this will not occur. In any event, exercise alone is more effective than diet alone for reducing weight.

Aerobic exercise results in the loss of fat by five mechanisms:

1 Research has shown that exercise trains the body to draw on its store of fat for energy.
2 Exercise builds muscle, which burns up more calories than fat does, even when you're resting.

Aerobic exercise causes you to burn up more calories, even while you are asleep.

3 Studies have shown that regular exercise increases body metabolism for up to twenty-four hours after a work-out. This means that even when not exercising (even when asleep in fact) you are burning more calories than you would if you did not exercise.
4 Exercise reduces appetite by stimulating the liver to release more sugar. This results in a higher blood sugar level which signals to the brain that you are not hungry.
5 Regular work-outs make the body less sensitive to stress, which can trigger overeating. Exercise does this by causing the brain to release endorphins, the body's calming chemicals.

Aerobic exercise is more effective for losing excess fat than dieting or any other kind of exercise.

Even if you don't want to lose any fat, if you exercise you can *eat more* without producing more fat.

In summary, research has shown that aerobic exercise reverses muscle turning to fat more effectively than dieting and better than any other type of exercise.

The Best Time to Exercise

There is no hard and fast rule here; it depends on what's convenient for you. Some like to exercise early in the morning when the air is fresh; they claim it gives them energy for the whole day. However, research has shown the early evening is the best time to exercise. This is for three reasons:

Early evening exercise produces the optimum results.

1 The whole day's *stress is released*, which induces a feeling of relaxation and vitality.
2 Sleep is improved, due to the release of stress, and that benefits the whole of the next day.
3 Studies have shown that the greatest fat loss and greatest muscle gain can occur with evening exercise. This is probably because appetite is reduced for about two hours after exercise. Eating less in the evening is especially beneficial, since body metabolism is lower in the evening, so you won't burn up the evening meal calories as easily as those of other meals.

How Often and How Long Should We Exercise?

To achieve a minimum fitness level you need to exercise for at least twenty-three minutes, three times a week. The duration of the exercise is important for two reasons:

To achieve a minimum fitness level you need to exercise for at least 23 minutes, three times a week.

1 Firstly, it takes into account the time it takes for your heart rate to reach 80 percent of your maximum heart rate (called your 'target heart rate'). This time varies for different exercises.
2 Secondly, you need twenty minutes of exercise at your target heart rate. For example, with jogging, it takes about three minutes to reach the desired heart rate (target heart rate), therefore you jog for twenty-three minutes.

The table below shows the recommended minimum times for exercises.

Table 1: Minimum Exercise Duration

Activity	Minimum time required	Activity	Minimum time required
Jogging	23 minutes	Treadmill	23 minutes
Skipping	23 minutes	Walking	28 minutes
Aerobics	23 minutes	Cycling (outdoor & indoor)	28 minutes
Chair stepping	23 minutes	Swimming	28 minutes

How Hard Should We Exercise?

You must exercise at your target heart rate. Below it you won't get fit and above it you will experience fatigue and muscle loss.

If you exercise below your target heart rate (see Table 2), you won't get fit. If you push yourself too hard, you will suffer from fatigue and muscle loss and you won't burn up any fat.

To know exactly how hard to exercise, you just have to take your pulse after exercise. You should aim for a pulse of 80 percent of your maximum heart rate (target heart rate). Table 2 below shows you how to find the 80 percent level for your age. For example, if you are forty years old, your heart rate (pulse) after exercise should be 146.

You may also use the following formula to calculate your target heart rate.

1 Subtract your age from 220.
2 Multiply that figure by 0.8.

Don't push yourself too hard or you will lose more than you gain. To get fit faster, exercise longer, not harder.

If you find after exercise, your pulse is more than six beats below your target heart rate, you'll need to go a little harder. If your pulse is more than six beats above your heart rate, you'll need to slow down a little.

Don't push yourself too hard, you will lose more than you gain. If you wish to get fit faster, exercise *longer*, not harder.

What if You're Fit Already?

If your pulse rate is below sixty at rest, you'll need to revise your target rate downwards, since you'll be pushing yourself too hard if you follow the above.

Your revised formula will be:

T.H.R. = (Maximum Heart Rate – Resting Heart Rate) multiplied by 0.65 + Resting Heart Rate.

Don't do the Same Exercise Every Day if Over Thirty-five Years Old

I recommend that you only exercise three days a week, spread over the whole week. Studies have shown that this provides all the benefits of aerobic exercise. Also, you are allowing the body to recuperate from the strain of exercise on the exercise-free days. Only if you wish to reach an athletic standard should you exercise more than this.

If you decide to exercise more than three days a week, do different exercises on alternate days. For example, jog on Mondays, Wednesdays and Fridays and do indoor circuit training or swimming on Tuesdays, Thursdays and Saturdays.

If you do the same exercise every day, you are putting stress on the same muscles every day and your body doesn't have enough time in between exercise periods to repair the stress. Your muscles will lose structure and become weaker. You may also develop a haggard appearance, as the body draws protein from the face to try to repair the overexercised muscles.

Table 2: Your Target Heart Rate

Age	80% of max. H.R. (Target Heart Rate)	75% of max. H.R. (Heart Disease History)	Maximum H.R.
20	160	150	200
22	158	148	195
24	157	147	196
26	155	145	194
28	154	144	192
30	152	143	190
32	151	142	189
34	150	140	187
36	149	140	186
38	147	138	184
40	146	137	182
45	143	134	179
50	140	131	175
55	137	128	171
60	128	120	160
65+	120	113	150

Eighty Percent of Target Heart Rate

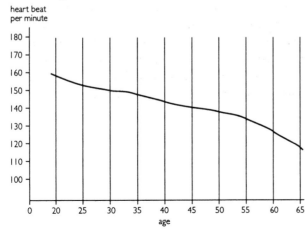

You can use the table or the graph to find your target heart rate. To use the table, find your age in the vertical column, and look at the corresponding heart rate in the next column. To use the graph, find your age along the bottom line and trace a line straight up the graph. From that point trace a line horizontally to the vertical line, and the point of intersection is your target heart rate.

How to Take Your Pulse

It's best to take the pulse at the radial artery in the wrist, using the middle finger. You'll find this artery on the thumb side of the wrist near the edge. Just touch the area – don't press, since you won't feel the pulse if you do.

Take the pulse for ten seconds only and then multiply this figure by 6. This is your heart rate per minute. We don't take the pulse for one minute or even fifteen seconds, since the heart beat will slow down considerably during this time, making the result inaccurate.

Increase Fitness Gradually

It's best to gradually work up to a high fitness level. If you jog, for example, spend the first month alternating jogging with brisk walking. Just jog slowly for a few minutes, then walk for a few minutes, and repeat this cycle for twenty-three minutes. Start with jogging, since this will quickly raise your heart rate to your target level. The next month you can jog for the whole period. Don't exceed your target heart rate.

If you are doing other exercises, apply the same principle of taking it easy for the first month. This gives your body time to adapt to the exercise.

Drink Water Before You Exercise

This will replace the fluid you lose in sweating and is especially important in summer. It is necessary to drink *before* you exercise, because this helps to keep your body temperature from rising while exercising.

You should drink about two glasses of water. Don't drink sugar drinks, such as soft drinks and sports drinks, since sugar interferes with absorption of water.

Don't rely on thirst to warn you of dehydration. During strenuous exercise 'thirst sensors' in the throat lose sensitivity and can fail to send out 'drink' signals.

Cooling Down After Exercise

Warming up before aerobic exercise is not essential, unless you are prone to injuries, since it is not a strenuous activity. If you're training at an athletic standard, that's a different matter.

To cool down after the exercise, just slow down whatever you are doing for a few minutes. If you are doing brisk walking, for example, then just walk slowly for a few minutes.

It's especially important after jogging to walk for a few minutes. Jogging causes blood to accumulate in the legs and walking assists the body to return the blood to the rest of the body.

How Will You Know You are Fit?

1 Your resting pulse rate will decrease, since your heart doesn't have to work as hard to pump the same amount of blood. After a few months your pulse should go down about 10 beats. For example, if your resting pulse rate is around the average of seventy beats per minute, it should reduce to around sixty beats per minute. Later it may go as low as fifty or less. When you are fit your heart will beat around 15 million times per year less than the unfit person. This greatly reduces stress on the heart and is probably the main reason why you will live a lot longer than the unfit person.
2 You will feel less tired after exercise and during the rest of the day.
3 You will need to work a little harder during exercise to reach your target heart rate. But because you are fit, you will not feel you are working harder.

When you are fit your heart will beat around 15 million fewer times per year than that of an unfit person. This reduced stress on the heart means that you are likely to live longer.

Don't Overexercise

I cannot emphasise enough the fact that you should not overexercise. Overexercise means:

1 Pushing yourself too hard; that is, exceeding 80 percent of your maximum heart rate.
2 Doing the same exercise more than three times a week if you are over thirty-five years old.

The results of overexercising are:

1 Loss of protein, since protein is needed to provide energy and repair tissue. This will cause loss of muscle structure and weak muscles.

2 Low energy level, since you are overtaxing your system.

If you wish to get fit fast, then exercise for longer periods.

Diet

It's advisable not to go on any special crash diet programme. Most of them are extreme and, at best, they don't work. Quite often they are also detrimental to health.

It's especially important not to go on a crash diet when you're doing an exercise programme. This is because the body requires a little more energy, and also an adequate supply of protein to repair muscle stress due to exercise. If you reduce carbohydrates too low, your body will use its protein supplies to produce energy. This means that your muscles will lose structure and become weaker. The same thing will happen if you go on a diet that is too low in fat: some of your protein will go to fat.

What if You are Sick?

If you are suffering from some illness which involves the whole system, such as a cold, it's best not to exercise until you have recovered. This is because your body needs plenty of rest to maximise its recuperative powers.

I would advise a brisk walk for no longer than half an hour a day. This is much less strenuous than the other exercises.

The Step Fitness Test

This test determines your level of fitness and how hard you should start exercising. You can also do this test once a month to see how you are progressing.

If you have heart trouble or are over thirty-five and have not exercised for over a year, you should have a stress electrocardiogram first. The test is as follows:

1 Obtain or make a stool 20 centimetres high, or use a step of about the same height.
2 Step up and down for three minutes at the rate of two complete steps in five seconds.
3 Sit down and rest for thirty seconds, then take your pulse for thirty seconds.

Check the table below to get your level of fitness.

Poor or Fair: Start doing aerobic exercise three times a week, twenty-three minutes a session, but take it easy for the first month.

Average or Good: Start doing aerobic exercise three times a week, twenty-three minutes a session. Exercise at your target heart rate.

Excellent: Just continue whatever you are doing!

Table 3: Fitness Level by Age (Heart Rate)

	Age 20–29 years	Age 30–39 years	Age 40–49 years	Age 50+ years
Men				
Excellent	34–36	35–38	37–39	37–40
Good	37–40	39–41	40–42	41–43
Average	41–42	42–43	43–44	44–45
Fair	43–47	44–47	45–49	46–49
Poor	48–59	48–59	50–60	50–62
Women				
Excellent	39–42	39–42	41–43	41–44
Good	43–44	43–45	44–45	45–47
Average	45–46	46–47	46–47	48–49
Fair	47–52	48–53	48–54	50–55
Poor	53–66	54–66	55–67	56–66

The Best Aerobic Exercises

These are jogging, brisk walking, swimming, aerobics, cycling (outdoor and stationary), skipping and rowing (outdoor and stationary). Other exercises such as isometrics, weightlifting or sports such as tennis, even if done vigorously, will not make you fit.

JOGGING

Advantages:
1 Very aerobic and time efficient.
2 Results in the fastest weight loss of all exercises.
3 Convenient – can be done anywhere.
4 Very little equipment needed – just good jogging shoes with shock absorbing inserts in them.

Jogging is an extremely efficient exercise. Most of the energy expended is used to produce fitness.

Disadvantages:
1 Too strenuous for the very unfit or those starting out when over sixty years old.
2 Stress injuries are common.

Jogging is my favourite exercise, because it is extremely efficient – most of the energy expended is being used to produce fitness – and you can change the scenery or make it a social outing. To relieve monotony, you can carry a pocket transistor radio with earphones too.

It's best to jog on grass, since this reduces the jarring effect of jogging on the body. Stay away from roads and footpaths, unless you have good jogging shoes with extra shock-absorbing inserts in them. This especially applies if you have any joint or back problems.

Don't jog on busy roads or within 20 metres of one. High levels of carbon monoxide from car engine exhausts can extend as far as 18 metres from roadways. One study showed that jogging for half an hour in heavy traffic is the same as smoking between ten and twenty cigarettes.

Many joggers, as well as getting the benefits of fitness, claim that they experience of feeling of euphoria (the 'runner's high'). Studies indicate that this is because running stimulates certain hormones called endorphins, which reduce pain and produce a pleasant mood.

Brisk Walking
Advantages:

Brisk walking is an excellent exercise and can be as aerobic as jogging. It has the lowest injury and drop-out rates of all forms of exercise.

1 Brisk walking is excellent exercise, especially if you find jogging too strenuous. It is also good if you are very unfit, if you are starting an exercise programme or if you're an older person.
2 It can be as aerobic as jogging if you do it vigorously enough.
3 It has a very low injury rate, since it's a low-impact exercise.
4 It is convenient because it can be done anywhere and at any time and can also be a social event.
5 Importantly, it has the lowest drop-out rate of all exercises.

Disadvantage:
Because brisk walking is not very strenuous, you will need to do it for longer than other exercises.

Brisk walking can be made as aerobic as jogging by carrying hand weights while walking. The weights should be no more than 3 kilograms and you still need to swing your arms to at least chest level. You can buy hand weights from sports stores. You can also wear a weighted belt to further increase the effectiveness. Don't wear a back-pack load, however, since I've found from experience with my patients that it can cause shoulder problems.

Swimming

Advantages:

1   Swimming develops all the body's major muscle groups, especially the chest and stomach muscles.
2   It has a very low injury rate.
3   The deep rhythmic breathing is very good for the lungs and therefore for general health.

Disadvantages:

1   You will not lose weight. The body will conserve its fat for warmth and buoyancy.
2   You need access to water.
3   It is not a sociable activity.
4   Eye and ear problems are common.

If you choose swimming, you must use a different target heart rate formula than the one given above for land exercise. This is because the heart rate is lower when swimming than with other exercises because your body does not have to work as hard to keep the temperature stable. Also, since you are horizontal, the heart doesn't have to work as hard to pump the blood against gravity.

So, for swimming use the following revised formula:

Target Heart Rate = (205 minus age) × 0.8.

I suggest you alternate two laps of overarm with two laps of breast stroke. This helps to prevent monotony and exercises more of the body's muscles.

Aerobics

This combines rhythmic exercise with music.

Advantages:

1   Aerobics can exercise all the joints and muscles of the body.
2   Music makes the exercise more enjoyable.

Disadvantages:

1   In high-impact aerobics injuries to legs and feet are common. In low-impact aerobics it is difficult to reach target heart rate.
2   Studies show that you will not lose weight if you just do aerobics.

Swimming develops all the body's major muscle groups but does not cause fat loss.

Cycling

Advantages:

1   Stress injury rate is low, since cycling is impact free.
2   It is pleasant and you can enjoy different scenery.

Disadvantages:

1   The equipment is expensive.
2   It can be dangerous on the roads.
3   You need to find a non-stop route to maintain target heart rate.

Outdoor Cycling

*   Buy a bike with ten gears so that when you are going uphill you're not straining yourself.
*   Always wear a good helmet

Stationary Indoor Cycling

*   This is just as effective as outdoor cycling. The main problems are that you have to do it quite strenuously to reach your target heart rate and that it quickly becomes boring.
*   It's best to combine cycling with other indoor activities such as skipping, rowing and chair stepping.
*   Make sure you buy a good exercise bike. It should have adjustable resistance and a heavy flywheel to give a smooth ride.

Skipping

Advantages:

1   Skipping is very aerobic.
2   It is not expensive; all you need are aerobic shoes and a rope.

Disadvantages:

1   Skipping is high impact so it has potential for stress injuries.
2   It is too vigorous for many people.

Tips

*   It's best to combine skipping with other exercises, since it is strenuous and high impact and the range of movement is small.
*   Make sure you skip on a soft surface, such as on carpet offcuts.
*   The handles should reach armpit level when you stand on the middle of the rope.

- The best technique is to alternate from foot to foot at about eighty jumps per minute. Don't jump with both feet at once; it is too stressful on the feet and shins. If you need to raise your heart rate more, lift your feet higher rather than jumping faster.

Rowing Machine

Advantages:

1 Rowing provides exercise for most of the body muscles, especially the chest, stomach, legs and back.
2 It has a low stress injury rate.

Disadvantages:

1 The equipment is expensive.
2 It must be done vigorously to achieve your target heart rate.

Tips

- These machines give similar benefits to rowing on water.
- Make sure you buy a good machine. It should have universal joints, so you can really exercise your chest muscles, and a sliding seat so that you can exercise the whole body.

Chair Stepping

This is a good indoor exercise, since it's just as aerobic as skipping, but without jarring impact. Just use an old chair, and if you're very unfit, start off with a low stool around 15 centimetres high.

All you do is step up and down from the chair. Here is the best way to do it:

1 Step on to the chair with the right foot.
2 Bring the left foot up too.
3 Bring the right foot down, and then the left foot.
4 After about one minute, reverse the sequence by stepping on to the chair first with the left foot.

Circuit Training

This is a variety of different indoor exercises. It has the benefit of preventing stress on one particular group of muscles and it can exercise all the major muscle groups. It also has the benefit of preventing boredom.

In circuit training you can do a combination of several of the following exercises:

The beauty of circuit
training is that it firms
the stomach and
develops the chest
while making you
generally fit.

Skipping, sit ups, push ups, stationary cycling, stationary
rowing and running on the spot.

Start with the most aerobic exercise, for example, skipping, since this will allow you
to attain your target heart rate quickly. Spend about two minutes with each exercise
and then repeat the cycle again until you've done about twenty-three minutes. This
is more enjoyable if you listen to music while exercising.

Highlights

1   Aerobic exercise is essential for
    maximum vitality and rejuvenation,
    since it increases the supply of oxygen
    and nutrients to all parts of the body.
    This makes you feel good, look good
    and stay younger – all this for about
    twenty minutes three times a week!
    It's an excellent time investment.

2   Aerobic exercise is more effective
    than dieting in losing *body fat.*

3   You need to do it for at least twenty-
    three minutes, three times a week.
    Optimum fitness comes from doing it
    for thirty-three minutes four times a
    week. The exact duration depends
    on the type of exercise (see Table 1,
    page 35).

4   You need to exercise at 80 percent of
    your maximum heart rate (see Table
    2, page 37). If your pulse is already
    below sixty, see the amended
    formula.

5   Take your pulse at the radial artery
    (wrist) for ten seconds after the
    exercise. Multiply this figure by

six to give you your *exercise heart
rate.*

6   You may like to take the *fitness test*
    (see page 41).

7   Increase your fitness *gradually.* Start
    off very easily the first month so that
    your body adapts to the exercise.

8   You'll know you're fit when your
    resting heart rate is less. You will also
    need to work harder to reach your
    target heart rate, but you will no
    longer feel tired after the exercise.

9   Remember to *cool down* after the
    exercise. Just slow down for a few
    minutes whatever exercise you are
    doing.

10 Drink two glasses of water *before* you
    exercise.

11 Choose whichever aerobic exercise
    appeals to you. The one you like best
    is the one you'll find easier to stick
    with.

Deep Sleep Every Night

'Chief nourisher in Life's feast…'

MACBETH

Sleep: The Most Important Factor in Vitality and Rejuvenation

Even though society emphasises nutrition and exercise as the main factors in well-being, in reality deep sleep has the greatest direct effect on vitality and rejuvenation. We never consider this, because we assume that sleep is a passive affair and that there is no way we can control its quality. This attitude is wrong. There are steps you can take to achieve high quality deep sleep which causes you to wake up fresh and full of vitality. You don't have to carry out all the sleep factors but the more you do, the deeper your sleep will be.

Incidentally, by following the principles in the rest of this book, such as good nutrition and exercise, you are also promoting deep sleep.

You can easily prove to yourself that sleep is more important than food. Those mornings when you wake up tired you can eat the most nourishing food in the world and feel no better. Your body needs deep rest and nothing can substitute for it. In fact, with poor sleep, the body's nervous and digestive systems do not function properly, and you will not digest the food properly. Your body is crying out for deep rest. When you wake up fresh, the day goes smoothly. You can even eat a bit of junk food, do no exercise, have stress, and you will probably get away with it (of course I don't recommend this). After a good night's sleep the nervous system is functioning so well that it can handle more abuse.

Why Sleep is the Most Important Factor
Sleep is essential for the rejuvenation of every cell in the body. It is especially important for the rest and rejuvenation of the nervous system, including the brain. This is

Sleep recharges the batteries and rejuvenates the brain.

because it is the nervous system which controls and co-ordinates all the other systems of the body, such as the digestive system, glandular system, immune system and reproductive system.

During deep sleep, nature restores and heals the body by eliminating toxins, tissue rebuilding, the replenishing of enzymes and so on. The mind is also given rest, and some stress is released by dreaming. In short, sleep recharges the batteries.

It must be emphasised that, if you are to attain the maximum rejuvenation from sleep, the sleep must be deep and unbroken. If your sleep is not like this, read the deep sleep factors and apply the factors which are relevant to you.

How Much Sleep do You Need?

The average adult requires between seven and nine hours a day. The exact amount depends upon the health of the individual, sleeping conditions and the energy expenditure during the day.

If you adopt the nutritional programme in this book, exercise and carry out the sleep factors which are relevant to you, after a few months you will need no more than seven to seven and a half hours sleep. This means you will have additional free time, even taking into account the time it takes to exercise.

Children need more sleep since they need extra energy for growth. People over sixty years old need less sleep.

Oversleeping is almost as bad as undersleeping, causing physical and mental sluggishness, reduced vitality and even depression.

Effects of Poor Sleep

1 Reduced vitality.
2 Increased irritability.
3 Looking tired and older. Sleep affects your skin, hair and eyes, as well as your general appearance.
4 Reduced life expectancy, since all your body systems require deep rest to rejuvenate themselves.
5 Reduced work efficiency and increased danger of work accidents.
6 More illnesses, since poor sleep reduces resistance to disease. This means more colds and infections. Studies have shown that sleep affects the immune system.

How to Sleep Deeply

Sleep is a natural function of the body, and therefore deep sleep is really dependent on the health of the *whole* body. This is why, when the health improves through correct nutrition and exercise, sleep will also improve.

Specifically, natural deep sleep depends upon the integrity of the sleep centre in the brain. The normal functioning of the sleep centre depends upon:

Deep natural sleep depends on the health of the whole body and the integrity of the brain's sleep centre.

1 Good *nourishment* of the sleep centre. Hence the importance of a good nutritional programme.
2 Good *circulation* to the sleep centre. This is best achieved by aerobic exercise and specific *yoga* positions.
3 Normal *nerve* supply to the sleep centre. The nerve supply to the sleep centre is from the cervical spine (in the neck). Yoga postures and neck exercises will improve the flexibility and mobility of the neck. If you have a neck problem, correct it first by visiting a chiropractor.

The Deep Sleep Factors

Good Nutrition

If you are following the nutrition principles in this book, you will be feeding the brain's sleep centre with high quality nutrients. Also, on this nutritional programme, the cholesterol lining your blood vessel walls will gradually decrease. This will result in an increased blood flow to the sleep centre, providing even more nourishment to the centre.

Certain foods will assist deep sleep. Some of these are:

- FISH
  Fish is very nutritious, with a high vitamin content (A, D & E) and also a high essential mineral content (iodine, fluorine, calcium). Fish in fact contains two to three times more fluorine than meat. Calcium is essential for the correct functioning of the nervous system, including the brain's sleep centre.

- VEGETABLES
  Vegetables also have a high vitamin content (B_1 and nicotinic acid) and a high mineral content (calcium and iron). Keep this in mind that vegetables should not be overcooked, since this will destroy a high percentage of these nutrients. Microwaving or steaming is the preferred way of cooking vegetables to minimise nutrient loss. Also, because vegetables are alkaline they have a relaxing effect on the nervous system. As a further advantage for sleep, vegetables are relatively easy to digest, so you are not wasting energy produced from sleep, on the digestion of food.

The evening meal should be light. A dish of fish and vegetables is ideal for a good night's sleep.

So, fish and vegetables make a good evening meal since as well as helping to give you a good night's sleep, they are also nutritious and good for weight control. Avoid desserts in the evening, since you won't wake up fresh after eating a heavy evening meal.

Sugar

I am referring to sugar in its simple forms, such as white, brown or raw sugar, honey, syrup, and the sugar in cakes, biscuits and processed foods.

Sugar is bad for sleep for four main reasons:

1 Sugar tends to excite the nervous system, causing irritability.
2 High blood sugar often causes itching of the skin. When this occurs at night time, it prevents continuous deep sleep because you partially wake up to scratch.
3 Itching can also be caused by *candida*, a yeast infection which is far more common that you may realise. Sugar will activate this condition and cause itching. Itching is an irritant to the nervous system and therefore prevents deep sleep.
4 The sugar addict eats excessive sugar during the waking hours. The body reacts to this later, during sleep time, by lowering the blood sugar. The problem is that the body does the job too well and the level goes too low. The brain, starved of its normal high sugar level, becomes irritable, just as in drug withdrawal symptoms.

The solution is to consume less sugar and sugar-rich foods and eat more *complex carbohydrates* (fruit, vegetables and grains), since they release sugar into the blood stream slowly and for a much longer time. Aerobic exercise also helps to control blood sugar levels.

Coffee and Alcohol

Avoid coffee and tea in the evening. They contain caffeine, a nerve stimulant which reduces the depth of sleep.

These drinks should be avoided in the evening as much as possible. Coffee contains caffeine, a nerve stimulant which will reduce the depth of sleep considerably. If you enjoy coffee in the evening, drink a decaffeinated form. It contains virtually no caffeine and tastes like the 'real thing'.

Tea and cola soft drinks also contain caffeine and should be avoided in the evening. Don't underestimate coffee or excessive tea, since caffeine is a strong drug and can be detected in the blood twenty-four hours after a drink.

Alcohol, especially in excess, is guaranteed to give you a bad night's sleep. It's true that alcohol has a relaxing effect and will make you get to sleep more easily. The problem is that it produces a drugged sleep, not a natural one, so you won't wake up feeling fresh.

Also, you will tend to wake up much earlier than usual because the body suffers withdrawal symptoms during the night, causing irritability in the nervous system. In addition, alcohol destroys vitamin B, which is important for a healthy nervous system and sleep.

Of course, there's nothing wrong with a glass of wine before your evening meal. This will have very little effect on sleep, since it's early in the evening, and the food will tend to absorb a lot of the alcohol.

Don't Drink too Much Fluid in the Evening

Drinking too much fluid in the evening will cause a full bladder during sleep. This will be relayed as discomfort to the nervous system. It will also cause you to get up during the night to relieve the bladder, resulting in broken sleep. Broken sleep disturbs the sleep cycle, resulting in your not waking up fresh.

Certain drinks, such as alcohol, coffee and tea, are what we call diuretics; that is, they stimulate the flow of urine. Try to avoid these drinks in the evening as much as possible.

Aerobic Exercise

Aerobic exercise, such as jogging and brisk walking, has a very positive effect on deep sleep. Firstly, the circulation to the brain's sleep centre is increased, thereby increasing the amount of nutrients and oxygen to the centre. Secondly, exercise releases stress, so the mind is relaxed for sleep. Early evening exercise is especially beneficial, since it releases the whole day's stress and produces a pleasant relaxing fatigue. This will induce a good night's sleep.

Studies have shown that less sleep is required when you are fit. You'll need at least half an hour less sleep a day. This will more than pay for the time it takes to exercise. Of course there are many other benefits of being fit which are discussed later.

Never exercise less than one hour before sleep, since the initial effect of exercise is stimulation, which will prevent you getting to sleep.

Aerobic exercise increases the blood supply to the brain's sleep centre. If done in the early evening, it also helps to release the whole day's stress, resulting in deeper sleep.

Yoga Exercises for Deep Sleep

There are two yoga exercises which have a positive effect on sleep. Since yoga works specifically on the nervous system and in particular on the brain, it's not surprising that it has a pronounced effect on sleep. The two exercises are the headstand and the spinal rocking exercise. Don't worry if you can't do the headstand, since the spinal rocking exercise is very effective on its own. It is best to do this exercise just before sleep. The headstand can be done any time during the day since its effect on the brain will last all day. Both exercises are described on pages 123–127.

The headstand works because an increase in blood is supplied to the brain's sleep centre. This nourishes the centre, correcting its functioning and normalising the sleep cycle.

The rocking exercise described on page 123 works by massaging the spinal joints and the muscles surrounding the spine. Since the spine is part of the central nervous system, this relaxes the whole nervous system. It will also correct minor displacements in the spine. So you're giving yourself a free spinal manipulation as well as improving your sleep. This exercise only takes about one minute.

There are two specific yoga exercises which will promote deep sleep.

Don't Retire too Late

Our sleep centre, and therefore our sleep cycle, is still programmed as it was thousands of years ago when we went to bed at sunset. As a result, the early hours of the night produce the greatest rejuvenation.

The best quality sleep is that taken between the hours of sunset and midnight. Our sleep centre, and therefore our sleep cycle, is still programmed as it was thousands of years ago, when we went to bed at sunset. The hours closest to sunset, that is, the early hours of the evening, produce the greatest rest and rejuvenation to the nervous system and the rest of the body.

By going to bed earlier, you can rise earlier. This is also an advantage, since the best hours for outdoor activities, such as work, exercise or reading, are the first few hours after the sun rises. The yogis state this is the optimum time for absorbing vitality (prana) from the air. This is the ideal time to do the deep breathing exercises.

So, if you go to bed late, not only do you lose high quality sleep, but also you can't get up early to take advantage of absorbing optimum vitality. This means you won't possess a high vitality level and you will age earlier than you should. It's a high price to pay for staying awake an extra hour or so in the evening, instead of rising earlier in the morning. Try to get to bed by 10 p.m., and then you can also rise earlier. You'll get much more done in the early morning, since your energy should be at an optimum level and you have fewer distractions, such as the phone ringing and other people moving around the house.

A good way to think about it is that by retiring early, you're getting *free* energy the next day.

Fresh Air in the Bedroom

The sleep centre requires a good supply of fresh air to function efficiently, so leave your bedroom windows open while you sleep.

Make sure your windows are open while you are sleeping. The sleep centre in the brain operates better when it has a fresh oxygen supply. If the windows are closed, there will be a build-up of stale air in the bedroom. The stale air consists mainly of carbon dioxide, the waste gas we are exhaling all the time. The carbon dioxide will tend to displace the dwindling supply of oxygen in the room.

The brain is a very greedy organ when it comes to oxygen. It demands more oxygen than any other organ in the body, and it will not function at its optimum level if the oxygen supply is reduced. This will cause you to wake up not feeling fresh.

Also, keep any *plants* away from the bed area. In the evening, plants give out carbon dioxide, which is what you don't want.

Firm Bed

For a good night's sleep your bed needs to be firm. You should also turn the mattress around from head to foot every two weeks to prevent sagging.

A firm bed gives a better night's sleep. Also, a bed which sags is detrimental to your back.

If your bed is nor firm and you don't feel like buying a new bed, just put a wooden board in between the base and the mattress.

About every two weeks (perhaps when you change the sheets), you should *turn the mattress around* from head to foot. This allows a more even distribution of weight on the mattress, instead of the same heavy weight of the pelvis on the same area of the bed. If you don't do this, the bed will sag where the pelvis lies every night.

In my practice, patients frequently ask me about *waterbeds*. There is nothing wrong with waterbeds, as long as they are filled almost to the top with water. Most people don't put enough water in, causing the bed to sag. This is bad for the back and you won't get a good night's sleep. In fact, if correctly filled, waterbeds are good for sleep and the back, since water distributes the pressure of the body evenly.

Position of the Bed

Surprisingly enough, this has an effect on a certain proportion of people. The yogis say the head should face north, since this aligns the body correctly with the earth's electromagnetic field. In one study which I am aware of, placing the bed in this position was found to cure insomnia in six out of ten people. Perhaps this only works on 'sensitive' people, or perhaps the people it doesn't work on need to correct other sleep factors as well.

> Facing the head of the bed north can help insomnia.

Hot Bath

This is an old-time favourite for relaxing before sleep. It really works, since the heat relaxes the muscles, which in turn *relaxes the mind*. This is an example of the body-mind relationship, in which one affects the other.

Don't have the water too hot, since this is enervating to the nervous system.

Putting bath salts in the water may make the bath more pleasant, but has no physiological effect on relaxing the muscles.

> The old-fashioned hot bath before bed really works.

Autosuggestion

If you have been sleeping badly for some time, your mind can convince itself to expect sleepless nights. This is an example of negative suggestion. It occurs at the subconscious level, and is therefore best corrected at this level.

The way to communicate with your subconscious mind is by autosuggestion. Just before sleep you are slightly drowsy; that is, your conscious mind is turning off. This is the ideal time to use autosuggestion, since there is no interference from the conscious mind. You are actually in a *natural hypnotic trance*. Any suggestion made at this time will go straight through to your subconscious mind without any interference from the conscious mind.

Here is the technique. When you are comfortable and relaxed in bed, just repeat silently to yourself several times:

'I'm falling into a deep, deep sleep. When I wake up, I will feel very fresh.'

> Just before you fall asleep you are in a natural hypnotic trance. This is the ideal time to use autosuggestion for deep sleep.

Repeat this positive suggestion to yourself *very slowly* and in the same tone, since this assists the trance state. With practice it will work.

Don't wait until you are falling asleep to repeat the suggestion, since you will most likely fall asleep before you even start.

Sleep Herbs

If you carry out all the above sleep factors, you shouldn't need to take any special sleep preparation. But you may need a little temporary help until your new sleep habits start working. Also, there are times when we have extra stress, and a herbal sleep formula will ensure that you get a good night's sleep.

Sleep herbs are safe and effective, but it's still best to use them only temporarily and not get into the habit of relying on them permanently. It's always best to find and remove the basic cause of poor sleep.

Sleep herbs are not habit forming, and do not have side effects, unlike sleep drugs. I suggest you stay away from sleeping pills, since they disturb the normal sleep cycle and produce a drugged sleep. This means you won't wake up fresh. Also, when stopped, your sleep will be worse.

There are several excellent herbal sleep preparations in health shops. Make sure the preparation contains the following herbs:

Valerian

Passiflora

Skullcap

Vervain

Herbs work gently and subtly and therefore may take a week or so to show effect. I suggest you take the preparation for at least a month to establish normal sleep.

Chamomile tea will also help produce a good night's sleep. Only drink half a cup, otherwise you may have to get up during the night, and that would defeat the purpose.

A herbal sleep preparation is useful until your new sleep habits start working or during periods of extra stress. Unlike sleeping pills, herbal preparations are not habit forming and have no side effects.

How to Dissolve Tension Before Sleep

Feeling tense before sleep will prevent deep sleep. There are three very effective ways of eliminating this tension:

1   Take a short walk and do some slow deep breathing while you are walking.
2   Take a hot bath.
3   Do the sleep relaxation exercise described on pages 162–163. The above will make you feel so relaxed that you'll probably fall asleep within a few minutes and sleep very deeply.

Sleep and Chiropractic

If your sleep is still not 100 percent satisfactory after applying the relevant sleep factors, I would suggest you visit a chiropractor. I have personally successfully treated thousands of cases of sleep problems using chiropractic. The effects are usually immediate and dramatic.

There are three reasons why chiropractic works in cases of poor sleep.

1 Deep sleep depends to a large extent on the muscles and the mind being relaxed. For muscles to be relaxed they must receive a normal nerve supply. If there is a misalignment in the spine (which often causes no pain), it will cause pressure on the nerve at the site of the misalignment. This in turn causes excessive nerve impulses to the particular muscles that nerve supplies. The result is *tension* in those muscles. Also, since there is a nerve connection from the muscles to the brain, the muscle tension will create a general feeling of mental tension or anxiety. This muscle and mental tension prevents deep sleep.
2 A spinal misalignment in the neck (again, there may be no pain) causes pressure on the nerves and blood vessels in the neck. Since these nerves and blood vessels travel to the brain, it means there is an interference to the brain's nerve and blood supply resulting in poor sleep.
3 If you suffer from *pain* in the neck, back, shoulders or legs, etc. this will also reduce the depth and possibly the duration of your sleep. Chiropractic would be the preferred means of treatment, since it removes the cause of the pain. Drugs tend to treat only the effects (symptoms), and are therefore delaying proper treatment. This means the condition is getting worse without you knowing about it, since the drugs are only masking the condition.

Chiropractic treatment often produces immediate and dramatic improvements to sleep.

What About Sleeping Pills?

If you are taking sleeping pills don't go off them immediately. Wait about one month to allow the programme in this book to work for you. Even after that, reduce them gradually over a period of about a month. This is necessary because complete and sudden withdrawal will cause more severe insomnia than before, due to withdrawal symptoms. During the month in which you are gradually reducing the drug, take a natural herbal preparation.

It's important to get off sleeping drugs, since tolerance eventually develops to the drugs. This means you will need to increase the dosage or change to a new drug. Also, these drugs have a detrimental effect on the brain's biochemistry, leading to even worse sleep problems. In the past, many sleeping pills contained barbiturates which produced serious side effects such as dramatic mood changes. The more modern sleeping drugs, the benzodiazepines, do not produce a hangover, but they

Sleeping pills produce a drugged, unrestful sleep. They are also addictive and produce side effects.

can be habit forming or addictive in as little as ten to fourteen days. Long-term use can lead to depression and other psychological symptoms.

At best, sleeping drugs treat the symptoms and not the cause of poor sleep, so they are really only sweeping the dirt under the carpet. It's better to carry out the sleep factors, since they treat the cause and have no side effects.

If You are Taking Other Drug Medication

Some medical drugs used for other conditions can produce side effects which affect sleep. For example, beta blocker drugs, used for high blood pressure, can reduce the quality of sleep. In most conditions it is better to correct your lifestyle, as directed in this book, and then gradually withdraw from the drugs. Do this in co-operation with your doctor, who can monitor the dosage. It must be kept in mind that the drugs are not curing the high blood pressure, they are merely treating the symptoms. In effect they are turning off the burglar alarm, since high blood pressure is nature's warning sign that something is wrong with the system.

Highlights

1 Deep sleep has the greatest direct effect on vitality and rejuvenation. During deep sleep, nature restores and heals the body. The nervous system, including the brain, is given a rest, and the body is recharged with energy.

2 Adults require between seven and nine hours sleep a night. If you carry out the deep sleep factors in this chapter, especially the nutritional and exercise factors, you will be able to reduce your sleep time by a half to one hour after a few months. Oversleeping causes physical and mental sluggishness.

3 Deep sleep depends upon good nourishment, good circulation and normal nerve supply to the sleep centre in the brain.

4 The deep sleep factors are:
  (a) *Good nutrition* (see pages 58–98). Reduce your sugar intake, especially in the evening.
  (b) *Coffee and alcohol.* Eliminate or reduce them in the evening.
  (c) *The evening meal* must be light and emphasise vegetables.
  (d) *Drink less fluid in the evening.*
  (e) Aerobic exercise such as jogging or brisk walking is especially beneficial if done in the early evening. Don't exercise less than one hour before sleep.
  (f) *Specific exercises for deep sleep.* These are the headstand (page 125) and the spinal rocking exercise (page 123). Don't worry if you can't do the headstand, since the spinal rocking exercise is very effective on its own.
  (g) *Don't retire too late.* The early hours of the evening produce the greatest rest and rejuvenation to the nervous system and the rest of the body.
  (h) *Keep the bedroom windows open.*
  (i) *Firm bed.* Rotate the mattress head to foot, about every two weeks.
  (j) *Position of the bed.* Some people get improved sleep when the bed faces north.
  (k) *Hot bath.* Very relaxing. It's most effective just before sleep.
  (l) Autosuggestion. Repeat the following silently to yourself several times: 'I'm falling into a deep, deep sleep. When I wake up, I will feel very fresh.' Repeat it very slowly and in the same tone.
  (m) *Sleep herbs.* These are safe and effective. It's best to use them as a temporary help until the other sleep factors start working, or during periods of extra stress.
  (n) *Chiropractic.* If you're still not sleeping deeply and waking up fresh, visit a chiro-practor to see if a spinal misalignment is the cause of your problem. Neck misalignments are a common cause of poor sleep, and may not be suspected since pain is often not present.

Nutrition for Reversing Ageing: The Basics

Introduction

The object of this chapter is to present the facts on nutrition and to simplify the subject. A practical approach is taken, so you can incorporate these facts immediately into your daily nutritional programme. You are shown how to achieve optimum nutrition without having to sacrifice the enjoyment of food. It is important to enjoy your food since this stimulates the secretion of saliva which is essential for good digestion. To be too restrictive with your diet is also bad for you psychologically, causing you to worry too much about food and make you feel that you are missing out.

Our diet is not really our own choice. It is conditioned by our parents and by society in general, and it is usually not the optimum diet for health and rejuvenation. We should really base our diet on scientific principles, since this will result in maximum vitality and rejuvenation. With the knowledge available today, we can do this.

Why Nutrition is Important for Rejuvenation

Rejuvenation depends upon a healthy nervous system (brain and spine), healthy glands and organs, fat-free arteries, a digestive tract which is free from putrefaction, and richly oxygenated cells. To obtain all this, you must supply all these tissues with adequate high-quality nutrients with a minimum of toxins.

The Four Secrets of Nutrition

I EAT SLOWLY
This causes a more thorough breakdown of the food, resulting in the release of more nutrients and hence better nourishment.

2 EMPHASISE RAW FOOD
Raw food such as fruit, salad, bean sprouts and raw nuts should make up about 70 percent of your total diet. Raw foods have no nutrient loss from processing and heating. If you eat raw food, it also follows that you will be eating less processed food, sugar and fat.

3 HAVE A BALANCED DIET
About 50 percent of your diet should consist of fruit since it is nourishing, easily digested and produces no toxins in the body. Vegetables and whole grains should comprise about 20 percent each, and high protein foods about 10 percent. Fat will take care of itself, since all foods contain some fat and we need very little.

About 50 percent of your diet should consist of fruit, since it is the most nourishing food, it produces no toxins and its digestion wastes virtually no energy.

4 REDUCE FAT AND SUGAR INTAKE
We consume far too much fat and sugar. Excess fat causes reduced blood flow to all parts of the body, resulting in disease and premature ageing. Especially reduce the saturated fats such as meat and dairy products. Excess sugar results in fatigue and sugar metabolic diseases and is converted to fat by the body, causing even more problems.

If you follow the above four recommendations your health and vitality will improve and you will look younger. In addition, you will lose excess weight since you will be better nourished and this will activate the brain to reduce your appetite. These recommendations will also prevent overeating, a major cause of premature ageing.

Excess fat and sugar cause premature ageing.

Processed Foods and Premature Ageing

Eating a lot of processed foods causes degenerative diseases and premature ageing.

Many of our degenerative diseases such as heart disease, cancer, strokes, high blood pressure, arthritis and dental decay are mainly due to the processing of natural foods, since much of their nutritional value is destroyed and they are loaded with harmful chemicals. These degenerative diseases are a major cause of premature ageing. Most fast foods are highly processed and contain a lot of fat, sugar and chemicals – a perfect recipe for premature ageing and chronic fatigue.

The processing of foods involves heating and the addition of chemical additives, which are discussed below.

1 HEATING FOODS
Heating destroys the enzymes – the life-promoting part of the food. This is done to ensure longer shelf life – no self-respecting weevil or other bug would want to eat dead food!

Food processing destroys 100 percent of the enzymes, the 'life force' of food, and involves more than 3000 chemicals.

2 CHEMICAL ADDITIVES
More than 3000 different chemicals are now used in food processing. They are used to create artificial flavours, colours and textures and as appetite stimulants. The latter is particularly bad since it leads to overeating processed foods and an addiction to them.

How to Reduce Processed Foods
1 Replace most of the processed foods you eat with fresh fruits, vegetables and wholegrain products.
2 Replace white bread with wholemeal bread.
3 Don't peel your potatoes, since the peel contains most of the nutrients, and cook them in their jackets.
4 When cooking, replace salt, pepper and spices such as M.S.G. with natural flavours from garlic, onions, herbs and lemon juice.

Optimum Food Combination

Incorrect food combination can lead to incomplete digestion, reducing the nourishment extracted from the food and to fatigue, because less energy is provided by the incompletely digested food.

There's no need for complicated rules on food combination. Food should be for enjoyment as well as for nourishment. Just follow the two simple rules below for optimum nourishment from the food you eat, and don't worry if you break the rules occasionally.

Optimum food combination is simple – just follow the two rules.

The Two Major Food Combination Rules

1   THE FEWER DIFFERENT FOODS EATEN AT ONE MEAL, THE BETTER
Eating a lot of different foods at one meal puts a big demand on the digestive system, resulting in reduced digestion, reduced nourishment and the formation of toxins. Also, different food groups require different enzymes to break the food down, and if too many enzymes are present, they may have an inhibiting effect on each other.

2   EAT FRUIT ON ITS OWN
This is for the following reasons:

- If fruit is mixed with other food, less nourishment will be extracted from it. This is particularly important since fruit is the most nutritious food.
- Fruit eliminates toxins from the body. This important function is very much impaired if other foods are eaten with it.
- Certain types of fruit don't mix well with other foods; for example, citrus fruits because they are acidic.

Other Vital Information

Salt
Salt is not a food, but rather a harmful chemical (sodium chloride). Contrary to popular opinion, it's not necessary to include salt in your diet. It cannot be digested or assimilated by the body and has no nutritional value. The body's salt requirements are very low and are satisfied by the salt in natural foods, especially vegetables.

Salt is harmful because it's a major cause of high blood pressure, it causes incomplete digestion of protein foods by inhibiting the secretion of a protein-digestion enzyme called pepsin and it causes irritability of the nervous system.

Salt is a harmful chemical and a major cause of high blood pressure.

To reduce your salt intake, stop adding salt to your food and reduce your processed food intake, since this contains a lot of salt. Check the labels on supermarket food.

Since salt deadens the taste buds, when you do reduce your salt intake you'll find that your taste buds will eventually enjoy the natural subtle flavours of food without salt.

Other Spices

It's best to use other spices, such as pepper, mustard and pickles, in moderation since they irritate the lining of the digestive system.

Replace spices with natural seasonings such as lemon juice, onions, garlic, other herbs or chilli, which has been found to have beneficial health properties such as increasing your metabolism, hence helping in weight control.

Milk and Milk Products

Commercially bought milk is highly processed, difficult to digest, mucus-forming and a contributor to respiratory problems.

Contrary to popular belief, milk is in fact a highly processed food. Milk and milk products should be used in moderation because they are difficult to digest (pasteurisation alters the structure of the sugar, lactose, and the protein, casein); mucus forming, which causes respiratory problems; and contain saturated fats.

Replace at least part of your cow's milk intake with soya milk and reduce your butter, cheese and cream intake. Yogurt is one of the better milk products, since the bacteria in it have partially digested the sugar and protein.

Fibre

THE HEALTH BENEFITS OF FIBRE
1 Fibre reduces your cholesterol level by mechanically and chemically removing the cholesterol from your intestines. The fibre in soya beans and oat bran is especially effective.
2 Fibre reduces blood pressure.
3 Fibre reduces heart disease by reducing cholesterol and blood pressure.
4 Fibre is necessary for bowel regularity and has been shown to help prevent cancer of the colon.
5 Fibre helps to regulate your blood sugar levels. This helps to prevent mood swings, obesity and diabetes.
6 Fibre assists in weight control. Fibrous foods hold water, creating bulk, and so fill up the stomach and make you feel satisfied.

THE BEST SOURCES OF FIBRE

All unrefined complex carbohydrates are good sources of fibre. These include fruit, vegetables and whole grains such as wholemeal bread and cereals. There is no need to put bran on your food, just include plenty of the above foods. This way you're getting fibre in the correct proportion to other nutrients and eating nutritious food at the same time.

The Fallacy of the Big Breakfast for Energy

Eating a large breakfast is one of the worst things you can do for your health and for reversing ageing, for the following reasons:

1 Early morning is when the body eliminates most of its toxins, but if most of the body's energy is being used for digestion instead of toxin elimination, a toxic build-up will occur.
2 The energy wasted on digesting a large breakfast will result in fatigue.
3 Because a large breakfast produces fatigue, many people drink coffee at breakfast time to give them a boost. This makes things worse, since coffee works by drawing on your already depleted energy reserves.

A big breakfast is detrimental to health and to reversing ageing.

Cooking Methods

Try to avoid boiling foods because this destroys most of the water-soluble vitamins and minerals, as well as the flavour. It's best to steam – using stainless steel cookware – or to microwave foods.

Alcohol

Alcohol is a very harmful drug unless it is used in strict moderation. If you wanted a recipe for brain damage, alcohol would be hard to beat. This is because alcohol not only kills brain cells, but also has a special affinity for the brain. Since the brain is the main centre for rejuvenation, it's especially important to be extremely moderate.

Excess alcohol is an ideal recipe for brain damage.

Alcohol does most damage when you go on a binge. Just one binge causes measurable permanent brain damage. Most of us have done this in the past, but now we have the scientific facts, there is no excuse to do it in the future.

To make drinking alcohol safer, eat some food beforehand so that alcohol will be absorbed more slowly, and intersperse alcoholic drinks with non-alcoholic ones.

The Effects of Aerobic Exercise on Nutrition

Exercises such as jogging, brisk walking and aerobics will increase the blood circulation to all parts of your body, including your digestive glands and organs. When

Aerobic exercise
results in increased
assimilation of
nutrients, reduction of
appetite and
conversion of fat to
muscle.

your digestive system is working better, you get better assimilation of food nutrients.

Aerobic exercise will also reduce your appetite and turn some of your excess fat into muscle, making you healthier and younger-looking.

Drinking Water

The importance of water is appreciated when we consider that our blood is 85 percent water and our brain 30 percent water.

How much water should be drink? The answer is very simple: drink when you are thirsty. Thirst is the body's way of telling you that it needs water. I also suggest that you drink one glass of water when you get up in the morning, preferably with a lemon squeezed in it. This helps the body eliminate toxins and also puts you in a positive water balance for the day.

Drink water only
when you are thirsty.
Fruits contain the
purest water and are
loaded with health-
promoting minerals.

Most of your water intake should come from fruits. Fruits contain the purest water and are loaded with health-producing minerals. Most books on health recommend six to eight glasses of water a day, but this is only relevant to the average person who eats a lot of meat, salty foods and not much fruit. They need the water to eliminate the waste products of meat and to reduce the salt concentration of the blood.

It is inadvisable to drink water ice-cold, since this causes irritation to the mouth and digestive tract as well as inhibiting the action of the digestive juices.

A Model Nutritional Proramme

There are two main considerations in producing a good diet:

1 IT SHOULD BE BASED ON SCIENTIFIC PRINCIPLES TO GIVE MAXIMUM NOURISHMENT

Avoid extreme diets, since they are detrimental to health and cause premature ageing.

2 KEEP IT SIMPLE

If you follow the general programme below, there will be no need to worry about counting calories, correct food combinations or the ideal proportions of the different food groups (fruits, vegetable, grain and protein). This detracts from the enjoyment of food and complicates life.

Breakfast

EARLY MORNING: FRUIT

Melons or oranges are excellent, since they clean the body out, or you may prefer fruit salad – you can include some canned fruit, but make most of it fresh.

LATER MORNING: CEREAL

Only if you have time and if you enjoy cereals. Make sure it's a wholemeal cereal and use soya milk rather than cow's milk. Use honey as a sweetener.

Lunch

SANDWICHES

Have salad-based sandwiches, or you may find banana sandwiches tasty – this way you'll be increasing your fruit intake and it's low fat. There's no need to butter your bread, since banana gives a smooth texture on its own. Banana and bread also make an ideal combination, since they are both carbohydrates.

Evening Meal

HIGH-PROTEIN FOOD AND VEGETABLES

High-protein foods include fish, meat, cheese, eggs, nuts, beans and soya bean products. Eat meat in moderation – fish is far healthier.

Vegetables should include salad, since raw food is more nutritious. Vegetables should be cooked by microwave, steaming or quick stir frying, since boiling destroys most of the nutrients.

Snacks and Tea Breaks

Fruit is best. Fruit snacks will help to bring your fruit intake close to the ideal 50 percent of your total diet.

Highlights

1 **Avoid extreme diets**. Base your diet on scientific principles.

2 **The four secrets of nutrition**. Eat slowly, emphasise raw food, have a balanced diet and reduce your fat and sugar intake.

3 **Processed foods and premature ageing**. Processing foods involves heating which destroys all the enzymes (the life of the food) and adding chemicals.

4 **How to reduce processed foods**. Replace canned food with fresh food, replace white bread with wholemeal bread and don't peel potatoes. Frozen food is better than canned food.

5 **Overeating**. This is a major cause of premature ageing. Prevent it by eating more nourishing food, eating slowly, spreading your food intake over several small meals and doing aerobic type exercise.

6 **Optimum food combination**. The two basic rules are to eat fewer different types of food at one meal and eat fruit on its own.

7 **Salt**. Salt causes high blood pressure, incomplete digestion of proteins and irritability of the nervous system. Reduce your salt intake by not adding salt to food and eating fewer processed foods.

8 **Other spices**. Replace pepper, mustard and pickles with natural seasonings such as lemon juice, onions, garlic and chilli.

9 **Milk and milk products**. Milk is processed by pasteurisation. Use it in moderation, since it's difficult to digest and highly mucus forming and it contains saturated fats. Replace it, at least in part, with soya milk. Yogurt is okay.

10 **Fibre**. Fibre reduces blood pressure, cholesterol and heart disease. The best source are fruits, vegetables and whole grain products.

11 **Don't eat a big breakfast**. This causes fatigue and toxins.

12 **Cooking methods**. Microwave or steam – don't boil.

13 **Alcohol**. In excess it causes brain damage. If you drink, eat food beforehand and alternate with non-alcoholic drinks.

14 **Aerobic exercise**. This results in increased nourishment and reduced appetite and turns fat into muscle.

15 **Drinking water**. Drink when you are thirsty and eat plenty of fruits, since fruit contains the most pure and mineral-rich water.

Nutrition for Reversing Ageing: The Details

Fruit: The Ideal Food

How Humans are Ideally Adapted to Eat Fruit

Human beings have several anatomical and physiological features which indicate that fruit is the most natural food for them; for example:

Fruit is the ideal food for human beings.

1 The colour, smell and taste of fruit is naturally attractive to us and its sweetness satisfies our natural desire for sweet foods.
2 Our digestive system, from the jaw and teeth structure to the length of the digestive tract, is ideally suited for eating fruit.
3 The human body cannot make vitamin C so we must ingest it in food. The only food with a high level of vitamin C is fruit.

Comparative studies of people eating diets restricted to one food group, such as fruit, grains or protein food, show that those on the fruit diet were the healthiest.

Why Fruit Reverses Ageing and Promotes Vitality

1 Fruit contains all the vitamins, minerals, carbohydrates and most of the protein and fat the body needs.
2 The digestion of fruit requires less energy than that of other food. In fact it requires virtually no energy, while at the same time fruit sugar (fructose) releases a lot of energy. You end up with a big net energy gain resulting in increased vitality.
3 Fruit is very low in fat so, if fruit represents around 50 percent of your total diet, your total fat intake is at a very safe level, decreasing the risk of heart disease, stroke and cancer. Fruit is obviously an ideal slimmer's food for this reason too.
4 Fruit eaten on its own eliminates toxins from the body. This effect is strongest if fruit is eaten between about 6 a.m. and 11 a.m. since this coincides with the

Eating fruit produces a large net energy gain, resulting in increased vitality.

body's eliminative cycle. To get the maximum benefit don't eat other food for about one hour after eating fruit in the mornings (You may drink freshly made fruit juices or carrot juice).

5 Fruit promotes healing because of its high nutritional value, its ability to eliminate toxins and its high contribution of energy. Some scientists believe that fruit has other, as yet undetected, factors which stimulate the body's own healing forces.

How Much Fruit Should We Eat?

Fruit is so important for vitality and reversing ageing that it should comprise up to 50 percent of your total diet.

Eat fruit early in the morning to take advantage of its toxin elimination effect, and wait for about one hour before eating other foods such as breakfast cereals.

Fruit is also ideal at morning and afternoon tea breaks, and for snacks at any time during the day.

Grains

Unrefined grains such as wholemeal bread, pasta, cereals and rice are an important source of nutrients and dietary fibre. Also, like fruit, they are complex carbohydrates and therefore provide an efficient and sustained energy supply.

Unrefined or Refined Grains?

Unrefined grains are superior since they contain more nutrients and fibre. Excessively refined grains such as white bread can eventually cause constipation and increase your chances of getting bowel cancer. Always buy wholemeal bread, preferably made from stoneground wholemeal flour.

Eat brown rather than white rice. When the outer husk is removed to produce white rice, the grain loses one third of its calcium content and about half of all other nutrients.

Why Grains are Important

1 Grains contain most of the vitamins and are especially rich in vitamin A, B and E.
2 Grains are a potent source of minerals, especially of calcium, phosphorous, magnesium, iron and zinc. The high phosphorous content is important since it's an important component of brain tissue, and fruit and vegetables are a poor source of phosphorous.
3 Grains are a good source of high-quality protein.

4   Grains promote age reversal by virtue of their rich supply of vitamin B and E, essential fatty acids and lecithin, which allows the body's tissues to better use oxygen. This also provides good protection against heart disease.

Grains promote age reversal by virtue of their high nutrient content.

Why Grains Should Only be Eaten in Moderation

Although grains are an important part of the diet, they should not be eaten in excess for the following reasons:

1   Most grains are acidic and produce an acidic state in the tissues and blood. In excess this promotes premature ageing and predisposes the body to certain diseases such as arthritis. The bones of ancient Egyptian mummies have been found to be riddled with arthritis and the ancient Egyptians were big bread eaters. The common cold virus and many other pathogens cannot survive in a non-acidic (alkaline) medium, which is produced by eating fruit and vegetables.
2   Grains are relatively hard to digest. This wastes a lot of the body's energy.
3   Grains need to be cooked, since they are hard to digest, and heating food destroys the enzymes – the life of the food – as well as vitamins and minerals.

Which Grains are Best?

Oats (as oatmeal porridge and muesli) and rice are preferable to wheat, since wheat is more difficult to digest and is quite a common allergy food. Oats are very nutritious and have healing properties – they are a nerve strengthener and reduce cholesterol levels.

Oats and rice are the two best grains.

Rice is also very nutritious and less acid forming than both wheat and oats.

This does not imply that you should never eat wheat products, but try to include some oats and rice in your diet at least once a week.

Sprouted Grains

Sprouted grains are far more nutritious than unsprouted, as their carbo-hydrate, protein and vitamin B content increases significantly. In addition, sprouted grains lose the acid-forming properties and instead produce a beneficial alkaline state in the body.

How to Ensure Your Grains are Fresh

Grains can spoil relatively easily and to prevent this take the precautions of buying grains only from shops with a fast turnover and storing them in airtight containers.

In summary, eat whole-grain products in moderate quantities. If you included grains in one of your daily meals, that would be adequate.

Protein: Where We've Gone Wrong

Proteins are the basic building blocks from which the body is made up. They maintain the body's continuing process of reconstruction and repair to keep bones, muscles and other tissues healthy. In fact everything, from the colour of our hair to our inherited talents, is determined by the way our bodies are genetically programmed to make proteins.

Proteins also make up the enzymes which act as catalysts for all the chemical reactions in the body. Some of the body's hormones, such as insulin, are also proteins. Proteins in the blood also contain antibodies which form the spearhead of the body's defence against infection.

We are making two basic mistakes with our protein intake; we are eating too much and too much of the wrong kind of protein.

The Harmful Effects of too Much Protein

Our excessive protein intake causes reduced fitness and contributes to arthritis, heart disease and strokes.

We eat too much protein for two main reasons. Firstly, the myth still exists that a lot of protein, especially meat, makes you strong and healthy. Secondly, we are now a more affluent society and can therefore afford to buy more meat and other high-protein foods. Here's why too much protein is detrimental to health.

1   The amino acids in excess protein are converted by the liver to fat. During this process nitrogen is released, which is eventually excreted in the urine. This puts stress on the kidneys.
2   One of the byproducts of protein metabolism is uric acid, a toxin. If excess protein is eaten, some of the uric acid is deposited in body tissues. This is a common cause of arthritis in the joints.
3   A high-protein diet causes reduced physical endurance for work and sports. This has been proved by many researchers, including Dr Irvine Fisher, whose research on a group of athletes found that when their protein intake was reduced by 20 percent there was a 33 percent increase in endurance. The explanation for this is that the excess uric acid has a toxic, paralysing effect on muscles and nerves.
4   High-protein diets can cause biochemical imbalances in the body and may produce vitamin B deficiency.
5   A high-protein diet is a common cause of heart disease and strokes, since most of our protein comes from meat with its high fat content. Studies have shown that a low-protein, mainly vegetarian diet, can prevent 97 percent of coronary heart disease.
6   Protein digestion requires more energy that any other food, so high-protein diets waste energy.

The Harmful Effects of the Wrong Type of Protein

The mistake we make here is to get far too much of our protein from animal sources such as meat and milk. Not only is vegetable protein of a higher quality than animal protein, but good health can be maintained on a smaller amount of it. This reduces cost, wastes less energy in digestion and creates fewer toxins.

Protein from vegetable sources such as soya milk, vegetables, lentils and nuts is superior to protein from animal sources for the following reasons.

1 Animal protein sources such as meat, eggs and milk create toxins in the body.
2 Vegetable proteins are easier to digest than animal proteins.
3 Many vegetable protein sources, such as nuts and salad, can be eaten raw. Raw food has a higher quantity of protein and other nutrients than cooked food.
4 Research has shown that a diet high in animal protein causes premature ageing. This is due to animal proteins, especially meat, producing toxins and acidity in the tissues, intestinal putrefaction and degeneration of the vital organs.

Diets high in animal protein such as meat and dairy products cause premature ageing.

The Best Non-Animal Protein Foods

1 Soya milk is a high-protein food which is also very nutritious, low fat and high fibre. You can use soya milk on your cereal, for milk shakes and whenever milk is required in a recipe. You can now buy soya milk in cartons in supermarkets.
2 Raw nuts are a rich source of protein and very nutritious. They mix well with raisins or sultanas and are ideal as an energy snack.
3 Legumes include foods such as beans, peas and lentils. Carob is a tasty, nutritious legume which makes a good chocolate substitute and can be bought in health shops.

The best non-animal protein foods are soya milk, raw nuts and legumes.

How Much Protein do We Need?

Most researchers recommend a daily protein intake of 30–40 grams. Many of us have around twice this much. Government health bodies tend to recommend around 56 grams a day, but this figure is based on incorrect superseded data and is not compatible with maximum health and age reversal.

If you do strenuous exercise, are under a lot of stress or are sick, you will need extra protein – about 50 grams a day. Try to get most of this from vegetable sources.

One advantage of obtaining some of your protein from vegetable sources is that you will need less protein than if all your protein came from animal sources.

Frequently Asked Questions About Protein

WHY DO WE ONLY NEED A LITTLE HIGH PROTEIN FOOD?
1 All food, including fruits, vegetables and grains, contains some protein.
2 The body stores protein reserves in the blood cells which can be drawn upon if a shortage occurs. This means it's not essential to eat high-protein foods such as meat every day.
3 The body can recycle some protein from the waste products of protein metabolism.

HOW DO I KNOW IF I'M GETTING SUFFICIENT PROTEIN?
As a rule of thumb, make one meal a day high in protein. For most people this is the evening meal, when they have some fish, meat or a vegetable protein dish.

IF I CUT DOWN ON MEAT CAN I GET SUFFICIENT PROTEIN?
The answer is definitely yes. Firstly, you need less protein than is commonly believed. Secondly, some vegetable foods contain more protein than does meat. For example raw nuts have twice the protein content of meat and soya beans contain more protein than prime beef. Another interesting fact is that the protein in potatoes is of a higher quality than the protein in meat, eggs or milk.

The Truth About Meat

Four Misconceptions About Meat

The strongest animals in the world eat no meat.

1 SINCE WE EAT MEAT EVERY DAY IT MUST BE GOOD FOR US, OR AT LEAST A NECESSARY PART OF OUR DIET
In reality all the research shows that meat reduces our health and fitness level as well as accelerating the ageing process.

2 MEAT MAKES US STRONG, SINCE WILD ANIMALS EAT MEAT AND THEY ARE VERY POWERFUL
The fact is that the strongest animals – elephants, horses, oxen and water buffalo, for example – all eat no meat. These animals also have the greatest endurance and live the longest.

The world's top boxers now refrain from eating meat for several days before a big fight, since it's been discovered that this helps them to perform better. Eating a lot of meat before a fight can cause boxers to become 'punch-drunk'.

3 WE REQUIRE ANIMAL PROTEIN FOR ENERGY

In fact our energy comes from fats and carbohydrates found in vegetables, fruits and grains.

4 AREN'T WE DESIGNED TO BE MEAT EATERS?

Although we are historically omnivorous (both plant and meat eating), our anatomical equipment – teeth, jaws and digestive systems – favours a diet of plant food. For much of human history people have subsisted on near-vegetarian diets and many in the world still live that way. The love affair with meat is less than one hundred years old – a result of the affluence of the 20th century.

Our love affair with meat is less than 100 years old.

Proof that Humans are not Designed to Eat Meat

1 Carnivores have long sharp teeth and their jaws move up and down only, for tearing and biting. We have molars and can move our jaws from side to side for grinding. Unlike carnivores, we have no strong claws for tearing meat.
2 A carnivore's saliva is acid so that it can digest animal protein. Human saliva is alkaline and contains ptyalin, an enzyme which digests carbohydrates.
3 A carnivore's stomach secretes ten times more hydrochloric acid, vital for animal-protein digestion, than the human stomach.
4 A carnivore's intestines are short, designed for the rapid processing of flesh which would otherwise rot. The very long human intestines are designed to process food for a long time. This is why, when we eat meat, putrefaction occurs. Our bodies are simply not designed to eat meat.
5 The liver of a carnivore can eliminate ten to fifteen times more uric acid, the waste product of animal protein metabolism, than the human liver. People who eat a lot of meat tend to suffer from chronic fatigue, arthritis and other conditions, due to the accumulation of uric acid in their bodies.

Our excessive meat consumption results in reduced health and fitness, fatigue, premature ageing and eventual disease.

Why Meat Should be Eaten in Strict Moderation

1 Because our long intestines are not designed to cope with meat, eating it causes intestinal putrefaction. That is, meat begins to rot in your intestines, releasing toxins into the whole body. This results in fatigue, premature ageing and eventually disease.
2 Meat itself contains a lot of toxins. Meat is animal muscle and muscle contains uric acid, a waste product of muscle metabolism.
3 About thirty-eight chemicals are pumped into meat to make it look and smell nice. Some of these chemicals are addictive and cause us to become addicted to meat. Keep in mind that meat is rotting flesh, and without chemicals added, the stench would be so overwhelming that no one would ever buy it. So we end up

Meat is rotting flesh and, without the thirty-eight preservative chemicals added, its stench would be so overwhelming that no one would buy it.

eating a rotting corpse and dangerous chemicals. Do you ever wonder why cancer is striking more and more people down in the prime of life?

4 Drugs such as arsenic, penicillin and stilbesterol are fed to animals and deposit in the muscle. We ingest these drugs when we eat meat. Stilboestrol has been shown to cause cancer, heart failure and reduced libido in males.

5 Meat contains a high level of pesticides from the spraying of animal fodder.

6 Animals often carry diseases which can be passed on to us when we eat meat. Farm animals contract an unusually high number of diseases due to over-population and a stressful environment. For example there are at least twenty-six diseases that we can pick up from poultry. Meat is also often found to contain worms and even malignant tumours. Cooking doesn't always destroy the worms and even when the tumours are cut away, the cancer is still in the system.

7 Meat does not rate very highly as a nutritious food. It's nutritionally unbalanced, containing excess protein but virtually no complex carbohydrates, fibre or calcium, and there are many vitamins missing. Since animals obtain their nourishment from vegetables and grains, when we eat meat we are getting our nutrients secondhand. These second-hand nutrients are lower in quantity and quality and constitute a more expensive way of obtaining nourishment.

One study showed that when meat was eliminated from the diet for one year, the body increased its oxygen intake by 39 percent and its blood flow by 50 percent.

8 Many research projects have confirmed that regular meat eating reduces your fitness. One study showed that when meat was eliminated from the diet for one year, the body increased its oxygen intake by an average of 38 percent and its blood flow by 50 percent. Top athletes now avoid meat, especially when doing intensive training.

As a further bonus, if you reduce your meat intake, you will become slimmer. A test group of 116 vegetarians weighed on average 15 kilograms less than a comparable meat-eating group. This is because vegetables are more nutritious and filling, so you eat less.

9 Excessive meat eating has been shown to contribute to mental and emotional imbalance. This is because meat contains adrenalin (stress hormone), toxins, chemicals and pesticides – all of which adversely affect our brains.

How to Reduce Some of the Harmful Effects of Eating Meat

Buy only lean red meat and free-range poultry.

Eat only lean red meats. Ask your butcher for lean meat and cut off any visible fat. Cook the meat on a suspended rack in your oven so that the fat will drop off.

Buy free-range poultry which are not fed chemicals and have more room to move around.

Conclusion

Eating meat causes premature ageing, reduces your fitness and is a major cause of diseases such as cancer, heart disease and stroke.

I'm not saying you should give up meat completely, unless you really want to. Why give up dishes you really enjoy? In any case the body can tolerate small abuses, especially if you are in good health from following the other health principles in this book.

What I do recommend is that you reduce your meat intake, since eating a large portion of meat every day is a major assault on the body. Replace some of your meat dishes with fish, eggs and other non-meat protein dishes. Try making Chinese dishes which consist mainly of vegetables with a few prawns or small pieces of meat for flavouring.

If you have trouble reducing meat, try reminding yourself before you buy it that it is the rotting flesh of a corpse which would look and smell terrible if it wasn't for the thirty-eight chemicals pumped into it!

Fats: The Good and Bad Fats

Fat's Vital Role
Fats have many important functions to play in the body and are vital for survival and good health. Fats form part of the wall surrounding every body cell. The body uses fat to insulate it against cold, as a shock absorber around bones and organs, to insulate nerves, to lubricate the skin, to help transport certain vitamins and as a reserve supply of energy.

Because of these vital functions, it is not advisable to go on extreme fat-reduction diets, as is suggested by some authors.

The Good Fats
As well as being nourishing, unsaturated fats have many health benefits, including the ability to lower blood cholesterol levels. Unsaturated fats are from two sources: vegetable oils (except for coconut and palm oil, which are saturated) and cold-water fish oils.

Monounsaturated Fats and Polyunsaturated Fats: Which are Best?
Nutritionists have been telling us for years that polyunsaturated fats are better for health, but recent research has shown this to be incorrect. Polyunsaturated fats can combine in the body with oxygen to form destructive free radicals, a major cause of premature ageing. Always use monounsaturated vegetable oils.

Monounsaturated oils such as corn oil and olive oil are healthier than poly-unsaturated oils.

Vegetable Oils

Corn oil is the best oil to use for frying.

The two best oils to use in your kitchen are corn oil for frying and olive oil for salad dressing. This selection is based on health benefits, taste and suitability. They are both monounsaturated and relatively unprocessed.

Even though vegetable oils have health benefits, I recommend that they be used in moderation for frying. This is because, being processed, they contain chemicals and cooking can make them carcinogenic if temperatures are high enough. (Therefore avoid deep frying, cook food for as short a time as possible and microwave or steam rather than frying.)

Since oils become rancid if exposed to sunlight, store your oil in the fridge or at least in a dark area.

Olive Oil

Olive oil is the king of oils – it is a potent factor in age reversal and the promotion of health.

This is the king of oils and deserves special mention. Research has now confirmed what Mediterranean people always knew – that olive oil is highly beneficial for health and helps you to stay young.

Olive oil is a rich source of the most active form of vitamin E, the alpha form which is a potent antioxidant. As an antioxidant it destroys free radicals and helps to reverse ageing. Studies also show that olive oil causes marked falls in blood cholesterol.

Use olive oil as a salad dressing or just take one tablespoon a day.

Olive oil helps to keep the arteries supple and contains the major fatty acid present in the oil of the skin glands. This accounts for Mediterranean people having smooth, slightly oily skin and shiny hair which remains dark for most of their lives.

Add to this the facts that olive oil is monounsaturated, can be purchased unprocessed (look for 'cold pressed' on the label) and is used unheated in salad dressing or on its own and you have a very powerful health promoter and age reverser.

If you can afford it, buy extra-virgin olive oil, since the vital antioxidants are preserved to give the oil maximum biological value. It's even better if it's been 'cold pressed'.

Cold-Water Fish Oil

The cold water fish include tuna, sardines, salmon, mackerel, red schnapper and whiting.

The body converts this oil into omega-3 fatty acids. It is these which produce the health benefits.

Omega-3 fatty acids reduce the level of fats and cholesterol in the body, as well as reducing the tendency of blood to clot. They are therefore useful in preventing and curing heart disease.

The fact that Eskimos have a diet high in cold-water fish explains why they have almost no heart disease.

The Bad Fats: The Saturated Fats

These are the animal fats, such as those in meat, dairy products and coconut and palm oil.

Highly processed oils are also saturated. This includes margarine, lard (used in frying fish and chips) and commercially prepared salad oil and mayonnaise.

About 99 percent of our fat comes from saturated fat sources. No wonder about half of all deaths are due to cardiovascular (heart and blood vessel) disease.

Why We Should Reduce Our Saturated Fat Intake

In general, we consume far too much saturated fat. About 40 percent of our diet is fat when it should be about half this amount. This has serious effects on our health, rate of ageing and lifespan.

A high fat intake is dangerous because fat lines the walls of the arteries and causes circulation to slow down. If the blood flow to the heart is reduced sufficiently, heart disease and eventually a heart attack may occur. If blood flow to the brain is reduced sufficiently, a stroke may occur. A long time before any disease shows itself, these organs will suffer gradually reduced function, resulting in declining health and premature ageing.

All your other tissues and organs are also affected by reduced blood circulation. This means your vision and hearing will deteriorate, your sex glands will work less efficiently and your joints will become increasingly arthritic. In other words you will age like the rest of the population. This ageing process can be reversed if you restore normal blood circulation to the tissues by adopting the principles in this book. The next section shows how you can reduce your saturated fat levels to help restore normal circulation.

How to Reduce Your Saturated Fat Levels

There are two main ways of achieving this:

1 Eat fewer foods high in saturated fats, especially such foods as meat, dairy products, margarine and fried foods. Read the labels on supermarket foods, since they often contain hidden fats. There is no need to be extreme and give up all high fat foods, just work at reducing your fat intake.

   You will also need to reduce your sugar intake, since excess sugar in the body is converted to triglyceride, a type of fat.
2 Aerobic exercise such as jogging and brisk walking will help to burn up some of your fat – both externally and, more importantly, inside your arteries. This type of exercise also increases the circulation to all parts of the body, further reversing the ageing process.

To reduce your saturated fat levels, eat less meat, dairy products, margarine and fried foods and do aerobic exercise.

Cholesterol – The Latest Research

Cholesterol is a fatty substance which has very important functions in the body. It is essential in the formation of cell membranes, nerve sheaths, vitamin D, sex hormones and as part of our defence against infection.

Cholesterol: the problem

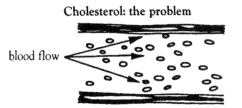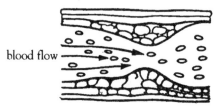

This silent killer turns healthy arteries into diseased arteries, reducing blood flow and increasing the risk of heart attack, stroke, angina, kidney failure, poor vision, lameness, gangrene and impaired sexual function in males.

Raised blood cholesterol levels are a major contributing factor in the development of 'hardening of the arteries' (arteriosclerosis).

Dietary Cholesterol is not the Problem

Cholesterol in food is not the problem; it is food high in animal fats which causes high cholesterol levels.

The latest research shows that cholesterol-rich food does not cause an increase in blood cholesterol levels. If dietary cholesterol is too high, then the liver makes less; if dietary cholesterol is too low, the liver makes more.

The Real Problem and Solution

The latest research shows that the real problem is twofold.

1 What does cause an increase in blood cholesterol is food high in saturated fat. So you need to cut down on foods such as meat, dairy products and fast foods. This effect is greater in males than females, so men have to be particularly careful with their saturated fat intake.
2 Part of the body's defence is to fight excess cholesterol; but a side effect of this is the production of free radicals. These free radicals build up as a plaque in the arterial wall, causing reduced blood flow to the heart and other organs.
3 Antioxidants such as vitamins A, C and E destroy these free radicals. It is best to get these vitamins from natural sources: vitamin A from green and yellow vegetables; vitamin C from fruits; and vitamin E from wholegrain foods and unsaturated oils.

Cholesterol-Lowering Drugs – Beware!

These drugs only lower the 'good' cholesterol produced by the body and not the 'bad' dietary saturated fat. Several studies have shown that while these drugs do slightly reduce the incidence of coronary heart disease, people taking them have a higher death rate from other factors such as suicide, homicide and car accidents.

Butter or Margarine?

BUTTER

Butter's main drawback is that it contains mostly saturated fat. As well as all the other bad effects of these fats, they can concentrate pesticides about five to ten times more effectively than vegetable oils. On the positive side, butter is relatively stable to light, heat and oxygen compared with vegetable oils. It's also easily digested and pleasant to taste.

Neither butter nor margarine are conducive to health or reversing ageing. Butter is the better choice but use it in moderation.

MARGARINE

Although margarine is advertised as high in essential polyunsaturated oils, these oils have been changed in the manufacturing process to become harmful and may contribute to cardiovascular disease. Margarine may also contain a number of additives, such as antioxidants, colouring, emulsifiers and flavourings, including M.S.G.

So which is best – butter or margarine? In terms of health, neither scores well. In terms of taste, digestibility and lack of synthetic processing, butter comes out in front easily. The only advantage of margarine over butter is that it's cheaper and spreads better. Don't use margarine in the belief that it's better for slimming or for your heart – it's no better than butter.

Whichever you choose, use it in moderation, since both contain high levels of saturated fats.

Sugar: Not a Sweet Story

It's natural to have a sweet-tooth – nature provided this so that we would be attracted to fruits! The problem is that we have perverted nature's design by eating concentrated, processed sugar, both on its own and in processed food.

Sugar is empty calories and studies show that excess consumption causes disease.

In western countries the average person eats one kilogram of sugar per week, or twenty-one teaspoons a day. This will certainly cause fatigue and mood swings and in many people it will eventually lead to diseases such as hypoglycaemia, diabetes, dental caries and obesity. Concentrated sugar can be described as empty calories which have a drug-like effect on the body.

What is Sugar?

When people talk about sugar, they are usually referring to sucrose, the most commonly used sweetener in households and food manufacture. It's also the most common sugar found in the plant kingdom and is obtained from sugar cane and sugar beet. Sugar from both sources is chemically the same.

From being a rarity in 1650 and a luxury in 1750, sugar became a virtual necessity by 1850. Since the turn of the century, sugar consumption has increased sixfold. Although consumption of sugar as a refined food has declined over the past forty years, presumably due to increased awareness of the need for a healthy diet, our consumption of sugar hidden in processed foods has risen by the same amount, so we are no better off.

It's easy to see why our sugar consumption is so high when we look at the sugar content of some popular foods and drinks. Just one can of soft drink, for example, contains about ten teaspoons of sugar, as does one slice of rich chocolate cake. One serving of ice-cream contains about six teaspoons of sugar.

The average person eats twenty-one teaspoons of sugar a day. Just one can of soft drink contains about ten teaspoons of sugar.

White, Brown and Raw Sugar

Raw sugar is coarse crystals obtained from the evaporation of clarified sugar cane juice. Brown sugar consists of raw sugar crystals coated with molasses syrup, which provides natural flavour and colour components. White sugar is made by dissolving the raw sugar crystals, removing impurities and crystallising the purified syrup.

Contrary to the view of some nutritionists, experiments show that raw and brown sugar have a significantly higher nutritional value than white sugar.

What's Wrong with Excess Sugar?

1 It causes diseases. Studies show there is a definite link between a high sugar consumption and disease. Our consumption of sugar has risen alarmingly over the past 200 years, and many diseases such as coronary heart disease and diabetes have become more common over the same period.

    Studies also show a link between sugar and obesity, dental caries, hyperactivity in children and fatigue.
2 It causes glycation, a reaction between the sugar and protein in your body. This process has been implicated in a number of diseases, such as eye cataracts, as well as in premature ageing.
3 It causes loss of vitamin B. Vitamin B is necessary for the digestion of sugar. The body depletes its storage of vitamin B to digest sugar, which contains none. Excess sugar also depletes the body's calcium supply.

How Excess Sugar Causes Problems

Excess sugar overworks the pancreas, causing it to lose some of its efficiency. The pancreas will begin to produce either too much or too little insulin. If it produces too little in response to high levels of blood sugar, diabetes is the result. If it produces too much insulin, then blood sugar levels are taken below the point where the brain can easily function. This is called hypoglycaemia.

Hypoglycaemia is now so widespread that it affects 10 percent of the population. Some of the common symptoms are feeling tired when you wake up, feeling weak if you miss meals and craving sweet things.

When you consider the typical day of the average person, you can understand why hypoglycaemia is so common. First there is a breakfast on the run of coffee or tea with sugar, and perhaps a sugary cereal. Driving to work is stressful and stress, like coffee, stimulates the adrenal glands to produce a rapid release of sugar. Then come the coffee-biscuit work breaks. Often there is a drink or two after work or with your evening meal, and alcohol has a very high sugar content. Then if you have a dessert the high sugar content further stresses your pancreas.

The result of excess sugar, coffee, alcohol and stress is hypoglycaemia and adrenal exhaustion. The situation is made worse since hypoglycaemia creates a craving for sweet things and a quick fix of coffee or alcohol.

The solution is to remove the cause – restrict all sugars, including honey, dried fruit and fruit juice, and reduce coffee and alcohol. It's also best to eat five or six small meals daily and to emphasise complex carbohydrates.

Hypoglycaemia now affects 10 percent of the population. Typical symptoms are feeling tired when you wake up, feeling weak if you miss meals and craving sweet things.

How to Reduce Your Sugar Intake

1   Read the ingredients on processed and packaged foods. The largest portion of sugar consumed is now hidden in processed foods and drinks bought from fast food outlets, supermarkets and bakeries.
2   Reduce the amount of sugar you add to food at the table, such as on cereals and in drinks.
3   Reduce your intake of foods with a high sugar content, such as sweets, cakes, soft drinks and alcohol.
4   Replace sugar with the sweet alternatives below.

Most sugar consumption is now hidden in processed foods and soft drinks.

The Sweet Alternatives

If, like me, you have a sweet tooth, there is no need to give up sweet things – there are several healthy sweet foods available. Also, indulging in your favourite sugar foods occasionally, for example on the weekend, will not cause any major problems.

If you have diabetes or hypoglycaemia, you should stay away from sugar and the sweet alternatives.

HONEY

Since much commercial honey is blended, heated, filtered and gathered from sugar-fed bees, it's best to buy your honey from a health shop or a beekeeper. Unrefined honey contains pollen and small amounts of vitamins, minerals and enzymes.

You can use honey in your tea, coffee, cakes and cookies and, since it is about twice as sweet as sugar, you will need only half the quantity. Honey gives food a pleasant taste, keeps your cakes moist and is a natural preservative. Use honey in moderation however, since it is made up of about 80 percent sugar.

CAROB

Carob is a natural sweetener with a chocolate taste. It is very nutritious, containing the B-group vitamins, vitamin A, vitamin D, phosphorus, magnesium, potassium, silicon, iron, some trace minerals, and three times as much calcium as milk. Carob is also rich in protein. It can be bought from health shops, either as solid chocolate (sugar free) or in powder form. It contains none of cocoa's harmful irritants and can be substituted wherever chocolate is required.

FRUCTOSE

Sweeter than sugar, fructose is the sugar which occurs naturally in fruit, vegetables and honey. It is far superior to commercial sugar (sucrose) since it does not rob the body of its mineral reserves or affect insulin production. It can be bought from health shops in packet form.

OTHER ALTERNATIVES

Other natural sweeteners which can be used are molasses, barley malt extract, concentrated apple juice, coconut and dried fruits such as dates, figs, sultanas and raisins.

Enzymes and Energy

What are Enzymes?

Enzymes are the body's catalysts. They speed up and make possible all the chemical activity in the body, indeed they speed up some chemical reactions several thousand-fold. They are essential for certain vital processes such as digestion, growth and reproduction, and they allow energy to be produced very rapidly.

Enzymes are present in every cell. There are over 600 enzymes in the body, each one with a different vital function.

Carob is a natural chocolate alternative and extremely nutritious. It contains three times as much calcium as milk.

The Discovery of Enzymes

The ancient Greek Pythagoras knew that raw food contained some factor which was not present in cooked food. He recommended raw fruits, raw goats' milk and unheated honey as ideal foods and medicines. In more recent time, a young Swiss physician called Dr. Bricher-Banner proved that powerful health-promoting curative factors in raw foods were destroyed by heating or processing. About forty years later, this was confirmed by scientists.

The Vital Functions of Enzymes

1   They are responsible for our body characteristics. The genes in the sex cells create enzymes which will determine a characteristic or an inherited trait in the new life to be.
2   They break down food into energy and living cells. Enzymes are very efficient. Without them food digested in three to six hours would take thirty years to release its energy.
3   Vitamins and minerals can only work in the presence of enzymes.
4   They are essential for autolysis; this is self-digestion of dead and diseased cells and their replacement with healthy cells.
4   They cause increased oxygenation of the body tissues; in fact, without enzymes oxygenation could not occur and we would quickly die.
5   They help in fighting disease, healing wounds and counteracting the adverse effects of drugs.

Enzymes are vital to survival and reversing ageing. They speed up some chemical reactions several thousandfold and vitamins and minerals cannot work without them.

The Source of Our Enzymes is Raw Food

The body makes only enough enzymes to keep ticking over. To have a high vitality level and reverse ageing, you need to tap the rich supply of enzymes which only exist in raw food. Cooking, canning and processing of foods destroys the enzymes they contain. Pasteurisation of milk also destroys the enzymes. Wet heat is especially destructive, to enzymes, so I suggest you use a microwave oven as much as possible, since it produces a dry heat and the cooking time is minimal.

The Rejuvenating Effects of a 70 Percent Raw Food Diet

1   It reverses ageing. The skin becomes tighter, resulting in fewer wrinkles and a natural face lift. The eyes become brighter and clearer, and the hair becomes thicker and more shiny. Greying hair starts to retain its natural colour. A high raw food diet is the most potent age reverser.
2   You become slimmer – the safe natural way. This is because raw food is very nourishing, low in calories and causes more efficient fat metabolism.

A diet high in raw food is the most potent factor in age reversal because of its rich supply of enzymes.

3 Improvement in brain function. Since the brain is better nourished, thinking becomes clearer, memory improves and you become calmer.

The Effect of Raw Food on Disease

It's important to prevent disease, since disease will accelerate the ageing process. Wild animals which eat only raw food do not get sick, but if they are put in a zoo and given cooked, processed food, they will become sick. Primitive people, such as the Hunzas and certain African tribes who eat mostly raw food, do not get the degenerative diseases of civilisation.

Raw food prevents and cures diseases by virtue of its enzyme content, its wide variety and abundance of nutrients, its low fat/sugar content and its ability to eliminate toxins.

Recent studies have shown that a diet high in raw food is effective in the treatment of sugar metabolic diseases such as hypoglycaemia and borderline diabetes, as well as for ulcers, obesity and even cancer – especially if the diet is high in carrot juice and foods containing chlorophyll, such as sprouts and wheatgerm.

Raw food is a very potent remedy for chronic fatigue. In one study of patients with chronic fatigue, about 80 percent were found to be deficient in potassium and magnesium. These patients were put on a diet high in raw food and most reported a considerable increase in their energy levels.

How to Increase Your Enzyme Intake

1 Include more raw food in your diet. This is the most effective way. It's not difficult to make around 70 percent of your diet raw – just eat more fruit (breakfast, tea breaks and snacks); have a big salad every day with fresh bean sprouts; make a glass of fresh carrot juice every day, and have some raw nuts for snacks or dessert. Fruits and sprouted foods (grains, seeds and beans) are the best sources of enzymes.
2 Eat more fresh foods. If you eat a lot of fruit, salad and bean sprouts, you are getting a lot of fresh food already. Buy fresh bean sprouts and keep them in the fridge. Buy frozen food in preference to canned food, since freezing does not destroy the enzymes, it only inactivates them. Canned food is heated, which destroys the enzymes.
3 Eat slowly. This causes better digestion of your food, resulting in the release of more enzymes.

Why Raw Juices?

1 Most of the nutrients are in the juice. To get the same amount of nutrients as are in one glass of carrot juice, for example, you would have to eat about

Raw food is a very effective remedy for chronic fatigue.

Try to make about 70 percent of your diet raw – fruit, salad, bean sprouts, raw nuts and carrot juice.

Canned food is 'dead' food, since heating has destroyed 100 percent of the enzymes.

three large carrots, which you are not likely to do. The juice is much pleasanter.
2 Juices eliminate toxins from the body faster than the whole fruit or vegetable.
3 Juices put less strain on the digestive system and require less energy for digestion. This means that the nutrients are assimilated better and there is a larger net energy gain.

Since juices are such a potent vitality and age-reversing factor, you may ask, why not eat all our fruits as juices? The reason is that the whole fruit or vegetable contains valuable fibre, which is essential for good health. Also, juices contain concentrated sugar, which if taken in excess, could lead to sugar metabolic disorders.

Why Fresh Juices?

Juices should be freshly prepared and drunk immediately to prevent loss of precious enzymes. As an example, orange juice loses one third of its enzymes after half an hour, and all of them after two hours.

The Two Best Juices

1 Lemon juice is the most effective for eliminating toxins. It's best drunk when you get up in the morning, at the time of the body's natural eliminative cycle. Just squeeze a lemon into a glass of water and don't eat or drink anything for at least half an hour after this.
2 Carrot juice is the most nourishing juice and also a powerful eliminator of toxins. The optimum time to drink this is about half to one hour after the lemon juice. Not only is this the best time to eliminate toxins, but also the body will extract maximum nourishment from the carrot juice, since there is no interference from other food. If you are pushed from time in the early morning, have your carrot juice half an hour or so before your evening meal.

Lemon juice is the most effective for eliminating toxins, while carrot juice is the most nourishing.

Ideally, about half an hour or so after your carrot juice, you should have some fruit for breakfast. Nutritionally, this is the best start to the day you could possibly have. You will feel alive all day and be rejuvenating yourself at the same time.

Carrot juice has a very important role to play in rejuvenation due to its high concentration of beta carotene. Your body converts the beta carotene into vitamin A, which, as an antioxidant, is so essential for the reversal of ageing.

The Magic of Sprouts

Of all the best vegetables, sprouts are the richest source of vitamins, minerals and enzymes. By a process of natural transmutation, sprouted food has a much greater nutrient content than the original food, as well as being easier to digest. For example when oats are sprouted, the vitamin B content increases by 1000 percent. When wheat is sprouted, the total vitamin content increases by 300 percent. Similarly when mung beans (bean shoots) are sprouted, the vitamin B content increases up to 500 percent and the vitamin A content by 200 percent.

The Best Sprouts to Eat

The best sprouts to eat, from a nutritional and taste point of view, are alfalfa and mung beans (bean shoots). Fortunately, both these sprouts can now be bought at supermarkets and fruit shops.

Highlights

Fruit – The Ideal Food

1 Fruit is the best food for reversing ageing and vitality because it is the most nutritious, it requires less energy to digest, it is low in fat, it eliminates toxins from the body and it has healing properties.
2 Up to 50 percent of our total diet should consist of fruit. Eat it early in the morning, at tea breaks and for snacks.

Grains

1 Unrefined grains are more nutritious than refined grains.
2 Grains are important because they are a rich source of vitamins, minerals, protein and lecithin which promotes age reversal.
3 Grains should only be eaten in moderation because they are acidic, hard to digest and need to be cooked.
4 Oats and rice are the best grains to eat.

5 Sprouted grains are more nutritious.
6 Ensure grains are fresh by buying from a shop with a high turnover and storing in airtight containers.

Protein: Where We've Gone Wrong

1 Protein is important because it is the body's basic building block, responsible for growth and repair, and it makes up the body's enzymes and some hormones.
2 Too much protein is harmful. Protein should only make up about 10 percent of our total food intake.
3 Replace part of your animal protein intake with vegetable protein such as soya milk, lentils (beans, peas, carob) and nuts. A diet high in animal protein causes premature ageing.
4 How much protein do we need? One high protein dish a day is sufficient.

The Truth About Meat

1 Humans are not anatomically,

physio-logically or biochemically designed to eat meat.

2 Meat should be eaten in strict moderation because it causes intestinal putrefaction, contains toxins, drugs, pesticides, can be contaminated with animal diseases, reduces fitness and can contribute to mental and emotional imbalance.

3 Reduce some of the harmful effects of eating meat by eating only lean red meats and buying free-range poultry, at least some of the time.

The Good Fats and the Bad Fats

1 Fats have many vital functions in the body, so don't go on extreme fat-reduction diets.

2 The unsaturated fats are the vegetable oils (except coconut and palm oils) and cold-water fish oil.

3 The saturated fats are the animal fats, such as those in meat, eggs, dairy products and highly processed oils (margarine, lard, commercial salad oil and mayonnaise).

4 Reduce your saturated fat intake because saturated fats reduce blood flow to the heart, brain and all tissues, resulting in premature ageing. To reduce your intake eat less meat, dairy products, margarine and fried foods and do aerobic type exercise.

5 To reduce blood cholesterol levels you need to eat less saturated fat and more foods high in antioxidants (vitamins A, C and E).

6 Butter and margarine are both bad for health, butter being slightly better. Use in moderation.

Sugar – Not a Sweet Story

1 Raw and brown sugar are more nutritious than white sugar. What's wrong with sugar? It causes disease – diabetes, hypo-glycaemia, cataracts, loss of vitamin B, and premature ageing.

2 Reduce your sugar intake by reducing processed foods, sugar added to food, sweets, cakes and soft drinks, and finally replace sugar with the sweet alternatives.

3 The sweet alternatives are honey, carob, fructose, molasses, barley malt extract, coconut and dried fruit.

Enzymes and Energy

1 Enzymes are essential for vitality and reversing ageing. Even vitamins will not work without enzymes.

2 The source of our enzymes is raw food. Processing, boiling and canning food destroys the enzymes. Cooking by microwave is the best way.

3 A 70 percent raw food diet reverses ageing, makes you slimmer and improves brain function.

4 Increase your enzyme intake by eating more raw and fresh foods and by eating more slowly.

5 Drink raw juices because most of the nutrients are in the juice, and because it eliminates toxins quickly and requires little energy for digestion.

6 The two best juices are lemon and carrot. Drink lemon juice first things in the morning and eat nothing for half an hour.

7 Sprouted food is very rich in nutrients. The two best are alfalfa and mung beans (bean shoots).

The Rejuvenation Foods and Supplements

The Rejuvenation Foods

In essence, all raw, fresh foods are rejuvenation foods, since they are a concentrated source of nutrients, especially enzymes, the life force of foods.

There are certain other foods which, by virtue of their contents, have a rejuvenating effect. These foods are discussed below.

Seafood

Fish has less toxins than meat and contains Omega-3 fats which lower blood cholesterol.

Seafood's rejuvenating effects are due to its rich supply of the following nutrients.

1. High-quality protein. Fish is a high-protein food which contains much fewer toxins than meat.
2. Good fats. Fish contains the omega-3 fats which actually lower your blood cholesterol level, resulting in younger, healthier arteries. This means your whole body becomes younger.
3. High mineral content. Fish eat seaweed, which has a very high mineral content. Fish is particularly high in calcium and iodine. Calcium is necessary to keep your bones young and iodine for normal thyroid gland function. The thyroid governs body metabolism, including fat metabolism, and therefore is important for weight control.

Try to eat fish at least twice a week. This will also help to reduce your meat intake. If you fry fish, try to use only a little oil.

Soya Milk

All soya bean products are beneficial to health, but soya milk is the tastiest and most versatile, since it can replace cow's milk on cereals and in recipes.

The soya bean is the most nutritious and easily digested food of the bean family, and has been used in China for 5000 years as a food and a component of medicines. Economically it is the most important bean in the world, providing vegetable protein for millions of people. It's one of the richest and cheapest sources of protein there is, since its yield of protein per hectare is nearly ten times that of chickens and almost thirteen times that of cattle.

WHY SOYA MILK IS SUPERIOR TO COW'S MILK

1 Soya milk is easier to digest. Pasteurisation of cow's milk alters the structure of the sugar (lactose) and the protein (casein), making it difficult to digest.
2 Cow's milk is highly mucous-forming in humans. Excess mucous in the body acts like a toxin and becomes an ideal medium for pathogens such as bacteria. This causes catarrh, colds and coughing and tends to lead to respiratory problems such as asthma.
3 Cow's milk contains saturated fats. Soya milk, being derived from a plant product, contains unsaturated fats and no cholesterol.
4 Soya milk is the best natural source of lecithin. Lecithin is an essential nutrient for health, vitality and rejuvenation.

    Lecithin has the following important functions: it is the main nutrient in brain nerve tissue and semen; it's vital in the structure of cell membranes; it's a natural emulsifier of fats and therefore prevents cholesterol build-up; it reverses hardening of the arteries, resulting in younger arteries; and it's a good source of the rejuvenating vitamin E and two B vitamins (choline and inositol), which slow down the ageing process.

Soya milk is now available in supermarkets.

> Soya milk is far superior to cow's milk.

Yogurt

Yogurt is milk fermented by bacteria called *Lactobacillus acidophilus*. Unlike plain milk, yogurt is not mucus forming since the bacteria break down the sugar and protein, making it easier to digest.

    Yogurt has been one of the principal foods of the Bulgarians for a long time, and is considered by many to be largely responsible for their unusual health, vigour and longevity.

THE REJUVENATING EFFECTS OF YOGURT

1 It prevents putrefaction in the large intestine. Yogurt causes an increase in the beneficial bacteria and a reduction in the harmful bacteria in the intestine. It's the harmful bacteria which produce putrefaction, causing poisons to be absorbed into the body.

Yogurt contains 35 percent more protein and 100 percent more calcium than milk and is far less mucous-forming.

Aspects of modern lifestyle such as smoking, excess alcohol, rich diets, stress and antibiotics can destroy the beneficial bacteria in the intestines. Eating yogurt helps to replace them.

2 It is far more nutritious than milk. Yogurt contains 35 percent more protein and 100 percent more calcium than milk.
3 The beneficial bacteria in yogurt help in producing vitamin B.
4 Yogurt heals stomach ulcers by neutralising excess hydrochloric acid in the stomach.

Eggs

Eggs have anti-ageing properties, including reducing wrinkles and increasing virility.

1 Eggs are a highly nutritious food with the following rejuvenating benefits.
2 They are rich in protein, vitamins and minerals, in particular vitamin B and iron.
3 They contain the amino acid cysteine, which reduces ageing, including wrinkles.
4 They increase virility due to the combination of cysteine and vitamin B.
5 They are rich in lecithin, which feeds your brain, nervous system and glands, the centres of rejuvenation. Lecithin also neutralises some of the cholesterol in eggs.

One survey of people in their eighties who displayed a high level of mental ability and an active sex life showed that all ate eggs daily. I would still advise moderation – about six eggs a week, due to the high saturated fat levels in eggs.

Broccoli

Nutritionists call broccoli 'the lean green nutrition machine'.

Broccoli is the most nutritious member of the cabbage family. One serving of fresh broccoli (55g/2oz) gives you about 90 percent of your daily requirements of vitamin A, 20 percent of vitamin C and 25 percent of fibre. It's also rich in vitamin B, calcium, phosphorous, potassium and iron. All this and only forty-five calories! No wonder broccoli is called the 'lean green nutrition machine'.

Broccoli has also been shown to give protection against certain forms of cancer.

Oats

Of all the grains, oats are the most valuable for rejuvenation and have been the staple diet of some of the hardiest races, such as the Scottish highlanders. They are extremely nutritious, containing rich supplies of protein, polyunsaturated fats, vitamins E and B, calcium, potassium and magnesium.

Oats possess potent therapeutic properties, such as reducing blood cholesterol, reducing blood pressure, normalising sugar metabolism and acting as a tonic for the nervous system. In one study eleven out of twenty diabetic men eating 100 grams of oat bran each daily stopped needing insulin shots. The tranquillising effect of oats is so powerful that some health practitioners are using it to wean people off addictive tranquillising drugs.

Raw Nuts

Nuts, like seeds, are tomorrow's plants and trees, so nature ensures that they are a very concentrated nutrient and energy source. They provide high-quality vegetarian protein, carbohydrates, vitamins, minerals and essential oils.

Nuts are high in fat content – some as high as 60 percent – but this fat is polyunsaturated and actually assists in lowering cholesterol levels as well as being beneficial to the brain and nervous system.

The almond is the king of nuts, being rich in protein, fat and vital minerals like zinc, magnesium, potassium and iron, as well as some B vitamins. Weight for weight, almonds have a third more protein than eggs.

Pine nuts have the highest protein level of any nut and make a tasty garnish for vegetarian dishes and salads, while hazelnuts have the lowest fat content of all the nuts. Brazil nuts are particularly rich in vitamin B_1 and magnesium.

Peanuts are really legumes. They are rich in protein and iron, but should be eaten in moderation, since their very high fat content could lead to weight problems.

Raw nuts can be hard to digest for many people. Years of faulty lifestyle has made our digestive system far from 100 percent efficient. For this reason, I strongly recommend that you eat ground nuts to ensure maximum assimilation of the nutrients and prevention of any digestive problems.

You can eat ground nuts on their own or in the form of nut butters or nut milks. Both are delicious and extremely nourishing, as well as being great favourites with children. Nuts can be ground in a coffee grinder. This is more nutritious than supermarket peanut butter, which usually contains a lot of salt, emulsifiers and preservatives. Nut butter can be used as a healthy spread and as a sauce for vegetables. To make nut milk, just soak almonds or cashews in warm water for one or two hours, pound them and then mix with water in a blender. This nut milk can be used whenever milk is required.

Because of their high fat content, nuts go rancid quite easily once shelled, and then they are a health hazard. Buy nuts in the shell where possible, store unshelled nuts in airtight containers in the fridge and eat them soon.

Olive Oil

Make sure you include this 'King of oils' in your diet.

Honey

Try to buy unprocessed honey from a health shop or a beekeeper, since processing removes the pollen and it is the pollen which gives honey its rejuvenation properties. In practice, it's more convenient to use supermarket honey as a sweetener and buy pollen from the health shop. Just sprinkle the pollen on your cereal, salad or whatever.

Nuts are tomorrow's plants, so they are a very concentrated source of nutrients and energy.

The almond is the king of nuts and contains a third more protein per weight than eggs.

Raw nuts can be hard to digest, so eat them ground for better assimilation.

Pollen increases vitality and stimulates the sex glands. Since pollen has been removed from honey during processing, buy your pollen separately from the health shop.

Pollen-rich honey has the following rejuvenating effects:

1 Increased vitality due to honey's pollen and fruit sugar.
2 It stimulates the sex glands. Pollen is the male germ cell of plants, and it secretes a hormone which stimulates the sex glands.
3 It is a germicide. Bacteria cannot survive in the presence of honey.
4 Honey has other medicinal properties; for example it is a mild laxative and sedative and it improves muscle tone and digestion.

Spices

There are three well-known spices which have rejuvenation effects: chilli, hot peppers and ginger.

CHILLI

1 It is rich in vitamins, minerals and enzymes.
2 It stimulates the circulation.
3 It assists digestion by stimulating the production of hydrochloric acid in the stomach.
4 It helps slimming by increasing the metabolic rate. Just a little chilli burns up to 70 calories.

Chilli, as well as being nutritious and stimulating the circulation, is an ideal slimmer's food since it speeds up the metabolic rate.

HOT PEPPERS

Red and yellow peppers contain four times more vitamin C than oranges do. Research has shown that capsicum (the active ingredient of hot peppers) breaks down blood clots.

GINGER

Ginger is used in about half of all Chinese herbal medicines. It has the following rejuvenation benefits:

Ginger is used in about half of all Chinese herbal medicines.

1 It stimulates the immune system.
2 It's an antioxidant.
3 It reduces cholesterol levels and blood clots.
4 It kills bacteria and fungi.

The Rejuvenation Fruits
While all fruits have rejuvenating effects, there are a few which deserve special mention.

1 **Apples**. Apples contain pectin which helps reduce cholesterol levels and protects us from pollution by binding to heavy metals like lead or mercury in the body and carrying them safely out. Apples are powerful detoxifiers, assist digestive problems and have antiseptic properties – many viruses cannot survive in apple juice. there seems to be some truth in the old expression 'an apple a day keeps the doctor away'.

> The saying 'an apple a day keeps the doctor away' has scientific validation.

2 **Avocados**. Avocados are almost a complete food, containing protein, carbohydrates, monounsaturated fats (the good ones), potassium and vitamins A, B, C and E. They are particularly rich in potassium, a deficiency of which can cause fatigue, depression and poor digestion, and have been shown to assist with stress and sexual problems.

   Studies show that avocados can reverse the ageing of skin. Substances in the pulp of avocados trigger DNA to produce more embryonal collagen – the type we start our lives with, producing smooth and wrinkle-free skins. In addition the vitamins A, C and E in avocados are antioxidants which destroy free radicals, also resulting in younger skin.

> Studies show that avocados can reverse the ageing of skin and alleviate fatigue and depression.

   Even though avocados are fruits, they combine very well with salad and protein foods. They also make a delicious milk shake (see below).

3 **Kiwi fruit**. Kiwi fruit is extremely nutritious. It contains twice as much vitamin C as oranges, more fibre than apples and twice as much vitamin E as an avocado. It's particularly rich in potassium, therefore helping to alleviate fatigue and depression.

4 **Dates and Figs**. These are both concentrated sources of nutrients and energy. They are a rich source of iron, potassium and calcium and are good for digestive problems. Bedouin Arabs travel for days across the desert with little more than a store of dates and figs.

   Dates and figs make a handy snack, but should be eaten in moderation because they have high concentrated sugar levels.

THE REJUVENATION DESSERT: AVOCADO AND CAROB MILKSHAKE

This is the most nutritious and rejuvenating cocktail that exists. It's also delicious – it tastes like chocolate mousse – and is simple to make. Being relatively low in calories, it's also good for weight control.

Just blend an avocado, one heaped teaspoon of carob or cocoa, one teaspoon of honey and one glass of milk (preferably soya milk). You can buy carob powder from the health shop.

If you can imagine all the nourishment of four highly nutritious foods in one combination, you can understand the health and rejuvenating effects of this cocktail.

The avocado reverses the ageing of skin and alleviates fatigue. Carob contains three times as much calcium as milk, not to mention a goldmine of other minerals and vitamins. Soya milk as stated previously, is rich in lecithin – the main nutrient in brain tissue and semen as well as reverses hardening of the arteries. Unprocessed honey contains pollen which increases vitality and stimulates the sex glands.

This healthy chocolate-tasting milkshake makes an ideal after-dinner sweet, since all the ingredients combine well with protein foods in your main dish.

The Rejuvenation Supplements

There are three important questions about food supplements: why do we need them? Which ones do we need? What is the best form in which to take them?

Why do We Need Vitamin and Mineral Supplements?

1 Poor soils. Due to the extensive use of fertilisers and poor farming methods, soils in many parts of the world have been depleted of vital trace elements. This causes produce from these soils to be nutritionally depleted.
2 Pollution. People and crops are increasingly subject to environmental pollution. This further depletes crops of micro-nutrients. We also need supplements to fight the effects of pollution on our bodies.
3 To help fight stress. In today's fast-pace, high-tech world we are subject to a lot of stress! Stress also depletes micronutrients.
4 To counteract drugs. Alcohol, nicotine and anti-inflammatory drugs such as aspirin cause a loss of vitamins in the body.
5 They are powerful antioxidants.

Ideally, if we are eating a nutritionally sound diet, we shouldn't need any supplements, but today's world is far from ideal. In addition, we are after more than just health – we want to reverse ageing, and this requires extra nutrients.

What Vitamin Supplements do We Need?

To reverse ageing we need to take antioxidants, since these destroy free radicals which are a major cause of premature ageing. The two most effective vitamin antioxidants are vitamin C and E. Vitamin C is also the vitamin we are most deficient in, due to depleted soils and the fact that our bodies use up a lot of vitamin C in fighting pollution.

The only other supplements we need are kelp as a concentrated mineral source, and garlic. These are discussed below.

Vitamin C

BENEFITS

Vitamin C is an antioxidant, gives some protection against cancer, accelerates wound healing, promotes immunity against disease, promotes regeneration of spinal discs, helps prevent heart disease, stimulates the adrenal glands (which are very important for rejuvenation), increases sex-hormone production and is a potent antitoxin.

Vitamin C also reduces facial wrinkles and promotes a smooth, healthy complexion. Scientists have shown that ageing, including facial wrinkles, is caused largely by destruction of collagen, the 'cement' which binds the body's cells together. Its destruction is mainly caused by lack of vitamin C and the sun's radiation.

You can see how important vitamin C is, and yet in one survey 90 percent of people tested for vitamin C were found to be deficient in it.

> Vitamin C reduces facial wrinkles and promotes a smooth, youthful complexion.

NATURAL SOURCES

Vitamin C is found in fruits and vegetables, especially citrus fruits, apples, kiwi fruit, strawberries, potatoes, cabbage, broccoli and tomatoes.

DOSAGE

You should take 1000mg, split into two tablets, each taken after a meal. The best form in which to take vitamin C is ascorbic acid. Tablets or pills are better than powder supplements, since nutrients are tightly bound together in this form and therefore protected against oxidation and going rancid.

Vitamin E

BENEFITS

Vitamin E is a potent antioxidant, it helps stress, it improves male and female fertility and virility and it improves the circulation. Improved blood circulation means that all parts of your body receive an increased blood supply, including your brain and glands, the two most important rejuvenation centres.

> Vitamin E improves the blood circula-tion to your two rejuvenation centres – the brain and the glands – and also improves virility and fertility.

NATURAL SOURCES

Vitamin E is found in wholegrains, wheatgerm, vegetable oils, leafy green vegetables and eggs.

Try wheatgerm on your sandwich bread, and include olives in your salad as a natural source of unprocessed, unheated vegetable oil, or you may just like to add olive oil.

DOSAGE

You should take 200 international units, split into two tablets, each taken after a meal.

The best form of vitamin E to take is d-alpha tocopherol acetate.

Minerals and Trace Elements

Trace elements are minerals of which only tiny traces are needed. The minerals in the body are sodium, chloride, potassium, calcium, phosphorous, magnesium, iron, copper, zinc and manganese. The trace elements in the body are iodine, fluorine, chromium, selenium and silicone.

Minerals, like vitamins, are an essential part of the diet and perform such important functions as building strong bones and teeth and forming a vital part of blood, hormones and enzymes.

NATURAL SOURCES

Sea food, all fruits and vegetables, eggs, soya milk and nuts.

I strongly suggest that you eat sea food at least twice a week since it's very high in mineral content.

MINERAL SUPPLEMENT: KELP TABLETS

Fish and kelp tablets are very rich in minerals.

Kelp is very nutritious seaweed which takes up a rich mineral supply from sea water. Seaweed has an almost identical chemical composition to human blood.

Kelp tablets can be bought from the health shop. One 1000-mg tablet a day after your main meal is sufficient.

Garlic

Garlic is the world's most popular herbal panacea. Even the AIDS virus does not grow well in the presence of garlic.

Garlic is both a food and a medicine. It's the world's most popular herbal panacea and world production now exceeds 2 million tonnes.

Garlic was cultivated long before recorded history. It is mentioned in the Bible (Numbers 11–5) and an Egyptian medical papyrus dating from about 1500 BC lists twenty-two different garlic preparations for ailments including heart disease, worms and tumours. Modern research has shown that garlic is effective for these conditions. The Roman army used it to fight infection and in fact the Roman legions were said to march on garlic.

The antiseptic properties of garlic were demonstrated during the Great Plague of Europe in the 17th Century. While millions died from this pestilence, it was observed that those who had stores of garlic in their cellars, by and large, survived.

During the two world wars garlic was taken by wounded soldiers with excellent results. It had come to their rescue as it had done for the Roman legions nearly 2000 years before.

The future of garlic is also looking very good. Recently it's been found that the AIDS virus does not grow well in the presence of garlic in tissue culture.

THE REJUVENATING EFFECTS OF GARLIC

1 It's an antibiotic. Allicin is the compound in garlic which accounts for its potent antibacterial effects.
2 It reduces heart disease. Garlic does this by lowering blood cholesterol levels and reducing blood-clotting tendencies.
3 It reduces high blood pressure. This is due to garlic's ability to remove cholesterol from the walls of the arteries and thin the blood.
4 It fights cancer. This is due to the sulphur compounds in garlic.
5 It stimulates the immune system. In particular garlic has been shown to activate natural killer-cell activity against cancer cells, with an increase of up to 50 percent against some tumour cells.
6 It increases endurance.
7 It stimulates cell growth and activity, causing a rejuvenating effect on the body.

HOW MUCH AND IN WHAT FORM SHOULD WE TAKE GARLIC?

Even just one gram (about one clove) of garlic per day has a beneficial effect on health, although for a maximum effect, I would recommend two cloves per day.

Raw garlic can be taken as a crushed clove mixed in your food, or as one 1000-mg tablet. To take cooked garlic, just cook the garlic with your food, or cook it on its own in a microwave oven for about half a minute.

Highlights

1 Seafood contains high-quality protein, the good fats and many minerals. Try to eat fish at least twice a week.

2 Soya milk is superior to cow's milk since it is easier to digest, non mucous-forming, contains the good fats and is a rich source of lecithin.

3 Raw nuts are very nutritious and contain the good fats.

4 Yogurt prevents putrefaction in the large intestine, is far more nutritious than milk and helps to produce vitamin B.

5 Eggs are very nutritious, help reverse ageing and increase virility. The lecithin in eggs feeds your rejuvenation centres.

6 Broccoli is very nutritious, very low in calories and helps prevent cancer.

7 Oats are nutritious. They are the best of all the grains for rejuvenation.

8 Pollen-rich honey increases vitality and stimulates the sex glands. You can buy pollen separately.

9 Chilli, peppers and ginger have rejuvenation effects.
   We need supplements because of poor soils, pollution and stress, to counteract drugs and because they are powerful antioxidants.

10 Vitamin C is an antioxidant and reduces facial wrinkles. Natural sources are fruits and vegetables. The dosage is 1000-mg, split into two tablets, each taken after a meal.

11 Vitamin E is also an antioxidant and improves circulation to all parts of the body, including the brain and glands, the rejuvenation centres. Natural sources are wholegrains, wheatgerm, vegetable oils and eggs. The dosage is 200 international units split into two tablets.

12 Kelp tablets are rich in minerals. Take one 1000-mg tablet a day.

13 Garlic is an antibiotic, reduces heart disease and blood pressure, fights cancer, stimulates the immune system, increases endurance and stimulates cell growth and activity. Take two cloves a day, either raw or cooked, or two 1000-mg tablets a day.

PART THREE

Specific Rejuvenation Techniques

Yoga: The Supreme Exercise System

This is not intended to be an exhaustive thesis on yoga – there are many excellent books on this subject. The aim of this presentation of yoga is to give only those exercises which give *maximum vitality and rejuvenation* with *minimum time expenditure*. It's geared for the busy westerner who wants the maximum return for time and effort. At the same time, to provide incentive to do the yoga routine, there is a brief discussion on how yoga works, its benefits and philosophy.

What is Yoga?

Yoga is unsurpassed as a means of self-improvement and attaining one's full rejuvenation potential.

Yoga is an ancient *natural* system of physical and mental culture, perfected over the centuries by philosophers and mystics in ancient India.

Yoga is designed to increase your vitality level and produce rejuvenation. It achieves this by rejuvenating your nervous system (brain and spine), organs and glands. Yoga has specialized in this subject for thousands of years and streamlined the methods to attain this aim.

In the advanced stages of yoga, superconscious states are attained which result in a feeling of bliss, deep peace and the emergence of psychic powers. That aspect of yoga is not discussed in this book since a personal teacher (guru) is necessary at this level.

Yoga is unsurpassed as a means of self-improvement and attaining your *full potential*.

Why Yoga?

Yoga works on the mind and the body at the same time, as well as exploiting their interdependence. No other system does this. Western psychology studies the mind, western exercise physiology studies the effect of exercise on the body, but there is no emphasis on the interrelationship of the mind and the body.

Yoga asanas (postures) and breathing deal with the physical body, but due to their effect on the brain, they also affect the mind.

Why not enjoy the benefits of modern science, but also do yoga to enjoy the benefits of vitality, rejuvenation and peace of mind as well?

A Brief Philosophy of Yoga

The yogis consider that we are all searching for happiness and that this is everybody's main goal. Even people who commit crimes such as stealing money are really searching for happiness. They are under the delusion that money gained by illegitimate means will bring them happiness.

Where we go wrong, according to the yogis, is that we try to attain happiness by chasing after temporary pleasures. We identify happiness with excitement. Excitement does not produce happiness since it is brief and there is always a long 'down' period after the excitement. The emptiness and boredom in our lives keeps us constantly searching for new excitement, so it becomes a bit like being addicted to drugs. The yogis state there is nothing wrong with pleasure, but that we should not live under the illusion that it will give us happiness and peace of mind.

The yogis were not prepared to settle for pseudo-happiness – they wanted the 'real thing'.

They devised meditation techniques to unfold our Higher Consciousness, which resulted in eternal bliss.

The yogis state that at some stage in our spiritual evolution over many lives, we will become dissatisfied with brief, temporary pleasures and start our quest for eternal bliss. They consider that nature's laws are so designed that we must evolve. The main mechanism nature uses in the early stages is pain. When we find that relationships, money or alcohol, for example, do not produce happiness or a sense of purpose, we will start looking more deeply into life. Yoga waits patiently for you to reach this stage.

In the later stages of spiritual evolution, pain is no longer needed to spur us on. Each stage of progress produces such peace and happiness that this entices us to go to a higher level of happiness. Thus, instead of pain, reward becomes the prime mover.

The above is a very brief indication of yoga philosophy, which is so comprehensive that it deals with every aspect of life and delves into the very nature of Reality. It is obviously beyond the scope of this book (see my book *Meditate to Rejuvenate* for a more in-depth discussion and how to unfold your Higher Consciousness).

How does Yoga Work?

The yoga postures are designed to rejuvenate the brain, spine, glands and internal organs. They work by increasing the blood and prana supply to these areas and by stimulating them with a gentle squeezing action.

Below is a general outline of how yoga as a whole works. (Details of how the yoga breathing exercises and particular asanas work are given later.)

The yoga asanas are designed to benefit the brain, spine, glands and internal organs and they are a tribute to the wisdom of the ancient yogis. Firstly, without the benefit of modern science, they fully understood the importance of the brain, spine, glands and internal organs to the wellbeing of the body and mind. In addition, they designed specific exercises which have dramatic effects on all these four aspects of the body.

The asanas were also designed with economy of time and effort in mind and most of them work on more than one aspect of the body at the same time. The 'twist' asana, for example, benefits the spine, adrenal glands, liver, pancreas and kidneys.

The yoga asanas benefit the organs and glands by several mechanisms. The actual position of the asana causes an increase in blood supply to the target organ or gland. The position also often produces a slight squeezing effect which massages and stimulates them. In addition deep breathing and visualising the target area sends an extra supply of rich oxygenated blood to the area.

Yoga's effect on the spine is to increase its flexibility. This ensures a good nerve supply to all parts of the body, since the nerves from the spine go to all the organs and glands.

Yoga breathing produces a huge storage of energy in the solar plexus area. This will cause the body to radiate vitality and, if any sickness is developing, the body can call upon some of this energy reserve to combat the disease.

Yoga breathing also improves brain function (intelligence and memory), as well as increasing the elimination of toxins from the system.

The total effect of yoga asanas and breathing is to produce a state of high vitality and rejuvenation.

The Benefits of Yoga

Here is a list of some of the benefits which will occur from practising yoga. Be patient, it will take time for yoga to show its effects. Within a few weeks you will feel calmer and your concentration will improve, but it will take a few months for rejuvenation of the glands to occur.

1 **Increased vitality** due to yoga's effect on the brain and glands.
2 **Look and feel younger**. Yoga reduces facial wrinkles and produces a natural 'face-lift'. This is mainly due to the inverted postures. In our normal upright position, gravity exerts a downward pull on our muscles. In time this causes our facial muscles to sag. By doing the inverted postures for a few minutes each day, we reverse the effect of gravity and use it to our advantage. The result is firmer facial muscles, which cause a reduction in wrinkles, and a natural face-lift.

   The inverted yoga postures often convert grey hair back to its natural colour and they will certainly delay the onset of grey hair. This is due to the inverted postures causing an increase in blood supply to the hair follicles in the scalp. Also, the increased flexibility of the neck produced by the asanas removes pressure on the blood vessels and nerves in the neck, causing an even greater blood supply to the scalp. The release of pressure on the nerves in the neck also causes the scalp muscles to relax, since the nerves in the neck supply the scalp muscles. This means that the hair follicles are better nourished and thicker healthier hair is the result.

   Yoga will take years from your face and add years to your life. As you get older, you will take on an *ageless* appearance and your friends will comment on how much better you are looking.
3 **Live longer**. Yoga affects all the important determinants of a long life: the brain, glands, spine and internal organs.
4 **Increased resistance to disease**. Yoga produces a healthy strong body with increased immunity against disease. This increased resistance extends from the common cold to serious diseases like cancer.
5 **Vision and hearing improve**. Normal vision and hearing depend to a large extent on the eyes and ears receiving a good nerve and blood supply. The nerves and blood vessels which supply the eyes and ears have to pass through the neck. As we get older, the neck becomes less flexible, like the rest of the spine, and there is a tendency for nerves and blood vessels to be encroached upon as they travel through the neck. This impairs the nerve and blood supply to the eyes and ears, affecting their function. Yoga postures and yoga neck exercises improve the condition of the neck, resulting in better eyesight and improved hearing.
6 **Mental/Emotional benefits**. Because of yoga's rejuvenation effects on the glands and nervous system, including the brain, yoga results in a positive

Within a few weeks you will feel calmer and have better concentration. Within a few months, rejuvenation of the organs and glands will start to occur.

Yoga will take years from your face and add years to your life. As you get older you will take on an ageless appearance.

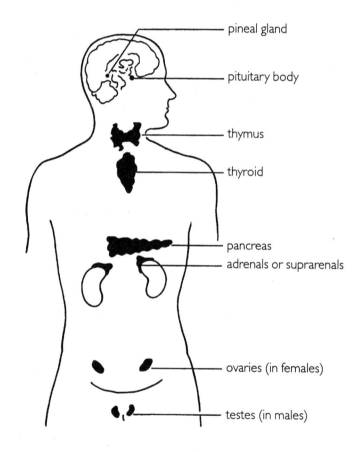

- pineal gland
- pituitary body
- thymus
- thyroid
- pancreas
- adrenals or suprarenals
- ovaries (in females)
- testes (in males)

Glands benefited by Yoga.

mental/emotional state. It will help you to feel more confident, enthusiastic and generally optimistic. You will also become more creative in your everyday life.

As you start to feel and look better and unfold more of your full potential, these positive mental and emotional states occur as a consequence.

Is Yoga a Religion?

It is important to stress that yoga is not a religion. It doesn't matter what your religion is or what your beliefs are. Yogis believe that all religions say basically the same thing – there is a Supreme Being and that there are different paths to attain spiritual illumination. Some religions emphasise devotion and prayer as the way, others ritual or good works. Most religions have an element of all of these methods in them.

The path of yoga is to unfold your full potential by a physical and mental culture system. The yogis claim that this is a sure way and does not depend on any external factors, such as ritual. The only variable factor is the time taken to attain the goal, and this depends on the constancy and intensity of practice.

There are several different types of yoga. The type presented here is a practical one called Hatha Yoga. This type has the greatest effect on vitality and rejuvenation.

The yogis consider Hatha Yoga not as an end in itself but as a preparation for doing a higher form of yoga, called Raja Yoga, which involves advanced meditation techniques. Raja Yoga is concerned with attaining the state of cosmic consciousness. This occurs when you are living at 100% from your Higher Consciousness, or if you like, from 100% of your full potential.

Is There any Age Limitation?

The answer is definitely no. The young are better at doing the physical postures, but most don't have the incentive to do yoga, since they are already young and energetic.

Yoga is really more for people over thirty-five. As people approach or are in middle age, they want to recapture the zest of youth as well as look younger. Yoga will do this for you. In fact, the older you get, the more enthusiastic you will be about yoga, and this will be your incentive to keep it up daily.

Of course, yoga will benefit all ages. If you are young and vital, it will keep you young and vital; if you are older, it will make you younger and more vital.

Yoga is for people of all ages but it has a special appeal for people over 35 who want to look younger and recapture the zest of youth.

Is a Teacher Necessary?

Not for the basic yoga course described in this book. For more advanced yoga techniques, an experienced teacher is essential, since you are dealing with very powerful forces within the body which have not yet been investigated by modern science. To play around with these forces is asking for trouble.

It is a good idea to go to a yoga class, since you can correct any faults you may have acquired. Also you will meet people with similar interests to your own and you can compare notes.

Will Yoga Benefit My Sleep?

Yoga will make you fall asleep sooner and improve the quality of your sleep so that you need less.

Yoga will benefit your sleep in three ways. Firstly, the quality of your sleep will improve because of yoga's beneficial effect on the nervous system, and in particular the brain. This results from certain yoga asanas increasing the blood supply to the sleep centre in the brain, which has the effect of normalising the sleep cycle.

Secondly, you will need less sleep because of the improved quality of your sleep, and because yoga increases the elimination of toxins from the body. On average, for every minute you put into yoga you will need one minute less sleep. This makes yoga an excellent time investment.

Thirdly, you will fall asleep in a shorter time. This is mainly because the body and mind are more relaxed.

Will Yoga Help Me Lose Weight?

The yoga postures cause fat loss by stimulating sluggish glands and increasing fat metabolism. The yoga breathing exercises cause fat loss by increasing the oxygen intake which burns more fat cells.

Most definitely. Yoga achieves this in two ways. Firstly, some of the asanas stimulate sluggish glands to increase their hormonal secretions. The thyroid gland, especially, has a big effect on our weight because it affects body metabolism. There are several asanas, such as the shoulder stand and the fish posture, which are specific for the thyroid gland. Fat metabolism is also increased, so fat is converted to muscle and energy. This means that, as well as losing fat, you will have better muscle tone and a higher vitality level.

Secondly, yoga deep breathing increases the oxygen intake to the body cells, including the fat cells. This causes increased oxidation or burning up of fat cells.

If you are not overweight, your weight will remain about the same. If you are underweight, you will gain weight. The weight you gain will be healthy firm tissue, not fat. That is, yoga will tend to produce the ideal weight for you. This is due to yoga's effect of 'normalising' glandular activity.

What is Yoga's View of Sex?

Yoga's view of sex is the same as of every other issue: *moderation*. Yoga considers sex to be a natural function, very beneficial in a loving relationship and, of course, essential for the continuation of the human race.

Yogi's warn against overindulgence in sex since they consider this will deplete the life force. They state that the sexual secretions contain very concentrated life force and nutrients, since they contains the seeds of life. Depletion of life force results in a reduced vitality level and reduced resistance to disease. It also retards progress from the practice of yoga.

The yogis consider that normal sexual function occurs when the reproductive system is in a state of optimum health. They have found that the most effective way of attaining this optimum health state is by doing yoga asanas and breathing exercises.

It's true that advanced yogis practise celibacy. They need every ounce of their life force for their quest for cosmic consciousness. They also know that the realisation of their goal produces eternal bliss, besides which the brief pleasure of sex pales into insignificance. Their minds have progressed so far that they are not prepared to settle for a watered-down version of happiness.

The most effective way to achieve healthy sex glands is by doing yoga.

Since Yoga Produces a Feeling of Peace, Will this Reduce My Productivity and Creativity?

Since your mind is calmer, you will act with more intelligence and waste less energy, so you will be productive and creative.

Also, yoga does more than just produce a feeling of peace. By affecting your brain, glands and internal organs, it produces a state of high vitality, which further increases your productivity and creativity.

Why Does Yoga Put so Much Attention on the Body?

Yoga does this for three reasons. Firstly, the yogis consider that the body is the temple of the soul and that it is therefore our duty to live by nature's laws and keep the body in top condition.

Secondly, the yogis' main goal of spiritual advancement will be impeded if the body is low in vitality and suffering from pains and aches. How can you give attention to higher matters when your consciousness is being dragged down to your body level by fatigue and pain.

Thirdly, due to the body-mind relationship, any improvement in the body will cause a corresponding improvement at the mental level.

Will Yoga Produce Psychic Powers?

If you practise yoga regularly, your intuition will develop due to increased 'refinement' of the brain. Intuition is called a psychic power since it operates outside the normal five senses. It is a higher form of intelligence which occurs instantly, without the normal slow thought process. Also, since intuition is a part of the Higher Self, it is always 100 percent correct, unlike the fallible decisions made by thinking.

One common sign that your intuition is developing is that you will start to know when the telephone is about to ring. Later, you will know who's ringing you. You will also notice that 'coincidences' will start to occur – far more than the laws of chance dictate. This is a sign your Higher Consciousness is starting to unfold.

Other psychic powers such as clairvoyance, telepathy and extrasensory perception usually only develop with more advanced forms of yoga. Yogis do not attach any importance to psychic powers, however. They consider them to be mere side effects on their journey towards cosmic consciousness and indeed, because of their attraction, a potential distraction to further progress.

Yoga's View of Nutrition

Yoga's main nutritional principle is to eat small quantities of high-quality food.

According to yoga, the basic principle of nutrition is to eat *small quantities of high quality foods*. The yogis define high quality foods as those which promote the life force of the body without producing toxins. The foods the yogis recommend are fruits, vegetables, whole grains and nuts. They do not go into great detail about nutrition, since they did not have the problems of food processing and polluted soils which we have today. Also, due to their practice of yoga, their bodies were in such a high state of health that food was not so critical to them, and any toxins formed in the body would be eliminated very quickly.

As you will see, yoga's principles of nutrition are very similar to what modern science has discovered in more recent times.

Meat

There is one food that the yogis advise to be cautious of: meat. Not all yogis are vegetarians, but they all recommend eating meat in strict moderation. The yogis state that meat, being animal flesh, has a low vibration rate and will lower the life force of the person eating it. This will cause a reduction in vitality and slow down your progress from yoga. Meat also contains toxins, especially lactic acid, which is a waste product of muscle metabolism.

Remember, those recommendations were given thousands of years ago. Meat is far worse today, since we now inject many toxic chemicals into the dead carcass to cover the smell of rotting flesh and to improve its colour and taste. Of course the body can handle a certain amount of abuse – it has mechanisms to eliminate toxins, but if you wish to eat meat, eat it in moderation. A full discussion of meat is given on pages 72–75.

Yogis consider fruit to have the highest life force of all foods and urge caution with meat.

Fruit

The yogi's favourite food is fruit. They consider fruit to possess the highest life force of all foods. Fruit is also very nutritious, raw, unprocessed and easily digested and it provides a quick and sustained source of energy with no toxins. It is no wonder the yogis favour fruit.

Vegetables

The yogis consider the green vegetables such as lettuce, cabbage, broccoli and so on, to have the highest life force of all vegetables.

Fresh Food

Yoga also stresses that food should be as fresh as possible. This means we should rely more on fresh fruits and vegetables than on frozen or canned foods. Frozen food is not so bad, since the enzymes are preserved, but canned food has been preheated, which destroys a lot of the vitamins and minerals and the enzymes.

Raw Food

The yogis also state that the greater proportion of our food should be eaten raw; for example, fruits, salad, raw nuts and sprouted grains. They consider that the cooking of food causes it to lose a lot of its life force, as well as its flavour. Because of this we need to add salt, spices and sauces, which often create more problems. Modern science is in complete agreement with this.

Yogis consider that cooking destroys a lot of the food's life force and we should therefore prefer raw food.

Food Temperature

The temperature of the food is also taken into consideration by yoga. The yogis state that food should neither be too hot nor too cold. They claim that very hot or very cold food or drinks can cause harm to the tissue of the throat. Modern science also agrees with this and considers that food and beverages which are too hot or cold may irritate the throat sufficiently to predispose it to cancer.

Alcohol

Yogis consider alcohol to adversely affect the brain. Scientific studies have verified this.

Yogis do not touch alcohol, since they consider it to lower the vibrations of their subtle body (astral body). This defeats the purpose of yoga, which is to increase the vibrational level so they can gradually unfold their Higher Self.

Yoga also considers alcohol to have an adverse effect on the central nervous system, and in particular the brain. The integrity of the central nervous system is considered very important by the yogis, since one of the goals of yoga is to improve the health of this system, and much of the progress of yoga is achieved via this vital communication system.

The increase in vitality which yoga causes cannot be duplicated by drugs.

Modern science agrees with yoga on this point, since alcohol is known to first stimulate and then shortly afterwards depress the central nervous system. This short stimulating period is why alcohol is considered to be a stimulant by many people. It is this effect which causes people to feel more 'alive' and talkative for a period. This period is short-lived, however, and is soon followed by the longer lasting depressing effect of alcohol. This is why alcohol is officially classified as a depressant.

Alcohol also causes poor sleep. Some people claim that alcohol 'relaxes' them, allowing them to sleep well. Science and experience say this is not the case. What these people mean is that alcohol gets them to sleep quickly, but the sleep is a drugged sleep, not a natural one so they wake up early and certainly not fresh. They then suffer for the whole of the next day.

Alcohol cannot compare with the effects of yoga. Yoga produces a natural stimulation without the depressing after-effect. Yoga also produces a general feeling of elation. The increase in life force produced by practising yoga cannot be duplicated by drugs.

This does not mean to say you must give up alcohol to have a high vitality level, or to make good progress with yoga, but if you do drink, drink in moderation, and this way you will avoid most of the depressing effects of alcohol, as well as prevent permanent brain damage.

Eat Slowly

The yogis place great emphasis on eating slowly; even more than on the type of food eaten. They claim that even nutritious food is not properly digested if eaten quickly. This means that, as well as not extracting all the nutrients from the food, you are also creating toxins in the body.

Even if you eat food which is not very nutritious, if it is eaten slowly and your digestive system is in good health from yoga exercises, your body will extract every last nutrient from the food, as well as eliminating all the toxins. Of course the intelligent way is to eat nutritious food and chew it slowly.

The yogis consider eating slowly to be even more important than the kind of food eaten.

Natural Change

As you progress in yoga, you will gradually lose your taste for rich and processed foods, as well as for drugs such as alcohol. You will desire more simple foods such as fruits. This will be a *natural*, gradual change – no effort is involved. The yogis attribute this change to yoga's effect on stimulating the life force, which results in a greater expression of the body's natural intelligence. In every sphere of life you will develop more attraction for natural things.

Yoga will cause you to lose your taste for rich and processed foods and for drugs such as cigarettes and alcohol.

Yoga's View of Disease

Yoga considers that most disease is due to insufficient life force, either in the body as a whole, or a blockage of life force to one part of the body. This leads to a lowered body resistance or immunity to disease.

When the whole body has lowered life force, the result is a lowered vitality level, poor health and susceptibility to any infection which is going around at the time. According to yogis, no infections would occur if the body's life force was high enough to fight off the infection. Pathogens (bacteria, viruses and so on) are a normal part of life and will only cause trouble when the body's resistance is too low to keep them in check.

The best way to increase the general life force of the body is by good nutrition, sufficient deep sleep, a positive mental attitude and yoga.

A blockage of life force to one part of the body, such as the thyroid gland, is usually caused by a slight misalignment of a vertebra which impinges on the nerve that travels to that particular organ. This causes an interference to the life force (called nerve impulses in modern terms) to the organ. This results in the organ not functioning at its optimum level (called functional disease). If the spinal misalignment is not corrected, the organ may develop pathology, which is then termed 'organic disease'. It is much more difficult to correct at this stage.

Yogis consider that most disease is due to reduced immunity. Medical science is gradually coming to the same conclusion.

The yogis were well aware of the relationship between spinal misalignments and health disorders.

The ancient yogis were well aware of the importance of the spine in relation to disease, since most of their asanas or postures were designed to make the spine more flexible to prevent spinal misalignments. Some of the asanas will even correct minor spinal misalignments.

The spine is so important for a high vitality level, good health and the correction of many health conditions that a whole science of healing has been developed to correct spinal misalignments. In fact, chiropractic is now the second largest healing profession after medicine and the fastest growing healing profession in the world.

Comparison of Yoga With Western Exercise and Sports

Yoga works on the whole system – the body and the mind – and in particular on the body's rejuvenation centres. western exercise systems tend to work on only one aspect of the body at a time and involve a net energy loss from physical exertion.

While western-type exercises such as weight lifting, isometrics, and especially aerobic exercises do have benefits, they cannot match the more comprehensive benefits of yoga. Yoga deals with the whole system, not just one aspect of it.

Yoga works on the body's *vitality and rejuvenation centres*, the brain, spine and glands. Even the cream of western exercises, the aerobic ones such as jogging, work mainly on only the cardiovascular system. They do not give any attention to the nervous system or the glands.

Yoga works on the mind as well while you are doing the physical exercises. When you do the asanas and yoga breathing, you are also concentrating on the part of the body which is mainly benefited. This increases your powers of concentration. The asanas and breathing exercises also have a calming effect on the mind.

With yoga there is no energy loss; in fact you gain energy from the stimulation of the brain and the increased intake of prana. Western exercises tend to expend a lot of energy and this can lead to fatigue, especially if you're unfit.

Yoga is a more *balanced* system of exercise. For example, weight lifting only works on certain major muscle groups, whereas yoga works on all the major muscle groups at the same time. This prevents the joint and muscle strain which frequently occurs with weight lifters.

Some people may argue that sports such as jogging cause us to breathe deeply, so there is no need to do special breathing exercises. In reality, sports tend to make us breathe quickly, with spasmodic jerky movements, and the increased oxygen intake is used to supply the energy to do the exercise. So, with western exercise, there is no net energy gain and no net oxygen gain; in fact you can end up with a net loss of both. This is why you sometimes feel tired after exercise. With yoga, there is a very substantial energy and oxygen gain.

One criticism of yoga by some fitness authorities is that it contributes nothing to cardiovascular fitness; that is, it doesn't benefit the heart and blood vessels. Nothing could be further from the truth. With brilliant economy, the ancient yogis designed the asanas and breathing exercises to benefit the heart and blood vessels at the same time as benefiting the brain, spine, glands, and other internal organs. Yoga benefits the cardiovascular system in two ways:

1 When doing the yoga breathing exercises, every time you inhale the diaphragm is pushed upwards and this gives a gentle massage to the heart. This causes a squeezing of the internal blood vessels of the heart, resulting in increased nourishment.
2 The headstand posture benefits the veins in the legs. By reversing the flow of gravity, the valves in the veins are given a rest. This prevents varicose veins occurring and will help to correct the condition if you already have it.

You may find yoga interesting and appealing, but remember it's actually doing it which brings results. The theory is only given to provide understanding and incentive – an ounce of practice is worth a pound of theory.

Yoga is an excellent time investment.

Yoga is so versatile and comprehensive that you can start at whatever level you're at and progress to whatever level you desire. It will help you realise your full potential – physically, mentally and spiritually. Remember, too, that yoga is an excellent time investment. After a few months, if you're doing about half an hour of yoga a day, you'll need about half an hour less sleep a day. This means yoga is costing you nothing in time, but giving you vitality and rejuvenation.

Highlights

1 Yoga is a *natural* system of physical and mental culture, designed to increase your vitality and produce rejuvenation.

2 Yoga is unsurpassed as a *self-improvement* system and for unfolding your *full potential*. No other system of physical or mental culture matches yoga in its benefits. Yoga works on the body and mind at the same time.

3 Yoga *philosophy* states that we are all searching for happiness, but we make the mistake of trying to find happiness through the senses, via brief external pleasures.

Yoga states that by unfolding the Higher Self through yoga practice, you will find deep and permanent happiness and you will even gain more enjoyment from external circumstances. This process of unfolding the Higher Self takes place over many lives, and in the initial stage, the motivation is suffering.

4 One of the main goals of yoga is to increase the body's supply of *prana*.

Prana is the essential basic energy of the universe. The highest concentration of prana is found in air, and therefore the yogis place great emphasis on correct breathing, and have devised special breathing exercises to increase the body's supply of prana.

5   Yoga *works* by dramatically increasing the health of the brain, spine, glands and internal organs. The result is to produce a state of high vitality and rejuvenation.

6   The benefits of yoga are: increased energy, looking and feeling younger, living longer, increased resistance to disease, rejuvenation of the glands, improvement of vision and hearing, deeper sleep, loss of excess weight, mental/emotional health and the development of intuition.

7   Yoga's view on *sex* is moderation, and that normal sexual function occurs when the reproductive system is in a state of optimum health. This is best achieved by yoga asanas and yoga breathing exercises.

8   Yoga's main principle of *nutrition* is to eat small quantities of high quality foods.

Yogis recommend eating mainly fruits, vegetables, whole grains and raw nuts, since they possess high life force, and eating meat in strict moderation or not at all.

Yogis also prefer food to be fresh, raw where possible, and not too hot or too cold.

Alcohol is considered to be bad for the health, as well as retarding progress from yoga.

The yogis place great emphasis on *eating slowly*.

9   Yoga is more beneficial than western exercises and sports, since it works on the *whole system* – specifically on the body's vitality and rejuvenation centres, the brain, spine and glands.

The Specific Rejuvenation Yoga Postures

A posture or asana is a certain position in which the body is held for a period of time, for the purpose of rejuvenating specific organs and glands as well as the spine. The posture should feel comfortable.

Although there are about eighty-four asanas commonly used by yogis, only about seven of them are considered essential for vitality and rejuvenation. They are presented in this chapter. It will only take you about 20 minutes to do the whole routine, including warm-up exercises, neck and eye exercises and rest periods. This is in line with the theme of this book: to give you the maximum benefits for the minimum time expenditure.

If you feel like investing more time in exercise, I suggest you consider doing some type of aerobic exercise (see pages 32–46). This is because doing extra asanas will only produce marginal benefits.

Origin of Asana Names

Many of the asanas have animal names, such as the fish posture and the cobra posture. This is because yogis devised their asanas partly by observing how animal instincts work in the wild. The yogis knew that when animals were sick they would only eat certain herbs and grasses. Similarly, animals would stretch and contract muscles in various postures instinctively.

Yogis also observed how animals relaxed. Cats, especially, were found to be experts in relaxation. On awakening from sleep, they instinctively stretch, arch the spine in both directions and then relax.

The yogis also based their asanas on a sound knowledge of human anatomy and physiology. They knew that placing the body in certain positions would stimulate specific nerves, organs and glands.

For example, the shoulder-stand posture causes the blood to be directed by gravity to the thyroid gland, and the tucking in of the chin causes a gently squeezing action on the gland. These two actions have a profound effect on the thyroid gland.

So yogis based their asanas on observation of animal behaviours and a sound knowledge of human anatomy and physiology.

How the Asanas Work

How the asanas work is based on five principles:

1 **The use of gravity**. The inverted postures such as the headstand, shoulder stand and the reverse posture take advantage of gravity to increase the flow of blood to the desired part of the body; in the headstand to the brain, in the shoulder stand to the thyroid gland and in the reverse posture to the gonads (sex glands).
2 **Organ massage**. The position of the asana causes a squeezing action on a specific organ or gland, resulting in the stimulation of that part of the body.
3 **Stretching muscles and ligaments**. This causes an increase in blood supply to the muscles and ligaments as well as relaxing them. It also takes pressure off nerves in the area.

    This stretching is involved in all the asanas, since it has such a beneficial effect on the body and in particular, the spine.

    The yoga routine described in this chapter, stretches all the joints from the neck to the toes. This relaxes all the muscles and ligaments of the body. Due to the body-mind connection via the autonomic nervous system, this stretching also causes *relaxation of the mind*, which occurs without any mental effort.
4 **Deep breathing**. While holding the yoga posture we breathe slowly and deeply, moving the abdomen only (abdominal or low breathing). This increases the oxygen and prana supply to the target organ or gland, thereby enhancing the effect of the asana.
5 **Concentration**. As well as breathing slowly and deeply, we also focus our attention on the target organ or gland. This brings the mind into play, and greatly increases the circulation and prana supply to the organ or gland.

    This concentration has the second benefit of increasing your general powers of concentration through regular practice. This benefits every aspect of your life. Your mind is less distracted and swayed by external events and you are therefore calmer and worry less. You will be able to solve day-to-day problems better and have more success in whatever activity you undertake.

What Asanas Will do for You

There are three very essential prerequisites for vitality and rejuvenation; a healthy central nervous system (brain and spine), healthy glands and healthy internal organs. The seven yoga asanas described in this chapter achieve these three prerequisites and more.

1 Healthy Central Nervous System (Brain and Spine)

Nerves from the brain and spine go to every tissue in the body and therefore the health of every tissue in the body depends upon the health of the brain and spine.

The headstand causes an increase in circulation to the brain, which stimulates the brain's nerve cells. This results in increased vitality and improved brain function (intelligence and memory).

Since the nerves from the spine go to all the organs and glands of the body, a healthy spine obviously plays an important role in vitality and rejuvenation. In fact, the spine is more critical to our wellbeing than the brain, since the brain is well protected by the cranium or skull bone. Where the spinal nerves leave the spine and pass through the intervertebral foramina is a very vulnerable area. If a vertebra is slightly out of place, it may cause the nerve to be 'pinched' in the intervertebral foramina. The spinal nerves do not have protection against mechanical insults as the brain does.

The ancient yogis fully understood the vulnerability of the spine and the tendency for slight spinal misalignments to occur. They also knew that if the spine was kept flexible by yoga asanas there would be much less chance of spinal misalignments. Some of the asanas will even correct some minor misalignments.

It's easy to test your spine's flexibility. The *spinal flexibility test* consists of bending over forwards while keeping your knees straight. At any age you should be able to touch the ground with your fingers. If you can't, and most of us can't, your spine has lost its youthful elasticity. The loss of spinal flexibility eventually causes the vertebrae to impinge on the spinal nerves. Since the nerves from the spine go to all the organs and glands in your body, this results in interference to the nerve supply to the organs and glands. This means your organs and glands are working at less than 100 percent efficiency. This impairs their function, and we call this *functional disease*. At this stage, the condition is reversible by skilful chiropractic manipulation of the spine and yoga asanas to help maintain the spine's flexibility.

If you do nothing to improve your spine's flexibility as you get older, your spine will deteriorate further and the spinal nerves will be increasingly impinged upon. This will lead to further deterioration of your organs and glands, until eventually their actual structure becomes diseased. We call this *organic disease*. At this stage not only is their function impaired, but their cells are actually dying. If the condition is too advanced, it is irreversible. It's at this state that many people go to doctors and

The spine needs even more attention than the brain because spinal misalignments happen frequently, whereas the brain is protected by the cranium.

are told that they have a disease of some particular organ. The cancer has not appeared overnight; in reality it has been developing for many years.

If you suffer from stiffness or pain in the spine (back or neck), I suggest you get your spine corrected by a therapist before you start yoga. Yoga will correct some of the minor spinal misalignments, but not long-term, major ones. Once misalignments are corrected, yoga will certainly help to keep your spine in top shape.

2 Healthy Endocrine Glands

The most important are the pituitary, pineal, thyroid, adrenal, pancreas and sex glands. The pituitary and pineal glands are situated in the brain, the thyroid is in the neck area, the adrenals and pancreas in the solar plexus area and the sex glands in the pelvic region.

The function of these glands is to secrete powerful hormones which control your growth, weight and size. They also determine your metabolism, vitality, sexual vigour and emotional state.

Since the *pituitary* and *pineal glands* are situated in the brain, the headstand has a powerful effect on them.

The *thyroid* gland secretes a hormone called thyroxine. If not enough thyroxine is secreted, you will become sluggish and fat. If too much thyroxine is secreted, you will suffer from nervous tension and become thin. Thyroid gland problems are very common and often go undiagnosed until the symptoms are very obvious. The shoulder stand is specific for the thyroid gland and will prevent and help cure thyroid gland problems.

The hormones secreted by the *sex* glands are important not only for sexual virility but also for sparkling eyes, smooth skin and a warm personality. The reverse posture stimulates the sex glands and therefore the production of the sex hormones.

The *adrenal* glands produce a variety of hormones. The medulla, or core of the adrenals, secretes adrenalin. This is known as the 'fight or flight' hormone because it prepares the body for the extra effort required to meet danger, cope with stress or carry out a difficult task. The area surrounding the medulla is called the adrenal cortex, and one of the hormones it secretes is called cortisone. Cortisone, as well as playing a key part in metabolism, is also vital to the functioning of the immune system. The twist posture is a powerful stimulant to the adrenal glands, causing them to release extra energy to boost your vitality level.

The correct functioning of the *pancreas* is vital to our health. The pancreas secretes two hormones, called insulin and glucogen, which help to balance the body's sugar level. If the pancreas is not working properly diabetes may develop. Diabetes results from a failure in the production of insulin, causing an increase in the blood sugar level. Diabetes is still a serious disease, since complications such as blindness, heart attacks or strokes may occur. To help prevent diabetes, it is

Yoga stimulates your glands resulting in vitality, sexual vigour, weight control and emotional balance.

recommended that you follow the nutritional principles outlined in this book, especially by avoiding concentrated sugar foods.

3 Healthy Internal Organs

As well as having a dramatic effect on the brain, spine and glands, most asanas also benefit the internal organs by massaging and stimulating them. This results in healthier internal organs which will function better and last longer.

Yoga postures stimulate our internal organs, causing them to function better and last longer.

As an example, the stomach lift raises the diaphragm, which massages the heart from below. This strengthens the heart muscle, resulting in better circulation and less chance of heart disease.

4 Healthy Digestive System

Even if we eat the most nourishing food, it still has to be digested and assimilated properly and the toxins have to be eliminated efficiently. As we get older the digestive system functions with gradually reducing efficiency. The asanas result in an improved blood and nerve supply to the digestive and eliminative systems, which in time will get them functioning at peak efficiency.

The stomach lift massages the digestive organs, as well as contracting and stretching them.

5 Healthy Joints

The stretching of the joints in asanas causes the secretion of a lubricant called synovial fluid. This is released into the joints and keeps them supple, as well as removing waste products. The result is to reduce stiffness, which will prevent arthritis or improve it if you already have the condition.

Stretching of the joints during yoga postures stimulates the release of a lubricant, synovial fluid, which helps to keep joints supple.

6 Healthy Skin

Stretching of the skin during the asanas causes stimulation of the skin cells. This results in firmer, healthier skin which won't sag or wrinkle.

Stretching of the skin results in a firmer skin which won't sag or wrinkle.

Contraindictions to doing the Asanas

There are certain medical conditions which made it inadvisable to do the inverted postures (headstand, shoulder stand and reverse posture). These are high blood pressure, dizziness, and serious eye problems. If you have any doubt, see your doctor before you start the asanas.

If you do have any of the above conditions, try to correct them, preferably by natural methods. For example, high blood pressure is often caused by poor nutrition, especially excess salt and fat, as well as lack of exercise. Follow the principles in this book on nutrition and aerobic exercise and this should bring your blood pressure down to normal. Check your progress with your doctor, and ask him to monitor your gradual withdrawal from any medication you are taking for the condition. From my experience as a practitioner, a lot of dizziness (vertigo) is caused by spinal misalignments in the neck. If you suffer from dizziness, see your chiropractor to see if it is coming from your neck.

What I'm saying is, don't despair if you have a medical condition. Most medical conditions can be corrected by natural means, such as correct nutrition, exercise and spinal manipulation. When you make good improvement, you can start doing the inverted postures, which will further improve your health.

The First Two Weeks

In some cases you may feel worse for up to two weeks after starting the asanas. This is because the yoga exercises cause the body to eliminate toxins, which spend some time in the blood before being eliminated. After this initial period of body cleaning, you will start to feel much better.

Some of the symptoms you may experience are a slight increase in your usual aches and pains, and a little stiffness. Your body may become slightly bloated and you may feel a bit drowsy during the day.

Of course the more toxic your body is, the more discomfort you will feel. But don't worry, you will soon feel much better.

It is quite common to feel sore in the back, neck and shoulder muscles for a couple of weeks. This is the result of your body resisting the exercises. Remember, you are using muscles and joints which have probably never been stretched properly before. To minimise any soreness, start gently and don't overdo it. Above all, *never give up*. Any discomfort will only be temporary and you will start to feel much better in a relatively short time.

Instructions for doing Asanas

Correct Sequence

The asanas must be done in the specific order in which they are described below. This is for very good reasons, and you will not get optimum results if you change the order.

First there is a yoga exercise to loosen up the spine before actually doing the main asanas. This is called the 'spinal rocking exercise'. As well as preparation for the main asanas, it is highly beneficial in itself. Then follows an exercise called the 'stomach lift'.

These are followed by the headstand, which is done first since it freshens the mind and makes the following asanas more effective. The headstand also needs to be followed by other asanas, to traction the neck after it has been slightly compressed by the headstand.

Next are the shoulder stand, reverse posture and 'plough'. These asanas, as well as having rejuvenation benefits to the body, also traction the neck.

Next is the forward posture which, like the three above, is a forward spinal flexion posture.

This is followed by the backward bending fish posture. This extension of the spine counteracts the four forward flexion postures just done. This leaves the spine in a balanced state, having stretched forwards and backwards, and prevents muscle strain.

The last posture is called the 'twist posture'. As the name implies, this posture twists the spine to the right and left.

After this the neck exercises are done to further improve the neck and remove any stiffness which may have resulted from doing the asanas.

The above procedure stretches and relaxes every muscle and ligament in the spine (including the neck).

We finish up with a short period of rest to allow the body to assimilate all the benefits produced by doing the asanas and to rest the muscles and nervous system.

While lying down resting, the eye exercises are done. This not only improves the vision but also has a relaxing effect on the whole body and mind, since eye tension will make you feel tense in general. This is due to the intimate connection between the eyes and the brain via the optic nerve.

For optimum results do the postures in the recommended sequence to stretch and relax every muscle in the body, from head to toe.

When to do the Asanas

It's best to do the asanas in the early morning or the early evening before the evening meal. Never exercise on a full stomach. Digestion of food requires a large part of the blood supply to be diverted to the stomach, and it is this blood supply

The best time to do the yoga postures is about one hour after getting up or in the early evening. Wait about 15 minutes before eating.

Preparation:
• Open windows.
• Wear loose clothing.
• Use a thick rug or about 2-cm-thick firm foam.

which you need to direct to various parts of the body when doing the asanas, so food in the stomach will greatly diminish their effectiveness. Before exercising, wait at least three hours after eating a main meal, about one hour after eating a light snack such as a piece of fruit and about half an hour after drinking juices. After finishing the asanas, wait about a quarter of an hour before eating, since the asanas are still rejuvenating the body for a short time after you finish exercising.

Don't exercise immediately after getting out of bed, since you'll be too stiff. Wait at least one hour. In fact the first few months you may find it easier to do the asanas before lunch or before your evening meal, since your joints will be more supple then.

It's not advisable to do the asanas before bed, since their stimulating effect may prevent you from getting to sleep easily.

Don't take a hot shower or bath immediately after yoga, since this draws blood away from the internal organs and glands to go to the skin. A shower which is just warm is all right, since this is neutral and will not affect the yoga exercises.

Where to do the Asanas and what to Wear

Make sure you have good ventilation in the room where you exercise. Open the windows, since it's essential to have a fresh supply of oxygen to gain the optimum benefit from the exercises. Of course, if you can do them outside in the garden, all the better.

It's best to do the asanas on a thick rug or about 2 centimetres of firm foam. Don't do them on the bed since it's too soft, or on the floor without some padding, since that would be too hard.

Wear loose clothing, since tight clothes will restrict the circulation to some areas of the body. This would defeat one of the purposes of the asanas, that of increasing the circulation to various parts of the body.

Basic technique:
• Slowly, with no strain.
• Breathe slowly and deeply with the abdomen only. When inhaling, push out; when exhaling, let it return.
• Concentrate on the main organ or gland (with your eyes closed).

Technique

The asanas should be done *slowly with no strain*. Take it particularly easy for the first two weeks, when you are stretching muscles which have probably not been used so much before. Keep in mind that yoga is different to western-type exercises and sports, where the more effort you apply, the more successful you are. With yoga you are not competing with anyone but aiming at gradual self-improvement.

Don't worry if you feel sore for a few days, as this will gradually disappear, and your muscles will be much healthier. The soreness indicates that those muscles have not been adequately used before and are in need of exercise.

While doing the asanas, breathe slowly and deeply with the abdomen only; that is, when inhaling slowly push the abdomen outwards, and when exhaling allow the abdomen to return to its normal position.

The mind is also brought into play as you concentrate on the organs and glands which the asana affects. To assist concentration, it's best to close the eyes while doing the asanas.

After each asana or group of asanas, you should rest for a short while. This allows the body to assimilate the effect of the asana, and gives the body time to withdraw the extra blood which had been directed to a particular organ or gland and return it to the general circulation. Then the body can send extra blood to another organ or gland when you do the next asana.

Be regular with your yoga sessions. You will not get good results if you frequently skip sessions. Aim for doing them six days a week and, when you are proficient, in the early morning, since you get it over with and don't have to try to find time later in the day. Also as the day progresses, many people become tired and you'll feel less inclined to do any type of exercise.

Finally, should you experience any unpleasant feelings, such as pain or dizziness, while doing a particular asana, stop doing that asana and try it again in a few months time when you're improved from doing the others. Your own body will tell you if a particular asana is not suitable for you at this stage.

While the first exercise, spinal rocking, is highly beneficial in itself, it is not an asana but a warm-up for the asanas. The stomach lift is also highly beneficial, but again it is not an asana. If you are pushed for time you may omit these two.

Be regular – aim to do the routine six times a week.

The Spinal Rocking Exercise

Technique
1 Lie on your back. Raise your knees and bend your head down. Put your hands under your knees, interlocking your fingers.
2 Gently rock back and forth on your rounded spine, imitating the swinging motion of a rocking chair. Feel for the massaging action on your spine. Use a mat, not a hard floor, and don't roll back too far on your neck.

Benefits of the spinal
rocking exercise:
• Greatly increases the
flexibility of the
spine.
• Massages the spine.
• Induces deep sleep.

Benefits
1 Makes the spine more flexible and youthful.
2 Massages all the vertebrae in the neck and spine.
3 If done on arising it helps to overcome the drowsiness and stiffness that people often feel on waking up.
4 It's also very beneficial just before sleep. The massaging action on the spine tends to relax the whole nervous system.

The Stomach Lift

Technique
The stomach lift really consists of two separate exercises.

First exercise. While standing with your feet slightly apart and your knees slightly bent, lean forwards a little from the waist and place your hands just above your knees.

Inhale deeply by pushing your abdomen forwards, and then exhale by pushing your stomach in. Don't take another breath; instead, push in your stomach even more, so that it becomes hollow, and hold your breath for about ten seconds.

Second exercise. Do the same as above but, instead of holding your stomach in after exhaling, rapidly push your stomach in and out ten times without taking another breath.

Benefits
1 This asana massages and tones up the internal organs in the abdominal area.
2 It also massages the heart, making it a stronger, more effective pump. Your circulation will improve and you will have less chance of having a heart attack.
3 It relieves constipation, gas and indigestion.
4 It tones up the nerves in the solar plexus region.
5 It reduces abdominal fat and strengthens the abdominal muscles.
6 It helps the correct functioning of the adrenal glands and sex glands.

The stomach lift benefits:
• The abdominal organs.
• The heart.
• The adrenal and sex glands.
• The stomach muscles.

Caution
Don't do this exercise if you have a hernia or serious heart or abdominal problems.

The Headstand

Technique
You must use extra padding for the headstand, so use a folded blanket or some extra form on top of your yoga mat. Don't use a pillow, since it's too soft.

If you don't feel very confident about going straight into the headstand, I suggest you do stage 1 first. Once you are confident with stage 1, you can go on to stage 2, which is the standard headstand.

If you wish to try it on your own, place a pillow lengthwise behind your head, in case you fall over backwards.

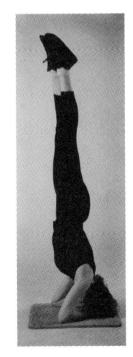

Stage 1, for Beginners:
1 Put your yoga mat into a corner, kneel down in front of it and place your interlocked fingers in the corner close to the walls.
2 Put your head into the hollow of the palms, rise off the knees and take a step or two towards the corner.
3 Lift one leg and place it in the corner against the wall. If you are a little unsure, ask a friend to hold the leg and put it in the corner. Now, just kick the other leg up. Stay there for about 15 seconds, trying to remain relaxed.
4 To come out of the headstand, just lower one leg at a time. Again, if you feel unsure, ask your friend to hold one of your legs while you lower the other.
   Start off in the headstand for about 15 seconds. Increase the time by 15 seconds every week until you are doing three minutes.

Stage 2, the Standard Headstand:

1 Kneel down on your yoga mat. Interlock the fingers of your hands and place them and your forearms on the extra padding on the yoga mat. Keep the elbows fairly close together.
2 Place the back of your head into the hollow of the palms (not on the palms or fingers). Rise up off your knees and take a step or two towards your head.
3 Inhale, and slowly raise the legs until they are vertical. Keep your back straight and try to relax. Breathe slowly and deeply from the abdomen.
4 Concentrate on the brain or the pineal gland between the eyebrows.
5 To come down, bend your knees and lower one leg and then the other. As for the beginners' stage, start off in the headstand for about 15 seconds and increase the time by 15 seconds every week, until you are doing three minutes.

Benefits

1 The headstand increases circulation to the brain, which causes improved brain function (intelligence and memory) and increased vitality and confidence.
2 It improves many ailments, such as 'nerves', poor eyesight and reduced hearing ability.
3 It stimulates the pituitary and pineal glands, which has a very beneficial effect on the whole body.
4 It promotes hair growth by increasing circulation to the scalp.
5 It helps to put the spine into correct alignment.
6 It restores the position of vital organs by reversing gravity.
7 The quality of sleep is improved. Poor sleep is often due to an excess of nerve impulses from the reticular formation to the cerebral cortex in the brain. The headstand causes an increase in circulation to the neck, which stimulates the baroreceptors in the neck. This calms the reticular formation down, causing reduced nerve impulses to the cerebral cortex. This results in a peaceful, deep sleep.

Because of the many benefits of the headstand, the yogis often refer to it as the 'king of the asanas'.

Caution

1 Don't do the headstand if you have high blood pressure. First get your blood pressure down by natural means such as good nutrition, aerobic exercise and the other asanas. Even just giving up salt and taking garlic daily (tablets or in cooking) will cause a substantial reduction in your blood pressure.
2 Atherosclerosis (blocked blood vessels) and any history of strokes are also contraindications to doing the headstand. You must improve your circulatory system first, before attempting it.

3   If you have any serious eye diseases, ask your eye specialist's advice about doing the headstand.

4   If you suffer from a neck injury or advanced arthritis in your neck, again you must improve your neck condition first. See your chiropractor, follow the nutritional principles in this book and do the other asanas to improve your neck. If you have a serious neck condition and you wish to get the benefits of the headstand, you can purchase an inversion apparatus, which gives you all the benefits without compression of your neck, in fact, this equipment produces traction of your neck, so your neck condition will actually improve.

Don't let any minor neck pain stop you from doing the headstand, since most of the weight of the body is actually supported by the forearms. There is very little pressure on the head and therefore very minimal compression of the neck.

The Shoulder Stand

Technique

1   Lie flat on your back. Inhale deeply while raising your legs and spine.
2   The body rests on the shoulders and the back of the neck. The body is supported by the hands, which are placed on the centre of the spine between the waist and the shoulderblades. Keep your spine and legs straight.
3   Breathe slowly and deeply with the abdomen and concentrate on the thyroid gland, which is in the hollow in the front of the neck where the neck joins the rest of the body. Stay in this position for about two minutes.
4   To come out of this posture, just bend your knees, curve your back and slowly return to lying on the floor. If you wish, you may go straight into the next posture (the 'reverse posture') instead of lying down.

Benefits

1   The main benefit of the shoulder stand is to get the thyroid gland working at peak efficiency. It's the thyroid gland which is mainly responsible for your correct weight and youthful appearance.
2   The shoulder stand also regulates the sex glands.
3   It gives a healthy stretch to the neck muscles.
4   It is beneficial for people suffering from poor circulation, constipation, indigestion, asthma and reduced virility. The yogis call this posture *sarvangasana*, which literally means 'all the body'.

Benefits of the shoulder stand:
• Weight control.
• Regulates the sex glands.
• Gives a youthful appearance.

The Reverse Posture

Technique

1 Lie on your back. Raise your legs and back, supporting your body by placing your hands under your hips. Make sure your legs are vertical and your toes pointed.
2 Breathe slowly and deeply from the abdomen and concentrate on the gonads (sex glands). In the male, these are in the testes, and in the female in the ovaries (see diagram on page 104). Stay in this position for about two minutes.

Benefits

Benefits of the reverse posture:
• Prevents premature ageing.
• Stimulates the sex glands.

1 The reverse posture produces optimum functioning of the sex glands.
2 It has a beneficial effect on the thyroid gland.
3 It produces vitality and rejuvenation due to stimulation of the sex glands and the thyroid gland.
4 According to the yogis, this posture prevents premature ageing and removes facial wrinkles. The headstand and shoulder stand also have this effect.

The Plough Posture

Benefits of the plough
posture:
• Spinal flexibility
• Improves the thyroid
gland, liver and
spleen

Technique

1 While in the reverse posture, bring both legs over your head until the toes touch the floor behind your head. Try to keep your knees straight. Stretch the hands out towards your feet.
2 Breathe slowly and deeply from the abdomen and concentrate on the spine, especially where you feel the stretch taking place. Stay in this posture for about one minute.
3 To come out of the posture, just slowly uncurl the spine. Don't worry if you can't straighten your knees. In fact if you're a beginner it will be virtually impossible for you to do this unless you do it later in the day. As the weeks go by, your spine will become more flexible and you will eventually be able to straighten your knees.

Benefits

1 This is the best posture for making the spine flexible. It stretches the spine as no other exercise can, opening up the spinal discs and stretching most of the spinal muscles and ligaments. This makes this posture very beneficial if you suffer from back or neck stiffness or arthritis in these areas. It also prevents these conditions. Since this posture rejuvenates the spine, and because the spinal nerves go to all parts of the body, it helps to rejuvenate the whole body.
2 It benefits the thyroid gland, liver and spleen.
3 It is very beneficial for indigestion and constipation.

The Forward Posture

Technique

1 Sit on the floor with your legs outstretched and your feet close together.
2 Take a deep breath, stretch your arms above your head, and then exhale while you bend your body forwards until you can grasp your ankles with both hands. Your forehead should touch your knees.

   Don't worry if you can't grasp your ankles or touch your knees with your forehead. Just stretch as far as you comfortably can and you'll find you'll gradually be able to go further.
3 Breathe deeply from the abdomen, and concentrate on the area within the abdomen.
4 Stay in this posture for about one minute.

Benefits of the forward posture:
• Stimulates abdominal organs and glands.
• Tones abdominal muscles.

Benefits

1 The forward posture stimulates organs and glands in the abdominal region, such as the kidneys, liver and pancreas.
2 It tones the abdominal muscles and stretches the hamstring muscles of the thighs.
3 It is very beneficial for cases of constipation, low back pain and sciatica. In fact, this posture is a specific for constipation.

The Fish Posture

Technique
1. Lie on your back with your knees bent.
2. Arch your back as much as you can while raising it off the ground by pushing the floor with your elbows. At the same time, throw your head backwards, resting the crown of your head on the floor.
3. Breathe deeply with the abdomen and concentrate on the thyroid gland.
4. Stay in this position for about one minute.

Benefits
1. The fish posture normalises the function of the thyroid, pituitary, pineal and adrenal glands.
2. This is the only posture in this sequence which bends the spine (including the neck) backwards. This is essential, to counteract the preceding asanas which bend the spine forwards. The result is to give a healthy stretch to the muscles and ligaments of the spine in the opposite direction.
3. This posture benefits people with asthma.

Benefits of the fish posture:
• Improves gland function.

The Twist Posture

Technique
1. Sit on the floor with both legs extended.
2. Cross your left leg and bend your right knee, placing your left foot just in front of your right buttock.
   Grasp the outside of your right ankle with your left hand, and bend your right arm and place it halfway up your back, so that the right hand reaches across to the other side of the back.

3 Take a deep breath and then slowly twist your back and your neck to the right as far as you can while you breathe out. Keep your spine vertical – don't lean to one side – and twist slowly, avoiding any jerky movements.

Stay in this position for two more breaths. Take another deep breath and, while exhaling, slowly return to your original position.

4 Concentrate on the stretching taking place in your spine.

5 Repeat the whole process, but in the opposite direction; that is, cross your right leg and bend your left knee, placing your right foot just in front of your left buttock.

Grasp the outside of your left ankle with your right hand, and bend your left arm and place it halfway up your back. This time you twist to the left.

Benefits of the twist posture:
• Stimulates adrenal glands, causing increased energy.
• Stimulates kidneys, liver and spleen.

Benefits

1 The twist benefits the adrenal glands, kidneys, liver and spleen.

2 It is very helpful for asthma, indigestion and constipation.

3 This is the only asana which twists the spine. The other asanas stretch the spine in the flexion (forwards) and extension (backwards). The twist completes the stretching of the spine so that now every muscle and ligament of the back and neck has been stretched in all directions.

Neck Exercises

The neck is given special attention by the yogis, since they realise that it plays a large role in health and vitality.

The neck is important for two main reasons. Firstly, since the nerves from the neck go to the eyes, ears and brain, a spinal misalignment in the neck can cause vision and hearing problems, as well as problems such as headaches and poor sleep. Secondly, since major blood vessels pass through the neck to the brain, a neck misalignment can put pressure on the blood vessels and reduce the blood flow to the brain. This is a very common cause of chronic fatigue.

The asanas and the following neck exercises improve the flexibility of your neck.

Benefits of the neck exercises:
• Improve vitality, sleep, vision and hearing.
• Prevent headaches, since the nerves and blood vessels in the neck go to the head and brain.

Exercise 1
Let your head drop forwards. Stay in that position for two seconds. Now let your head drop backwards. Stay in that position for two seconds. Repeat this exercise twice more.

Exercise 2
Turn your head to the right as far as you can. Now push a little further and hold it there for two seconds. Repeat to the left. Do twice more.

Exercise 3
Let your head drop sideways towards your right shoulder. Hold it there for two seconds. Repeat to the left. Do twice more.

Caution
A lot of books include the neck roll exercise, in which the neck is rolled around clockwise and then anti-clockwise. This exercise is not recommended, since it jams the side joints of the neck, which can cause inflammation.

Eye Exercises

The yogis also attach special importance to eye exercises, for two reasons.

Firstly, a lot of eye problems in later life are due to a loss of tone in the eye muscles. These muscles become rigid, and this loss of elasticity reduces the ability of the lens of the eye to focus at different distances. It also causes the eyesight to become weaker. These exercises tone the eye muscles up and keep them elastic. If you

The yoga eye exercises improve eyesight by toning the eye muscles and making them more elastic.

already have eye problems when you begin these exercises, you will find your eye-sight improving after a few months.

Secondly, any eye tension present will tend to produce a general feeling of tension, due to the eye's connection to the brain via the optic nerve. What happens is that eye tension produces an increase in the nerve impulses in the eye muscles. This increase in nerve impulses travels along the optic nerve and bombards the brain, causing a general feeling of tension and anxiety. The eye exercises will reduce tension in the eye muscles, as well as reduce general tension.

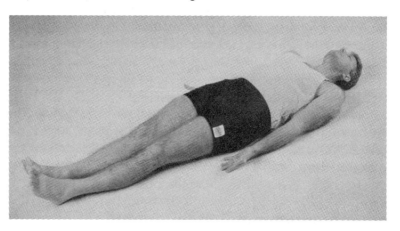

It's best to do these eye exercises while lying down after you've finished the asanas. This way you're resting after the asanas and doing the eye exercises at the same time, thus reducing the time taken to do your yoga routine.

When doing the eye exercises keep your eyes open and don't move your head.

Exercise 1
Move your eyes upwards as far as you can, and then downwards as far as you can. Repeat four more times. Blink quickly a few times to relax the eye muscles.

Exercise 2
Look to the right as far as you can, and then to the left as far as you can. Do this five times, then blink a few times.

Exercise 3
Look upwards to the right corner and then downwards to the left corner. Then look upwards to the left corner and then downwards to the right corner. Repeat four times, then blink a few times.

Exercise 4
Roll your eyes in a clockwise direction and then counterclockwise. Do this five times then blink the eyes for at least five seconds.

When rolling the eyes, make as large a circle as possible, so that you feel a little strain as you do the exercise. This stretches the eye muscles to the maximum extent, giving better results.

Exercise 5
Close your eyes as tightly as you possibly can. Really squeeze the eyes, so the eye muscles contract. Hold this contraction for three seconds, and then let go quickly.

This exercise causes a deep relaxation of the eye muscles, and is especially beneficial after the slight strain caused by the eye exercises. Blink the eyes a few times.

Exercise 6
This exercise is called 'palming' and is very relaxing to the eyes. It's an ideal way to finish off the eye exercises.

Just cup the palms of your hands over your eyes and keep your eyes gently closed. Stay in this position for about one minute.

Highlights

1 The asanas presented here are those which the yogis consider essential for vitality and rejuvenation. This streamlined routine will take you only about twenty minutes.

2 These asanas will produce a healthy central nervous system (brain and spine), healthy glands, healthy internal organs, healthy joints and healthy skin.

3 If you suffer from high blood pressure, dizziness or serious eye problems, you should not do the inverted postures (headstand, shoulderstand and reverse posture) until these conditions improve.

4 A small proportion of people feel worse for up to two weeks after starting the asanas. This is because the yoga asanas cause the body to eliminate toxins. After this you will start to feel much better.

It is common to feel muscle soreness after the first few sessions, too, because you are stretching muscles which haven't been used before. Just do the asanas gently with no strain. To minimise any soreness for the first two weeks, do the asanas later in the day (before lunch or the evening meal) when the joints are less stiff.

5 Always do the asanas in the sequence indicated.

6 The best time to do the asanas, once any initial soreness is overcome, is in the early morning or in the early evening before the evening meal.

Never exercise on a full stomach. Wait at least three hours after eating a main meal, about one hour after eating a light snack and about half an hour after drinking juices.

After finishing the asanas, wait about a quarter of an hour before eating.

7 Do the asanas in the garden or in a room with the windows open. Use a thick rug or about 2 centimetres thickness of firm foam and wear loose clothing.

8 The asanas should be done slowly with no strain. Breathe slowly and deeply with the abdomen only. When inhaling, push the abdomen out, and when exhaling allow the abdomen to return to its normal position.

Concentrate on the particular organs and glands which the asana affects. Keep your eyes closed.

After each asana or group of asanas, rest for a short while.

Aim to do the asanas six days a week. Don't skip sessions; it is regularity which produces results. If you experience any pain or dizziness when doing a particular asana, stop doing it and try it again in a few months time.

The Three Vitality and Rejuvenation Breathing Exercises

Prana

To understand how yoga breathing works, it is necessary to understand the yogi's concept of prana. The beneficial effects of yoga can be explained by the increase in blood circulation and oxygen to the brain, glands and internal organs, but the yogis say this is not the full explanation of yoga's effects. Advanced yogis, who are clairvoyant, can see a subtle energy flow in the body. This energy flow occurs in non-physical energy channels which yogis call 'nadis'. These are the same channels acupuncturists work on when they stick needles into the skin, although the acupuncturists call them 'meridians'. The ancient Chinese acupuncturists and Tai Chi masters were also aware of this subtle energy, which they called 'chi'. It is identical to prana.

The yogis' concept of 'prana' (meaning 'absolute energy' in Sanskrit) was also familiar to the ancient Chinese acupuncturists and Tai Chi masters, who called it 'Chi'.

Modern science has not yet detected this subtle energy, since it is a non-physical entity and cannot be perceived by the five senses. This does not mean that prana does not exist, it's just that science has not yet invented sensitive enough instruments to detect it.

Occultists in all cultures and ages have maintained that there exists in the air, water, food, sunlight and everywhere, a substance or principle from which all activity, energy, power and vitality were derived. They used different names for this force, but the basic concept remains the same. In Sanskrit, 'prana' means 'absolute energy'.

Prana is the essence of all motion, force or energy, and is manifested in gravitation, electricity and all forms of life.

We are constantly inhaling air charged with prana and extracting the prana from the air for the body to use for its various functions.

The yoga breathing exercises described here in this book, allow us to extract a much greater supply of prana, resulting in increased vitality.

In normal breathing we absorb and extract sufficient prana for the normal body functions, but by doing yoga breathing exercises, we extract a much greater supply of prana. This extra prana is stored away in the nerve centres, producing vitality and a reserve of energy to be drawn upon when necessary. The psychic powers of advanced yogis are largely due to their knowledge and intelligent use of this stored-up energy.

Even the simple yoga breathing exercises described in this book will produce a storage of prana and will cause you to radiate vitality.

Prana, once it enters the body, is taken up by the nervous system and our supply is gradually diminished by our activities and even by our thinking. This means that constant replenishment of prana is necessary.

Even the messages transmitted from the brain to all parts of the body along the nerves, called nerve impulses by modern science, are known by the yogis to be just another manifestation of prana. Without it the heart couldn't beat, the lungs couldn't breathe and none of the other organs could function.

The main storehouse of prana in the body is the solar plexus, which lies just behind the stomach at a level just above the navel. Even the brain draws its prana supply from the solar plexus and yoga breathing takes advantage of this important point.

According to yoga teaching, fresh air has the greatest concentration of prana which can be directly used by a man. Mountain air, being the freshest, has the greatest concentration of prana of all, and that is the main reason why advanced yogis retire to the Himalayas to practise yoga.

Even though science has not yet discovered the yogis' prana, there's no need for you to wait until science catches up! Apply this ancient knowledge now and reap the benefits.

The Role of Oxygen

Why Oxygen is so Vital

Oxygen is the most vital nutrient for our bodies. It is essential for the integrity of the brain, nerves, glands and internal organs. We can do without food for weeks and without water for days, but without oxygen, we would die within a few minutes. This point was not lost on the yogis, who realised the vital importance of an adequate oxygen supply thousands of years ago. It made them develop and perfect various breathing techniques, which they turned into a science. They discovered that different techniques would produce different predictable and repeatable results. They also developed an elaborate philosophy to explain the results.

You may still think that food is more important than air, but remember food can only be properly used by the body when it is oxidised or broken down by oxygen; that is, food is useless without a plentiful supply of oxygen.

Oxygen is especially important for the *brain*. The brain requires more oxygen than any other organ of the body, and if it doesn't get enough the result is fatigue, mental sluggishness, negative thoughts, depression and so on. You can easily verify this for yourself by going into a room with poor ventilation where the air is stale – after a few minutes you will not feel very well. This is especially true if people have

Oxygen is the most vital nutrient for our bodies. It is essential for the integrity of the brain, nerves, glands and internal organs.

been smoking in the room. Smoking results in carbon monoxide being released into the air. This poisonous gas has a higher affinity for red blood cells than oxygen, so it displaces oxygen in the body

A good oxygen supply is critical for the brain, and the brain is by far our most important organ. This is well demonstrated in old and often not so old people, who often become senile and vague because oxygen to the brain is reduced by clogged arteries. These people get irritable very quickly and alcohol affects them markedly, since alcohol reduces their already small oxygen supply.

Poor oxygen supply affects all parts of the body. Due mainly to faulty lifestyle, the oxygen supply is reduced to all parts of the body as we get older. This is the major reason why so many of us need reading glasses and suffer hearing decline in old age.

When an acute circulation blockage deprives the heart of oxygen, a heart attack is the result. If this occurs to the brain, the result is a stroke.

For a long time lack of oxygen has been considered a major causative factor in cancer. Even as far back as 1947, Dr F. Windesch of Germany showed that when oxygen was withdrawn, normal body cells could turn into cancer cells.

Similar research has been done with heart disease. Dr. Finney, of Baylor University in Dallas, infused oxygen into the diseased arteries of monkeys and in eight weeks reversed arterial disease.

Since oxygen is so critical to our wellbeing, why not increase the supply to our body and especially to the brain? This was the basis upon which the yogis devised their potent breathing exercises. These exercises are especially important for people who have sedentary jobs and spend most of the day in offices. Their brains are oxygen starved and their bodies are just 'ticking over'. They feel tired, nervous and irritable and are not highly productive. To make matters worse, they sleep badly at night, so they even have a bad start to the next day. This situation also lowers their resistance to disease, so they catch colds and any other 'bugs' going around.

> The brain requires more oxygen than any other organ. If it doesn't get enough, the result is fatigue, mental sluggishness, negative thoughts and depression and, eventually, vision and hearing decline.

> Research has shown that lack of oxygen is a major cause of heart disease, stroke and cancer.

Oxygen Purifies the Blood Stream

One of the major secrets of vitality and rejuvenation is a purified blood stream. The quickest and most effective way to purify the blood stream is by taking in extra supplies of oxygen from the air we breathe. The breathing exercises described in this chapter are the most effective methods ever devised for saturating the blood with extra oxygen.

Oxygen burns up the waste products (toxins) in the body, as well as recharging the body's batteries (the solar plexus). In fact, most of our energy requirements come not from food but from the air we breathe.

By purifying the blood stream, every part of the body benefits, as well as the mind. Your complexion will become clearer and brighter and wrinkles will begin to fade away. In short, rejuvenation will start to occur.

> The yoga breathing exercises produce vitality and rejuvenation by saturating the blood with extra oxygen.

Medical science agrees with the yogis on the importance of oxygen. Scientists have discovered that the chemical basis of energy production in the body is a chemical called Adenosine Triphosphate (ATP). If something goes wrong with the production of ATP, the result is lowered vitality, disease and premature ageing.

Scientists have also discovered that oxygen is critical for the production of ATP; in fact, it is its most vital component.

What's Wrong With the Way We Breathe

We need to breathe more slowly and deeply. Quick shallow breathing causes oxygen starvation which leads to reduced vitality and premature ageing.

Our breathing is too shallow and too quick. This means we are not taking in sufficient oxygen and eliminating sufficient carbon dioxide, so our bodies are oxygen starved, and a toxic build-up occurs. Remember, every cell in the body requires oxygen and our level of vitality is just a product of the health of all the cells.

Also, shallow breathing does not exercise the lungs enough, so they lose some of their function, causing a further reduction in vitality.

Animals which breathe slowly live the longest; the elephant is a good example.

How Have We Developed the Habit of Fast, Shallow Breathing?

1 There are several reasons for this. The major reasons are as follows:
2 We get too emotional too easily. We get excited easily, angry easily, and most of the rest of the time we suffer from anxiety due to worry. These negative emotional states affect the rate of breathing, causing it to be fast and shallow.
3 We are in a hurry most of the time. Modern life is fast paced, and our movements and breathing follow this pattern.
4 Modern technology leads to less physical activity. This means there is less need to breathe deeply, so we develop the shallow breathing habit.
5 Modern life increasingly involves working indoors and exposure to pollution. Both these conditions lead to less pure air, which cause the body instinctively to inhale less air in order to protect itself from pollution. The body just takes in enough air to tick over.
6 The increasing stress of modern living also tends to make us breathe more quickly and less deeply.

In summary, our modern unnatural lifestyle is the root cause of our poor breathing habits. The solution is to consciously breathe more deeply and slowly, especially when walking where the air is relatively fresh, and also to do the deep breathing exercises shown later.

Primitive humans lived under more natural conditions. Living was mainly out-doors and involved activities such as walking and hunting. This made them natural good breathers.

The Effects of Shallow Breathing

1 Reduced vitality, since oxygen is essential for the production of energy in the body.
2 Increased disease. Our resistance to disease is reduced, since oxygen is essential for healthy cells. This means we catch more colds and develop other ailments more easily. It is believed by many authorities that lack of sufficient oxygen to the cells is a major contributing factor in cancer, heart disease and strokes.
3 With our 'normal' sedentary way of living, we only use about one tenth of our total lung capacity. This is sufficient to survive and just tick over, but not sufficient for a high vitality level, long life and high resistance to disease.
4 The ancient yogis knew the importance of correct breathing and developed techniques not only to increase health and life span, but also to attain superconscious states.

The Medical Viewpoint on Fast, Shallow Breathing
Modern science agrees with the ancient yogis on the subject of shallow breathing. According to a recent editorial in the *Journal of the Royal Society of Medicine*, fast, shallow breathing can cause fatigue, sleep disorders, anxiety, stomach upsets, heart-burn, gas, muscle cramps, dizziness, visual problems, chest pain and heart palpitations.

It has also been discovered by medical science that a lot of people who believe they have heart disease are really suffering from improper breathing.

Why We Should Breathe Through the Nose

The first rule for correct breathing is that we should breathe through the nose. This may seem obvious, but a large proportion of the population breathe principally through the mouth. Just stop for a moment, and see how you breathe. If your mouth is open, there is a good chance you are a mouth breather. To break the habit just keep your mouth closed and you'll automatically breathe through the nose. Your health will benefit considerably. If you have children, instruct them to do the same. Mouth breathing in children can affect the development of the thyroid gland and predispose them to infection of the tonsils. Of course the tonsils can easily be removed but, contrary to medical opinion, they play an important role in health.

Some people breathe through the mouth, causing health problems and lowered vitality. To break this habit, just keep your mouth closed and you will automatically breathe through your nose!

The tonsils are lymphatic glands situated at the entrance to the throat and their function is to fight infection before it gets deeper into the body. Once the tonsils have been removed, you have lost an important defence mechanism. Even the mental development of a child is affected adversely by mouth breathing.

The nose has various defence mechanisms to prevent impurities and excessively cold air entering the body. At the entrance to the nose, a screen of hairs traps dust, tiny insects and other particles that may injure the lungs if you breathe through the mouth. After the entrance of the nose, there is a long winding passage-way lined with mucus membranes, where excessively cool air is warmed and very fine dust particles that escaped the hair screen are caught. Next, in the inner nose are glands which fight off any bacilli which have slipped through the other defences. As if this isn't enough, the inner nose also contains the olfactory organ – our sense of smell. This lets us know if there are any poisonous gases around or if there is any off food present which may injure our health.

The yogis even give further reasons why we should breathe through the nose. They believe that the olfactory organ has another function: the absorption of prana from the air. You can demonstrate the prana-absorbing function for yourself quite easily.

Next time you are at the beach or in the mountains where the prana level is high, breathe deeply through the nose a few times. You will notice a light, fresh feeling come over you. Allow the feeling to go and then breathe through the mouth. You won't feel the same refreshing feeling as when you breathed through your nose. You're breathing in the same air, so obviously the nose is extracting something from the air which the mouth isn't.

If you breathe through the mouth all the time, as many people do, you are cheating yourself of all this free energy (prana). The Yogis say this is a major factor in lowered resistance to disease and impairs the functioning of your vital glands and nervous system. Add to this the fact that pathogens can enter the lungs via mouth breathing, and you can see that it's impossible to be healthy, not to mention vital, if you breathe through the mouth. If not already doing so, start the habit of breathing through the nose now, and instruct your children to do the same.

How the Breathing Exercises Produce Vitality and Rejuvenation

Deep breathing produces the following benefits:

1 Improvement in the quality of the blood due to its increased oxygenation in the lungs. Increased oxygenation of the blood aids the elimination of toxins from the system.

2 Increase in the digestion and assimilation of food. This is due to digestive organs such as the stomach receiving more oxygen and therefore being more efficient, and also to the fact that the food is oxygenated more.

3 Improvement in the health of the nervous system, including the brain, spinal cord, nerve centres and nerves. This is due again to the increased oxygenation and hence nourishment of the nervous system. This improves the health of the whole body, since the nervous system communicates to all parts of the body.

4 Rejuvenation of the glands, especially the pituitary and pineal glands. This is because the brain has a special affinity for oxygen, requiring three times more oxygen than does the rest of the body. This has far-reaching effects on our well being.

5 Rejuvenation of the skin. The skin becomes smoother and a reduction of facial wrinkles occurs.

6 The movements of the diaphragm during the deep breathing exercise massage the abdominal organs – the stomach, small intestine, liver and pancreas. The upper movement of the diaphragm also massages the heart. This stimulates the blood circulation in these organs.

7 The lungs become healthy and powerful, a good insurance against respiratory problems.

8 Deep, slow, yoga breathing causes a reduced work load, and therefore less strain, for the heart. This means a more efficient, stronger heart which will perform better and last longer. It also means reduced blood pressure and less heart disease.

   The yoga breathing exercises reduce the work load on the heart in two ways. Firstly, deep breathing leads to more efficient lungs, which means more oxygen is brought into contact with blood sent to the lungs by the heart. This means that the heart doesn't have to work as hard to deliver oxygen to the tissues. Secondly, deep breathing leads to a greater pressure differential in the lungs, which leads to an increase in the circulation, thus resting the heart a little.

9 Deep, slow breathing assists in weight control. If you are overweight, the extra oxygen burns up the excess fat more efficiently. If you are underweight, the extra oxygen feeds the starving tissues and glands. In other words, yoga tends to produce the ideal weight for you.

10 Relaxation of the mind and body. Slow, deep, rhythmic breathing causes a reflex stimulation of the parasympathetic nervous system, which results in a reduction in the heart rate and relaxation of the muscles. These two factors cause a reflex relaxation of the mind, since the mind and body are very interdependent. In addition, oxygenation of the brain tends to normalise brain function, reducing excessive anxiety levels.

The breathing exercises cause an increase in the elasticity of the lungs and rib cage. This creates an increased breathing capacity *all day*, not just during the actual exercise period. This means all the above benefits also occur all day.

The three yoga breathing exercises reverse ageing by:
- Increasing oxygenation of the blood.
- Increasing the assimilation of food.
- Rejuvenating the nervous system.
- Making the skin smoother and less wrinkled.
- Making the heart stronger and more efficient.
- Relaxing the mind and body.

The Yoga Complete Breathe

This method of breathing is essential in order to do the three yoga breathing exercises described later. It's quite simple, it just takes a little practice.

The complete breath is a combination of three methods; high breathing, mid breathing and low breathing.

High Breathing

This type of breathing is also called 'collar bone breathing'. It's done by raising the ribs, collar bone and shoulders. This is the least desirable form of breathing since the upper lobes of the lungs are used and these have only a small air capacity. Also the upper rib cage is fairly rigid, so not much expansion of the ribs can take place. This form of breathing is quite common, especially among women, probably because they often wear tight clothes around the waist which prevents the far superior abdominal breathing. It's a common cause of digestive, stomach, constipation and gynaecological problems.

The yogis consider that high breathing causes diseases of the respiratory system and tends to lead to the bad habit of mouth breathing.

Mid Breathing

This is also known as 'rib breathing'. This is better than high breathing, but far inferior to low breathing and the yoga complete breath technique.

With this form of breathing, the ribs and chest are expanded sideways.

Low Breathing

This is also called 'abdominal' or 'diaphragmic' breathing and is far more effective than high or mid breathing.

To do low breathing, when you inhale you push the stomach gently forwards with no strain. When exhaling you allow the stomach to return to its normal position.

This type of breathing is far superior to high or mid breathing for four reasons:

1 More air is taken in when inhaling, due to greater movement of the lungs and the fact that the lower lobes of the lungs have a larger capacity than the upper lobes.
2 The diaphragm acts like a second heart. Its piston-like movements expand the base of the lungs, allowing them to suck in more venous blood. The increase in the venous circulation improves the general circulation.
3 The abdominal organs are massaged by the up and down movements of the diaphragm.

4 Low breathing has a beneficial effect on the solar plexus, a very important nerve centre.

Yoga complete breathing includes all three types of breathing methods to gain the maximum possible benefit. It brings into play the whole lung capacity, as well as all the respiratory muscles and takes maximum advantage of the respiratory mechanism.

The yoga complete breath is the basic technique of all the different types of yoga breathing, and therefore should be mastered before you learn the specific breathing exercises.

Keep in mind that this type of breathing is only done when you do the breathing exercises. The rest of the time you should be doing low breathing by pushing the stomach out slightly when you inhale, and then just letting the stomach fall back to its original position when you exhale. Also, make sure you are breathing through your nose and not your mouth.

The yoga complete breath technique brings the whole lung capacity into play and is the basis of the three specific breathing exercises.

The Yoga Complete Breath Technique
Maximum benefit is gained if you sit with the spine erect while doing the breathing.

Inhaling
First, push the stomach forwards as you breathe in.

Second, push the ribs sideways while still breathing in. The stomach will automatically go inwards slightly.

Third, lift the chest and collar bone up while still breathing in.

Even though this is described as three separate processes, it should be done in a smooth, continuous rhythm with each part following smoothly on from the previous part. Try to avoid any jerky movements.

Exhaling
First, just allow the collar bone, chest and ribs to relax – the air will go out automatically.

Second, when all the air seems to be out, push the stomach in slightly to expel any remaining air in the lungs.

Exhaling is a more passive affair, except for the second stage when the stomach is pushed in slightly.

Basic Instructions for the Breathing Exercises

Basic technique:
- Do twice a day: before breakfast and before the evening meal.
- Don't eat for about 15 minutes afterwards.
- Open windows.
- Sit very straight.

1 Find a quiet place where you won't be distracted. This can be outside or inside. If doing the exercises inside, make sure the window is open to allow plenty of fresh air into the room.

2 Sit on a chair or if you prefer, cross-legged on the floor. Make sure you sit very *straight*. Unless your spine is erect, some of the benefits of the breathing exercises will be lost. Don't sit in a tense fashion, just straight and relaxed.

3 Breathe deeply and slowly, without strain. Breathe smoothly and quietly.

4 You should do the exercises on an empty stomach. Wait at least three hours after a heavy meal, and about one and a half hours after a light snack, such as fruit. This is for two reasons. Firstly, a heavy meal will reduce your concentration. Secondly, food in the stomach causes some of your blood and oxygen supply to be diverted to the stomach for digestion. This will reduce the blood and oxygen available for directing to the brain while you are doing the breathing exercises.

5 To gain maximum benefit, do the exercises twice a day, in the early morning before breakfast, and in the early evening. It's best not to eat for about fifteen minutes after the exercises.

You are now ready to do the three deep breathing exercises. They are the rhythmic, retention and alternate nostril breathing exercises. The yogis consider these to be the three most potent breathing exercises for vitality and rejuvenation, and they are completely safe.

The Rhythmic Breathing Exercise

Benefits of the Rhythmic Breathing Exercise
The yogis claim that by rhythmic breathing you bring yourself into harmonious vibration with nature and attunement to the rhythm of the universe. This assists the unfolding of latent powers.

Everything in the universe is in vibration, from the atom to the planets themselves. In all vibration there exists a certain rhythm, so rhythm pervades the universe. The movement of the planets around the sun, the ebb and flow of the tide, all follow rhythmic laws.

Our bodies are also subject to rhythmic laws called biorhythms and these are currently being researched. Sleep and waking periods also have a rhythm. Sleep itself is governed by the sleep cycle, a definite series of stages which occur when we sleep. The waking period also has precise cycles of varying metabolic rates which differ between individuals. For example, some people are wide awake early in the morning, while others reach their peak efficiency in the afternoon or evening.

The fast, jerky tempo of life in the cities tends to upset our natural rhythms. This causes a loss of equilibrium, resulting in irritability, tension, mood swings and general nervousness. Some people are very sensitive to this negative external influence, which may result in mental instability or nervous breakdown. The yogis say that the deep rhythmic breathing exercise will allow the body to re-establish its own natural rhythm and attune us more to the cosmic rhythm. This will protect us from any negative external influences.

The deep rhythmic breathing exercise, by falling in with the rhythm of the body, also allows the body to absorb a lot more oxygen than just normal deep breathing.

Benefits of the rhythmic breathing exercise:
- Increased oxygen supply (even more than deep breathing).
- Re-establishes the body's own natural rhythm.

Technique

1   Sit up straight, either on a chair or cross-legged on the floor. Let your hands just rest on your lap.

2   Inhale slowly and deeply for eight seconds. Push your stomach forwards to a count of four seconds, and then push your ribs sideways for a count of two seconds, and then finally lift your chest and collar bone upwards for a count of two seconds. This makes a total of eight seconds.

3   Don't breathe out immediately; instead hold the breath (called retention) for four seconds.

4   Exhale slowly for eight seconds. For the first six seconds just allow the collar bone, chest and ribs to relax, so the breath goes out automatically. For the last two seconds, push the stomach in gently, to expel all the air from the lungs.

5   Keep the stomach in this position for four seconds before you take the next breath.

Do the above exercise three times the first week, and add one more round each week, until you are doing seven breaths. It's best to build up the number of breaths gradually, because if you are not used to doing yoga breathing and you overdo it, you will purify your system too quickly. This will cause your body to release toxins from your tissues into the blood circulation too quickly, resulting in unpleasant symptoms such as headaches, skin rashes and fatigue.

The yogi rule for rhythmic breathing is that the units of inhalation and exhalation should be the same, while the units for retention and between breaths should be half that of inhalation and exhalation; that is, a ratio of 2:1:2:1.

Sometimes beginners find that inhaling for eight seconds is too difficult. If this is the case, inhale for six seconds, hold the breath for three seconds, exhale for six seconds, and pause for three seconds before taking the next breath. In a few weeks you will easily be able to do 8:4:8:4.

Try to feel the rhythm of the vibratory motion throughout your whole body. This will eventually come with practice.

Rhythmic Breathing with Visualisation

The rhythmic breathing exercise is made much more potent if you use visualisation while doing the breathing.

Visualisation works on the principle that whatever you concentrate on, an extra supply of oxygen and prana (life force) will be directed to that area. The secret of successful yoga is combining the exercise with visualising the specific area the exercise affects.

The technique is simple. When you breathe in, visualise the prana accumulating in the solar plexus area, just above the navel, behind the stomach. The solar plexus is where the body stores its energy. When you retain the breath and breathe out, visualise the prana going to the brain. Just concentrate on the brain area.

The visualisation technique achieves two things. Firstly, it produces a reserve of energy in the solar plexus, thereby increasing your general energy level. Secondly, since some of the stored energy is directed to the brain, brain function and vitality are increased.

The Retained Breath Exercise

Physiologists claim that the air breathed in should remain in the lungs for ten to twenty seconds to maximise the gaseous interchange in the lungs. The yogis devised an exercise in which the breath is retained for four times the duration of inhalation (about twelve to sixteen seconds) thousands of years ago. They claimed this exercise would take maximum advantage of the air inhaled.

Benefits of the Retained Breath Exercise

1 It provides the optimum supply of oxygen to the body. Even jogging and other aerobic exercise doesn't achieve this, since the breathing is quick and shallow and there is no retention of oxygen.
2 The air which has remained in the lungs from previous inhalations is purified.

3   There is increased oxygenation of the blood.
4   The retained breath gathers up some of the waste matter of the body and expels
    it on exhalation.
5   The lungs increase their elasticity and capacity and become more powerful. This
    allows benefits to be enjoyed all day, not just during the exercise.
6   The exercise builds a bigger, more powerful chest and prevents or helps to
    correct sagging breasts in women.

Technique
1   Sit up straight.

2   Inhale for four seconds. Push your stomach forwards to a count of two seconds
    and then push your ribs sideways for one second, and finally lift your chest and
    collar bone upwards for one second. This makes a total of four seconds.

3   Hold the breath for sixteen seconds. If you find this is difficult at the start, just
    hold for eight seconds, and gradually over a period of a few months build up to
    sixteen seconds.

4   Exhale for eight seconds. For the first six seconds, just allow the collar bone and
    ribs to relax, so the breath goes out automatically. For the last two seconds push
    the stomach in gently to expel the air from the lungs.

Do this exercise only once the first week, and add one more round each week, until
you are doing three rounds.

   The yogi rule for the retention breath is that exhalation should be twice that of
inhalation, and retention should be four times that of inhalation; that is, a ratio of
1:4:2.

   Use visualisation as with the rhythmic breathing exercise.

The Alternate Nostril Breathing Exercise

With this exercise, we breathe through only one nostril at a time. The logic behind
this exercise is that normal breathing does alternate from one nostril to the other at
various times during the day. You can easily prove this to yourself. Just squeeze one
nostril closed with your thumb and try breathing through just the one nostril.
Repeat this procedure with the other nostril. You'll find it much easier to breathe
through one of the nostrils than the other. One of the nostrils will always be partially
blocked, so we are always breathing through mainly one nostril.

Benefits of the
retained breath
exercise:
• Optimum supply of
  oxygen.
• Air which has
  remained in the
  lungs is purified.
• Greatly increased
  lung elasticity and
  capacity which
  allows the benefits
  to be enjoyed all day.
• Builds a powerful
  chest and corrects
  sagging breasts.

Benefits of the
alternate nostril
breathing exercise:

• Optimum
functioning of both
sides of the brain –
the logical and the
creative.

• Produces a balanced
personality.

• Calms the mind.

In a healthy person the breath will alternate between nostrils about every two hours. Because most of us are not in optimum health, this time period varies considerably between people and further reduces our vitality. According to the yogis, when the breath continues to flow in one nostril for more than two hours, as it does with most of us, it will have an adverse effect on our health. If the right nostril is involved, the result is mental and nervous disturbance. If the left nostril is involved, the result is chronic fatigue and reduced brain function. The longer the flow of breath in one nostril, the more serious the illness will be.

The alternate nostril breathing exercise restores the normal breathing pattern between nostrils and raises our health and vitality levels.

Benefits

The exercise produces optimum function to both sides of the brain: that is optimum creativity and optimum logical verbal activity. This also creates a more balanced person, since both halves of the brain are functioning properly.

The yogis consider this to be the best technique to calm the mind and the nervous system.

The Scientific Confirmation

Medical science has recently discovered something which was known by the yogis thousands of years ago: the *nasal cycle*. Scientists have recently found that we don't breathe equally with both nostrils, that one nostril is much easier to breathe through than the other at any particular time and that this alternates about every three hours.

The yogis claim that the natural period is every two hours, but we must remember these studies were done on people who, like the rest of the population, do not have an optimum health level.

Scientists also discovered another very important fact – that the nasal cycle corresponds with *brain function*. It was found that the electrical activity of the brain was greater on the side opposite the less congested nostril. The right side of the brain controls creative activity, while the left side controls logical verbal activity. The research showed that when the left nostril was less obstructed, the right side of the brain was predominant. Test subjects were indeed found to do better on creative tests. Similarly when the right nostril was less obstructed the left side of the brain was predominant. Test subjects did better on verbal skills.

Medical science has not quite caught up with the ancient yogis yet. The yogis went one step further. They observed that a lot of disease was due to the nasal cycle being disturbed; that is, if a person breathed for too long through one nostril. To prevent and correct this condition, they developed the alternative nostril breathing technique. This clears any blockage to air flow in the nostrils and re-establishes the natural nasal cycle. For example, the yogis have known for a long time that prolonged breathing through the left nostril only (over a period of years) will produce a tendency to asthma. They also know that this so-called incurable disease can be greatly helped by teaching the patient to breathe through the right nostril until the asthma is improved, and then to prevent it recurring by doing the alternate nostril breathing technique. The yogis also believe that diabetes is caused to a large extent by breathing mainly through the right nostril.

Medical science confirms the rationale of the yoga alternate breathing exercise.

Technique
Close the right nostril with your right thumb and inhale through the left nostril. Do this to the count of four seconds.

Immediately close the left nostril with your right ring finger and little finger, and at the same time remove your thumb from the right nostril, and exhale through this nostril. Do this to the count of eight seconds. This completes a half round.

Inhale through the right nostril to the count of four seconds. Close the right nostril with your right thumb and exhale through the left nostril to the count of eight seconds. This completes one full round.

Start by doing three rounds, adding one per week until you are doing seven rounds.

Deep Breathing When Walking

This is a time-economical way of doing additional deep breathing to gain extra vitality. Inhale to the count of four steps (one step = one movement each of the right and

Do some deep breathing while walking to gain extra vitality with no extra time cost.

left leg), retain the breath to the count of two steps, exhale to the count of four steps, and pause for two steps before taking the next breath.

If you walk slowly, the above will be difficult, so just inhale for two steps, retain for one step, exhale for two steps, and pause for one step.

Don't do this walking breathing exercise on busy main roads, since the pollution from cars will counteract any benefits.

Incentive to do the Deep Breathing Exercises

Oxygen is the most vital food of all. It's also free and has no calories in it, which makes it ideal for the budget conscious and people trying to slim.

While aerobic exercises such as jogging are very beneficial, they are not sufficient for optimum vitality and rejuvenation. Deep breathing is also necessary, for two reasons. Firstly, with aerobic exercise some of the energy gained in the exercise is lost in supplying energy to do the exercise. With deep breathing there is no energy loss. All the oxygen taken in is used for vitality and rejuvenation. Secondly, there is no deep breathing during aerobic exercise, since the body has to breathe quickly in order to supply the muscles with energy for the exercise. This means you lose many of the benefits of deep breathing. The main benefits from aerobic exercise come from the training effect, which produces a healthier heart and blood vessels and increased circulation.

It makes sense to do both aerobic exercise and the deep breathing exercises. This gives you *all* the benefits of deep breathing and fitness and would provide a much more comprehensive insurance policy for a long, sickness-free life. It will also give you a high vitality level and younger looks.

From the viewpoint of western physiology alone, without considering yoga philosophy, the deep breathing exercises are extremely beneficial to our wellbeing.

Remember that oxygen, as well as being the most vital nutrient, is free and has no calories – so take advantage of it by doing the breathing exercises!

Highlights

1 Deep breathing exercises are necessary since our breathing tends to be too shallow, which reduces our vitality level and makes us more prone to disease.

2 The main cause of shallow breathing is our modern way of life which is too fast, anxiety producing, provides mostly indoor work and reduces our physical activity.

3 Oxygen is the most vital nutrient for our bodies and is especially important for good brain function. The deep breathing exercises will increase the supply of oxygen to the body, resulting in increased vitality, better brain function and staying younger longer.

4 You should breathe through your nose and not your mouth all the time. Mouth breathing will reduce your vitality and make you more prone to disease. If you do breathe through your mouth, you can break the habit simply by keeping your mouth closed.

5 The breathing exercises produce vitality and rejuvenation by increasing oxygenation of the blood, aiding the digestion and assimilation of food, causing a healthier nervous system, rejuvenating the glands and skin, making the lungs more powerful and the heart more efficient and stronger, controlling weight, relaxing the mind and body and causing us to become more attuned to the rhythm of the universe.

6 It is essential to learn the yoga complete breath, since this is the basis of the yoga breathing exercises.

7 The three most effective deep breathing exercises are described: the rhythmic breathing exercise, the retained breath exercise, and the alternate nostril breathing exercise.

How to Release Stress and the Supreme Relaxation Exercise

Why Deep Relaxation and Stress Release are Necessary

Tense muscles produce lactic acid which causes fatigue and premature ageing.

Your body will function better if the body and mind are relaxed. The brain and nerves function better, which in turn affect the whole body. Also, relaxed muscles accumulate less lactic acid than tense muscles. Lactic acid is a waste product of muscle metabolism, which in excess can cause fatigue and premature ageing.

Dis-ease is a very accurate descriptive word. It implies that illness is due to not being at ease (that is, having tense muscles and nerves).

Since your body functions better when relaxed, you will also live longer. Tense people tend to have high blood pressure and stress is a proven contributory cause of both heart disease and cancer. All these diseases are major causes of premature death.

Overactive nerves and tense muscles sap your energy even while you are asleep, so that you don't wake up feeling fresh.

When your body is relaxed and your mind is free from stress, you will certainly look and feel better. You will have more vitality and look younger. Overactive nerves and tense muscles sap your energy, especially when you consider that this occurs for twenty-four hours – even while you are sleeping.

When the nervous system is free from stress, the mind is also clear and intelligent and we perceive the world as a joyful place and appreciate life more. Like a current running through a filament, when joy enlivens the nervous system, the whole system lights up and radiates vitality and youthfulness.

Since a stress-free mind is clear and intelligent, it is also the basis of success in all areas of life – business, career, relationships, etc. Success results in satisfaction, making you even happier. This further increases your vitality and youthfulness.

Why Sleep does not Usually Produce Enough Rest

A lot of people think that a night's sleep is sufficient rest for the day. This is only the case if you sleep very deeply and for long enough. Most people do not sleep deeply for seven to eight hours. They go to bed unrelaxed and the muscles remain tense throughout the sleep period. This tenses the mind in turn, and so the whole system is tense. Consequently they don't feel relaxed and fresh when they wake up. This is usually made worse by tossing and turning and dreaming.

Deep relaxation is different however, since you are completely still and your muscles are totally relaxed. There is no energy wastage from tight muscles and an overactive nervous system. In fact ten minutes in a state of deep relaxation is more beneficial than a night's sleep spent in tossing and turning! Of course you still need sleep, but to totally relax the nervous system and muscles, it needs to be supplemented by a short period of deep relaxation.

Later you will be shown the best techniques for releasing stress and producing deep relaxation, but first we need to understand the nature of stress.

The Nature of Stress

Most people consider stress to be some external factor which causes discomfort. In reality, studies have shown that stress is mainly an internal factor; that is, it's how we personally react to a situation which causes the discomfort, not the external situation itself.

One person may react to a situation by considering it as a problem and worrying about it. Another person considers the situation as a challenge and looks forward to solving the problem. The external situation is the same, and yet one person experiences stress and the other person doesn't. Obviously stress is an internal factor and depends on your attitude rather than the event itself. The solution is to think positively in any situation, since most potential disasters don't happen anyway, and you are better off taking positive steps to prevent or remedy the problem than worrying about it. Shakespeare was right when he suggested that nothing is really good or bad, it's just our thinking which makes it so.

Recent research by Dr Richard Lazarus and a group of his colleagues at the University of California, indicated that frequent, minor stressors are more harmful than one particular major stress. Such minor stressors are things like getting stuck in traffic jams or frequent arguments with your partner. Frequent minor stresses are more harmful because they are cumulative and there is little time in between them to recover.

Why the Body Cannot Cope with the Stress of Modern Life

A certain amount of tension and stress is vital for everyday life. We must respond to challenges and danger with a certain degree of tension, otherwise we would achieve nothing.

When the nervous system is free from stress, we perceive the world as a joyful place and radiate vitality and youthfulness.

Our sleep is usually not deep or restful enough, so we need to do the deep relaxation exercise.

Ten minutes of the deep relaxation exercise is more beneficial than a night's unrestful sleep.

The best way to prevent stress is to think positively in every situation.

Studies show that stress is mainly an internal factor; that is, how we react to a situation rather than the situation itself.

The body reacts to stress – whether emotional (perceived danger) or physical – by activating a series of mechanisms, collectively known as the fight or flight response, which prepares us either to fight or to run. When this happens, a series of physiological reactions occur:

1 Our muscles begin to contract, thereby fortifying our 'body armour'. We are now more protected from bodily injury.
2 Our metabolism speeds up, providing more strength and energy with which to fight or run. The heart rate and the amount of blood pumped with each beat increases.
3 Our rate of breathing begins to increase, providing more oxygen to the brain and muscles.
4 Our digestive system begins to shut down, diverting more blood and energy to the large muscles needed to fight or run.
5 Arteries to our arms and legs begin to constrict and our blood begins to clot more quickly, so that less blood would be lost if we were wounded or injured.

We are designed to cope with *acute* stress, not the *chronic* stress of modern life. When these stress mechanisms are chronically activated, the same responses that are designed to protect us can become harmful, even lethal. Arteries constrict not just in our arms and legs but also inside our hearts. Blood clots are more likely to form inside our coronary arteries. Both these factors may cause a heart attack.

In the old days stress was mainly physical, and therefore the response was physical: fight or flight. After a physical challenge, the body relaxed and the person was probably all the better for the incident. Physical exercise and relaxation are health promoting. The problem nowadays is that the stress is mainly emotional, so that the body is not physically exhausted and therefore does not relax afterwards.

The types of stress we suffer from today are financial problems, relationship problems and the fast pace of life. This can lead to stress symptoms such as headaches, high blood pressure and chronic fatigue.

How to Tell if You Have Stress Overload

The following are common symptoms of stress overload:

1 Over-reacting to minor problems, such as excessive anger or impatience.
2 Increased use of alcohol, coffee or tobacco.
3 Overeating or loss of appetite.
4 Disturbed sleep.
5 Reduced work efficiency and reduced decision-making ability.

6 Physical symptoms such as headaches, indigestion, ulcers, neck tension, teeth grinding, skin conditions and heart palpitations. These conditions are called psychosomatic disorders.

Stress can cause many physical disorders such as headaches, ulcers, skin conditions, heart disease, high blood pressure, colds and reduced immunity.

Physical Diseases Caused by Stress

Physical diseases caused or aggravated by stress (psychosomatic diseases) are well documented.

The most significant physical effect is the suppression of the body's immune system. In one study of students during stressful examinations, antibody levels were found to be lower than normal, making them more susceptible to infections. Other studies have shown that aggressive Type A personalities catch more colds than the more relaxed Type B personalities.

Studies have also found a strong connection between heart disease and stress.

Stress is also a factor in many skin disorders. In a recent Swedish study, psoriasis sufferers showed higher levels of stress hormones than healthy subjects when subjected to stressful tests.

Another study showed that people with high blood pressure had higher levels of adrenalin and noradrenalin, the stress hormones, than did subjects with normal blood pressure when given a word-matching test.

Studies have also shown a strong correlation of high stress levels with sexual problems.

Are the Effects of Stress the Same for Men and Women?

A study of 311 male and 171 female executives revealed that men and women respond to stress differently. Male executives with stress-related problems suffered more from physical illnesses, such as ulcers and heart disease, while women suffered more from mental disorders, such as excessive anxiety and depression.

But men and women with stress-related illnesses also had some similarities such as alcohol abuse and compulsive work habits. They also tended to have a sedentary lifestyle, which does not help stress.

What Distinguishes People who Manage Stress Successfully?

University of Chicago researchers did an eight-year study on how managers coped with stress. It was found that those who handled stress well had three personality traits in common: commitment, control and challenge. They were enthusiastic about their work and tended not to give up in the face of obstacles. They also felt they could influence events at their company and even turn situations to their advantage. They also viewed change as stimulating rather than stressful.

How to Relax and Achieve More

You may claim that you don't get time to relax – you have a full life. The fact is, if you don't find time to relax, you are reducing the quality of your life and eventually the quantity. Even if you are busy, you can learn to do things in a relaxed manner. Here's how to do it:

1 **Don't rush.** Slow down. You'll get the work done just as quickly, since you'll make fewer mistakes. Rushing around really isn't productive – it's just nervous tension which wastes your energy and produces fatigue. Also put less effort into your activities. Most of us use more effort than is necessary for a particular activity. This extra effort drains even more of your energy supplies. In short, learn to take it easy.
2 **Mental detachment.** Become mentally detached from your work. This doesn't mean that you don't put your best into the job. It means you don't worry about the result. Just apply the cause and the results will take care of themselves. You will actually achieve more, since you won't have worry interfering with doing your best. Establish goals without worrying about results.
3 **Positive, pleasant thoughts.** These types of thoughts have a relaxing effect on the nerves and muscles. They tend to make you happier, and a happy person is a more relaxed and successful person. The relaxed nerves and muscles make you feel better and will tend to encourage pleasant thoughts naturally, without effort. A beneficial cycle is created.

   Unfortunately it also works the other way. If your thoughts are mainly negative and unpleasant, this causes tension in your nerves and muscles. This increased tension affects the mind and the mind becomes more negative – a vicious cycle is set up. Fortunately, this vicious cycle can easily be broken; just change your thoughts to positive, pleasant ones. Prevent Stress. Try to avoid situations which produce stress, such as financially over committing yourself.

How To Release Stress

Exercise

People usually exercise to increase their fitness, but many people notice a release of stress and a feeling of relaxation after exercise.

Many studies have shown that exercise does reduce anxiety levels and depression. One recent American study compared the effect of stress on two groups of students. One group had completed a fourteen-week aerobics program; the other had not. When each group was asked to solve a set of mostly unsolvable problems, the exercise group displayed a much lower level of muscle tension and anxiety than the non-exercise group.

Studies show that exercise reduces anxiety levels and depression.

Laughing

Laughing has long been known to release stress, as well as being enjoyable. Research verifies this fact. Laughing increases respiratory exchange and heart rate, as well as stimulating the production of beta-endorphins, the same chemicals which produce the runner's 'high'. In fact, laughing can be regarded as 'internal jogging'.

Research shows that laughing stimulates the production of beta endorphins, the same chemicals which produce the runner's 'high'. In fact laughing can be described as 'internal jogging'.

Crying

Studies show that crying reduces stress. In one study, a group of people with stress-related disorders was compared with a group of healthy people of similar age background. One major difference found was that the healthy group was not ashamed to cry, whereas the sick group regarded crying as a sign of weakness or loss of control. In a survey, 73 percent of men and 85 percent of women questioned stated that they felt better after crying.

Social Relationships

Many studies have shown that separation from other family members – especially death and divorce – are the most stressful events in life. Fortunately it also works the other way – support from people around you can have an equally powerful effect in reducing stress.

Studies have shown that social support causes an increase in lifespan, reduces stress following the loss of a loved one, speeds recovery from surgery and heart attacks and alleviates the symptoms of asthma and other disorders. One study examined 109 people living near the Three Mile Island nuclear plant at the time of the disaster in 1979. It was found that those residents who received little or no support from friends and neighbours suffered the most stress-related problems.

Relaxation Techniques

Studies show that people who practise a relaxation technique or meditate have lower stress levels.

Studies show that people who set a little time aside each day to practise a relaxation technique or meditate have lower stress levels. Studies also show that these people have lower blood pressure and a reduced incidence of heart disease (see the deep relaxation techniques later).

Colour

The colours blue and brown reduce stress.

Choosing the right colour for your surroundings can reduce stress. Colour often works in a very subtle way, so you are influenced subliminally (below the threshold of consciousness).

Scientific research has shown that red is the most stimulating colour and can increase your stress level, as indicated by greater blood pressure, pulse and brain wave activity.

If you wish to produce a calming effect and reduce stress, you should surround yourself with blues and browns.

Recreation

Vary your activities and don't spend too long on any one activity.

This is a very apt word, since it literally means to re-create; that is, to change activity and become more creative. If you spend too long on any one activity, even if you enjoy it, stress will occur. Vary your activities and spend some time doing such things as sport, gardening, reading, hobbies, and socialising.

If you need to spend a long time on one particular activity, take small breaks and do something else.

Don't view recreation as a waste of time. If you work too hard and do not have enough recreation, stress will occur and you will be less productive in your work. Recreation is actually a good investment as well as being enjoyable.

Increase Your Vitality Level

If you increase your vitality level you can handle stress – just follow these steps.

This is probably the main factor in coping with stress. If your vitality level is high, you can handle stress and you'll tend to view events more as a challenge, rather than stress. If you're feeling good, life takes on a different perspective. If stressful situations do arise, you have the energy and clarity of mind to overcome them. You can't always avoid stress, but you can increase your vitality level so that you are better able to cope with it.

To increase your vitality level, just follow the principles outlined in this book. Pay particular attention to the chapter on sleep – good sleep has the greatest immediate effect on your vitality level.

Make sure your nutritional programme is sound, too. Try to avoid processed foods, since the chemicals in them can affect your brain function, and good brain function is essential for stress management. Avoid too much sugar, either as a sweetener or in foods, since it has been shown to produce hyperactivity of the nervous system as well as fatigue. Both of these symptoms will make stress management more difficult. Also avoid excess meat, since it contains a lot of chemicals, and the toxins in it will make you more irritable and aggressive. Your body is also taking in adrenalin which the animal produced due to the fear of death. All these factors will reduce your ability to handle stress. Overeating should also be avoided, since the excess food draws extra blood from the brain to the stomach for digestion. This produces fatigue, further reducing your stress-handling ability as well as your general health.

Set Realistic Goals

Regularly – at least once a year – stand back and take a long hard look at your life. Assess the past and present in terms of what you have achieved in various fields, and what it has cost you in terms of strain and tension. Think of the future in terms of what you would like and what you are realistically able to achieve.

The 'mid-life crisis', when stress disorders peak, is usually caused by setting unrealistic goals in life.

One of the most common causes of stress if people's failure to see that the goals they have set themselves are beyond them. They need to readjust their sights. Ambition is a necessary and constructive quality, but if stress disorders are to be avoided, it needs to be tempered with an ability to give up and change direction if it becomes clear that an achievement is impossible. The so-called 'midlife crisis', when stress disorders peak, is usually caused by unrealistic goals in life.

How not to Reduce Stress

People often turn to quick fixes to relieve their stress. These can produce a short, temporary relief, but they usually increase stress levels in the long run. Below are a list of the quick fixes commonly used:

Quick fixes such as coffee, cigarettes, alcohol and tranquillisers actually increase stress levels.

Coffee and Cigarettes

The caffeine in coffee and the nicotine in cigarettes both stimulate the body's neuroendocrine system. This is also what stress does. The result is increased blood pressure, pulse rate and anxiety. The initial pleasant stimulation experienced is achieved at the expense of using up the body's energy reserves. Also, gradual tolerance develops which diminishes the stimulating effects.

Alcohol, Tranquillisers and Sleeping Pills

These have the opposite effects of coffee and cigarettes. They depress the body's neuroendocrine system. Initially they do relieve stress, but over a long period they will cause increased anxiety and depression. They also slow reaction time and impair coordination and judgement. Tolerance can develop to these drugs and they can become addictive. Also, their excessive use can cause diseases of the liver, nervous system and other body parts.

Coffee and alcohol in strict moderation will cause no harm, but keep away from cigarettes, tranquillisers and sleeping pills. If you are taking tranquillisers or sleeping pills, gradually reduce the dosage, with the co-operation of your doctor.

Note: Keep in mind that all of the above five drugs will reduce the quality of your sleep, so your body will be less able to cope with stress, thus defeating the very purpose of the drugs. If you drink coffee, try to limit yourself to just one cup in the morning, to minimise its effect on sleep. If you drink alcohol, drink just before your evening meal, since the food in your stomach will reduce the effect of the alcohol on your sleep.

The Physical Deep Relaxation Exercise

This relaxation exercise is based on an ancient yoga technique and is the most effective way to relax your body.

This deep relaxation technique is very simple, but also very effective. It's based on an ancient yoga technique.

Firstly, make sure you have a quiet place where you won't be disturbed for around ten minutes or so. Wear loose clothing so that you will not be distracted by any discomfort while you are relaxing. Make sure, too, that you are neither too cold nor too hot.

It's best to do the exercise on the floor, with a rug underneath you if you wish.

1   Lie flat on your back with your arms alongside your body. Make sure you feel comfortable.
2   Breathe slowly with your abdomen. On inhaling, push your abdomen forwards and on exhaling, just let your abdomen fall back to its normal position.
    Concentrate on establishing this slow, relaxed breathing pattern for a few minutes.
3   The next stage is to relax your muscles. Tense your right foot and toes for about three seconds and then quickly let go. Do the same with your left foot and toes.
    Next, tense your right leg for three seconds, let go and repeat with your left leg.
    Next, clench your right fist tightly and at the same time tense your right arm for about three seconds. Let go and repeat with your left fist and arm.
    Next, tense your shoulders and upper back for three seconds and let go.
    Repeat this process for your neck, then your face, and finally your eyes. For the face, just screw your face up. For the eyes, close them as tightly as possible.
4   Now become aware of the body parts you have just relaxed, and feel if there is any tension left in them. If any part is still tense, repeat the contraction/relaxation for that particular part, and mentally tell the area to 'let go'.

5   Just lie there for a few minutes, breathing slowly and enjoying the relaxed feeling. If any thoughts arise in your mind, don't try to stop them – just let them go.

6   Just before you get up, raise your arms above your head and stretch your whole body for a few seconds. Stretching is a very effective muscle relaxer.

7   When you stand up, shake your hands for a few seconds and then shake each foot. This releases any residual tension that may be left. this completes your deep relaxation technique.

Don't expect to be an expert the first time you try this. With practice you will get even better results. Once you are proficient in the technique, ten minutes of practice will make you feel better than several hours of sleep. Normal sleep is not as restful as you may think. During sleep you are tossing and turning, as well as experiencing mental tension from any unpleasant dreams. All this causes muscle tension, which is one reason why many people don't wake up feeling fresh in the morning. The deep relaxation exercise is just the opposite to this. Instead of muscle tension you consciously relax your muscles, and there are no unpleasant dreams to cause mental tension. This is why such a short period of deep relaxation can be more restful than several hours of normal sleep.

Regular practice of the deep relaxation exercise will cause you to cultivate a more detached outlook on life. This will make you a happier as well as a healthier person. You will cease to identify yourself so closely with external events, which allows you to see things more clearly and objectively. You will sleep better and start to look younger.

Scientific tests show that this technique does much to reduce muscle tension. It also relieves stress symptoms such as tension headaches, anxiety, hypertension and insomnia.

The relaxation effect extends beyond the practice period. Studies have shown that with regular practice, you can stay in the relaxed state for several hours.

The best times to do the deep relaxation exercise are after your yoga session, when you are feeling tired or tense or just before sleep if you are having trouble sleeping. If you do it before sleep, it's best to do it in bed in case you fall asleep.

Mental Deep Relaxation Exercises

The mental deep relaxation exercise combines the ancient wisdom of yoga with the modern technique of self-hypnosis and takes you to deeper levels of relaxation.

This exercise is best done immediately after the physical deep relaxation exercise. It takes you to a deeper level of relaxation and is extremely effective and economical with time. The exercise combines the ancient wisdom of yoga and the scientific method of self-hypnosis.

1 Do the physical deep relaxation exercise to relax your muscles.
2 When you breathe slowly, put your attention on the rising and falling of your abdomen. This concentrates your mind and distracts you from other thoughts.
3 Concentrate your attention on the body parts you have previously relaxed, and instruct them mentally to relax. Go through each body part one at a time and repeat the mental instruction several times.
4 Next, concentrate your attention on your heart beat and mentally instruct it to calm down. Repeat this for about one minute. Don't worry, your heart won't stop.
5 Now repeat the following autosuggestion several times to yourself:

'I'm feeling very relaxed. My eyes are feeling very heavy and tired. I'm now going into a state of deep, deep rest.'

Your mind will now be in a state like a light hypnotic trance. This means your conscious mind has been partially turned off, allowing any suggestions you make to go straight to your subconscious. This is the time to break any bad habits such as smoking. Just mentally repeat a sentence about the habit to yourself several times; for example, 'I will not smoke any more cigarettes'.
6 Whether you choose to use your relaxed, trance-like state for breaking habits or not, just lie there for a few minutes enjoying the peaceful deep rest state.

Highlights

1 Deep relaxation periods and stress release are necessary, since muscle tension and mental stress will eventually cause disease and premature ageing.

2 Sleep does not always provide sufficient rest, since most people do not sleep deeply because of muscle tension, worries, dreams and tossing and turning. With the deep relaxation exercise, your muscles are relaxed and you are completely still.

3 To live a more relaxed life and achieve more, slow down, put less effort into your activity, cultivate mental detachment and think positive, pleasant thoughts.

4 Stress is an internal rather than an external factor; that is, how we react to a situation causes the discomfort, not the external situation itself.

5 The following are common symptoms of stress overload: over-reacting to minor problems; increased use of alcohol, coffee and tobacco; overeating or loss of appetite; disturbed sleep; reduced work efficiency and decision-making ability; and physical symptoms such as headaches and neck tension.

6 Stress can actually cause physical (psychosomatic) diseases by suppressing the body's immune system and increasing susceptibility to heart disease, infections and cancer.

7 The best ways to release stress are as follows: exercise, laughing, crying, social relationships, relaxation techniques, the right colours, avoiding stressful situations and recreation.

8 *Don't* reduce stress with coffee, cigarettes, alcohol, tranquillisers or sleeping pills. These are 'quick fixes' which increase your stress level in the long run.

9 Learn to do the physical and mental deep relaxation exercises, since they are very effective in releasing stress and take only a short time.

Using Your Shower for Rejuvenation

The Therapeutic Use of Water

Water is the most universal and the most ancient of all remedial agents, dating back to the days of the early Egyptian and Assyrian dynasties. The early Spartans enacted laws making cold-water bathing compulsory, while under the Romans the therapeutic use of water reached a peak. In Japan, the cold bath has been used for healing for over 900 years.

Two personalities stand out in the history of the therapeutic use of water. The first is Hippocrates, the 'Father of Medicine'. He successfully treated a great variety of maladies with water therapy, including fevers, ulcers and haemorrhages. He had an excellent understanding of the physiological properties of water. The second is Vincent Priessnitz, an Austrian farmer's son who observed that sick animals tried to get to streams and rivers to bathe in running water. In the early 1800's he built a water treatment establishment which could deal with 1,000 patients at a time – a forerunner of the modern hydrotherapy spas of Europe.

The Benefits of the Hot/Cool or Cool Shower

When the proper procedure is followed a hot shower followed by a short cool shower, or a cool shower alone, will rejuvenate the whole system. In particular, it will produce the following benefits:

1 Stimulation of all the glands, especially the adrenal glands.
2 Increased vitality due to stimulation of the adrenal glands and the brain.
3 An increase in the blood circulation and all the benefits which follow from this.
4 Stimulation of the nervous system, including the brain and spine.

The hot/cool or cool shower, when the correct procedure is followed, will rejuvenate the whole system.

5 An increase in body metabolism, including increased efficiency in burning up excess fat.
6 An increase in your blood count. More blood cells in circulation mean more oxygen in the system and also more resistance to infection.
7 An increase in muscle and skin tone. Your muscles and skin will be firmer, giving a younger, healthier appearance.

How Water Treatment Works

When the body is warmed up, either by a hot shower or exercise, the blood vessels in the skin expand, increasing their capacity to take blood. To fill these expanded blood vessels in the skin, blood rushes from the deeper tissues of the body to the skin. When a brief cool shower is then taken, the skin blood vessels contract, causing even more warm blood to go back to the deeper tissues. At the same time, the brain records this coolness in the skin area and compensates by sending fresh warm blood from the liver into the circulation. This causes fresh warm blood to go to all parts of the body. This flushing of the deeper tissues of the body with extra fresh warm blood causes a general feeling of warmth throughout the body, even though a cool shower has been taken. It also causes a feeling of vitality and freshness.

This warm glow and feeling of vitality will last all day if the proper technique is followed, as described below. The technique also shows how to stimulate the powerful nerve centres of the spine, including the solar plexus.

The Vitality/Rejuvenation Shower Technique

It's very important to follow these instructions exactly in order to get maximum benefits.

There are two basic techniques you can use: one from yoga and the other a modern western technique. Both work equally well, so try both to see which suits you better. They are based on the same principles, but have slight variations in procedure.

The rejuvenation shower will produce a warm glow and a feeling of vitality all day.

The Yoga Shower
Since this involves a cool shower only, without warming up with a hot shower first, it is necessary to do some aerobic (fitness) exercise first to warm up. This can be a jog, a brisk walk, aerobics or just running on the spot for a few minutes.

Next take a cool shower for a few minutes. Make sure the water is cool and not cold. Cold water is unpleasant and can be a shock to the body not used to it. Over a

Make sure that the shower is cool, not cold, and run the water slowly.

period of a few months you may gradually make the water cooler, allowing your body to adapt to completely cold water. It's also best to run the shower *slowly*, so as not to cool the body excessively. To warm yourself up in the shower, rub your body vigorously with your hands or a course cloth. This also enhances the physiological effect of the shower. To further increase the effectiveness, breathe deeply while taking the shower.

After the shower, rub the hands vigorously over the body several times. There is something in the human hands which cannot be duplicated by a towel. Continue the deep breathing while you are doing this. Don't dry yourself, just leave a little moisture on the surface of the skin.

Next, dress *immediately* in warm clothes. Don't worry, you won't feel cold. In fact you will experience a pleasant feeling of warmth all over the body and radiate a magnetic glow. This is what the yogis call the 'warm reaction'. It's an indication that your whole body is being rejuvenated and makes you feel good all day.

To further intensify the effect, the yogis do a little exercise immediately after dressing, such as a couple of minutes running on the spot.

If you find cool water too daunting, start with water which is just warm and gradually make the water cooler.

The Modern Western Method

The basic difference from the yoga method is that with the western method a hot shower is taken before the cool shower, and after the shower the body is dried vigorously with a towel.

Exercise before the shower is not necessary with this method since the body is warmed up with the hot shower, although aerobic type exercise before the shower will increase its effectiveness.

Firstly take a hot shower for two to three minutes. During this time you may wash with soap and then rinse. Next turn the shower to cool – as cool as you can take – and make sure you run the cool shower slowly. Only run the cool shower for about thirty seconds, and rub the body vigorously with the hands while taking it. Don't run the cool shower for more than about thirty seconds, since it's a rule of hydrotherapy that the hot shower should last between four and five times longer than the cool shower. If you run the cool shower for too long, the body will cool down too much and you will lose some of the benefit.

After the shower, rub the body almost dry with your hands and then dry completely with a thick towel. After this, dress warmly immediately.

After dressing, spend two or three minutes doing light exercise to increase the effect. This can be running on the spot or any other exercise.

As with the yoga shower, you will experience a peculiar warm glow which will last all day and indicates that rejuvenation is taking place.

The Streamlined Method

I have devised a more streamlined version of the two techniques which has a similar effect but is quicker, and you don't need to shower the whole body with cool water.

All you do is direct slow-running cool water on the scalp and face for about ten seconds only, and then run cool water on the lower half of the spine, at the level of the navel, for about ten seconds. This area of the spine is where the solar plexus is located. This can be done with or without a hot shower first. Make sure you follow the other procedures as described in the yogi shower or the western method, depending on whether you take a hot shower first or not.

Cool water on the head stimulates the brain, the most important nerve centre and organ in the body. Cool water stimulates the solar plexus, which is the second most important nerve centre in the body – in fact it is regarded by the yogis as a second brain. It is composed of white and grey matter similar to that of the brain, controls the main internal organs and plays a much more important role than is recognised by modern science. The yogis consider the solar plexus to be the great central storehouse of prana (life force). 'Solar' as a good name for this powerful nerve centre, since it radiates strength and energy to all parts of the body. Even the brain depends upon it as a storehouse of prana.

To increase the effect of the shower, just do two or three minutes running on the spot or a similar exercise. Again, this method is a synthesis of ancient yoga and modern science and is very time economical.

If you have heart trouble, don't use cold water, since the stimulation may be excessive. Instead use water which is just cool, and make sure you are feeling warm first.

Highlights

1 A hot/cool or cool shower, following the correct procedure, will produce the benefits of stimulation of all the glands and the nervous system, increased vitality, blood circulation, blood count, body metabolism and skin and muscle tone. In short, rejuvenation.

2 This technique works by producing a 'warm reaction' due to a flushing of the deeper body tissues with extra fresh warm blood. The result is a warm glow which will last all day. It indicates that rejuvenation of the body is taking place.

3 The yogi shower: First, do aerobic type exercise for a few minutes to warm up (jogging, running on the spot, etc.). Take a cool (not cold) shower for a few minutes. Run the shower slowly. Rub your body vigorously with your hands while under the shower. Breathe deeply. After the shower, rub the body with your hands again several times. Don't dry yourself. Dress immediately in warm clothes. Next, exercise for a couple of minutes to warm up (running on the spot or a similar exercise).

4 The western technique: Take a hot shower for two to three minutes. This can be your normal daily shower using soap. Exercise before the shower is not essential, but it will increase the effect. Then turn the shower to as cool as you can take for about thirty seconds. Run the shower slowly and rub the body vigorously with the hands. After the cool shower, rub the body almost dry with the hands and then dry vigorously with a thick towel. Dress warmly immediately. Last, do two or three minutes exercise to increase the effect.

5 The streamlined method: Exercise, take a hot shower or do both first. Run slow cool water onto the scalp and face for about ten seconds, and then onto the lower half of the spine at the level of the navel for about ten seconds. Dry vigorously with a towel and dress immediately. This technique stimulates the brain and the solar plexus, resulting in increased vitality and rejuvenation of the internal organs.

6 The western method or the streamlined method can be done in the morning, making you feel good all day, or any time as part of your normal shower.

Super Brain Power

It has been estimated by scientists that we only use about 5–10 percent of our true brain potential. This chapter will show you how to use more of that potential. Since we've got where we are now by using only 10 percent at most of our brain potential, imagine how much more we could achieve with an increase of just another 10 percent. We would be more intelligent, creative and productive and the scope of our lives would increase enormously.

If we had a machine which worked at only 10 percent of its potential, we would waste no time in getting it to perform better. The tragedy is that most of us go through our entire lives living at only 10 percent of our potential either because we don't know that this is the case or because we don't know what to do about it.

We use only about 5–10 percent of our true brain potential.

Why the Brain is the Most Important Organ for Vitality and Rejuvenation

The brain is the most important part of the *nervous system*. It has nerve connections to every cell of the body via the spinal cord and autonomic nervous system. It controls the activity of every organ in the body. This means that if the brain is not functioning at its optimum level, the rest of the body will suffer.

1 The brain is the source of *intelligence,* the most important aspect of life, since our thoughts and actions depend upon this faculty. If we can improve the functioning of the brain, we can increase its intelligence.

Even to carry out the vitality and rejuvenation principles in this book, requires the intelligence to realise how important they are, since our wellbeing and success depend upon them. The correct application of the principles requires intelligence too. As your intelligence increases, as it will if you carry out these principles, you will appreciate their importance even more and be more motivated to carry them out.

Since the brain controls the activity of every organ and gland in the body, if the brain is not functioning at its optimum level, rejuvenation cannot occur.

There is no aspect of life which does not require intelligence, and therefore every aspect of our life will improve when intelligence increases. Business success, work performance and relationships are all dependent on intelligence.

3   The brain contains a very important gland called the *pituitary gland*. This is the master gland of the body, since it controls all the other glands, including the thyroid, adrenal and sex glands (gonads).

The thyroid gland secretes hormones which are vital to metabolism and normal growth. If the pituitary gland is not working properly, the thyroid gland will also suffer. You may become overweight and mentally sluggish.

The adrenal glands have many functions. They produce steroid hormones for metabolism and adrenalin for energy. They also help to reduce inflammation and fight allergies. A defect in the secretions of the adrenal glands, caused by a malfunctioning pituitary gland, can reduce our resistance to disease and also produce chronic fatigue.

The sex glands, as well as being important for normal sexual function and reproduction, secrete hormones which produce the 'magnetic personality' when the glands are working properly. Again, this depends partly on the correct functioning of the pituitary glands.

The pituitary gland also influences the pancreas, which secretes the hormones insulin and glucogen. Insulin aids the body in using the sugar in the blood for energy (insulin is lacking in people with diabetes). Glucogen promotes the release of sugar from the tissues. Since the pituitary gland is part of the brain, when the brain is made to function better, naturally the pituitary gland will also benefit.

4   The brain contains another very important gland called the *pineal gland*. Modern science still knows very little about this gland, and the only function yet discovered is the secretion of a hormone called melatonin. This hormone causes the concentration of pigment in the cells of the skin and is therefore important for the skin's protection from the sun.

The yogis believe that this gland has a more important function, not yet discovered by science. The yogis say that this is the physical organ responsible for the development of higher consciousness, intuition and spiritual evolution. This gland corresponds to the *ajna chakra*, one of the spiritual energy centres in the spine. The yoga breathing exercises stimulate the pineal glands.

As with the pituitary gland, when brain function is improved, the pineal gland will benefit also.

5   Vitality and rejuvenation are largely a *product of the brain*. The brain is where you feel vitality and youthfulness, so it's very important that the brain itself is in good shape.

The brain contains the pituitary gland, the master gland of the body which controls all the others, including the thyroid, adrenal and sex glands.

The brain is where you feel young and vital.

How To Revaitalise The Brain

Revitalising the brain depends to a large extent on optimising brain function. This is achieved by the general vitality and rejuvenation measures mentioned elsewhere in the book, but they need to be understood in relation to the brain.

Deep Sleep

This has the greatest effect on revitalising the brain. During deep sleep, the brain is rested and recharged with energy. It's essential to get deep unbroken sleep and enough of it. To learn how to achieve deep sleep, see pages 47–59.

Deep sleep has the greatest effect on revitalising the brain, since it rests and recharges it.

Increased Oxygen to the Brain

The best way to increase oxygen to the brain is by doing the yoga breathing exercises described on pages 144–152. Next to sleep, this has the greatest effect on revitalising the brain by increasing the supply of oxygen to it. The importance of the oxygen supply to the brain is indicated by the fact that the brain uses 20 percent of the total oxygen requirements of the body. An increase in oxygen to the brain via deep breathing improves brain function, including intelligence and memory.

Yoga breathing exercises saturate the brain with revitalising oxygen.

Intellectually handicapped children have improved after being on a deep breathing programme. The late Doctor Philip Rice, who dedicated his life to these children, found that many of them were suffering from oxygen starvation of the brain. He found that a child's IQ could be increased by the deep breathing exercises. Dr Rice also believed that many juvenile delinquents could benefit from deep breathing exercises.

Aerobic exercise will increase oxygen to the brain indirectly, by increasing the flow of oxygenated blood. Even though you are breathing much faster and taking in more oxygen during aerobic exercise, this will not benefit the brain very much because most of the extra oxygen taken in is used by the muscles to produce energy to carry out the exercise. Deep breathing exercises are so effective because the extra oxygen is not used up by muscles and benefits every cell of the body.

Increased Blood Supply to the Brain

An increase in blood supply to the brain will cause an increase in food nutrients as well as oxygen. This results in an increase in vitality and brain function (intelligence and memory).

There are two main ways of increasing the blood supply to the brain. These are aerobic exercise and the yoga headstand.

Aerobic exercise increases the blood supply to all parts of the body, including the brain. There is a technique to send even more blood to the brain when doing aerobic exercise. After you finish your exercise, just bend forward as if you are trying to touch your toes. This will cause the increased blood supply from the aerobic exercise to be directed to the brain. With this technique, you are taking advantage of the force of gravity to further benefit your brain. As a fringe benefit, the face will also receive an increase in blood supply and look healthier and younger as a result.

The yoga headstand is a specific posture for increasing the blood supply to the brain. In the normal upright position, gravity tends to favour the flow of blood in the direction of the feet away from the brain. In the inverted position of the head-stand, there will be an increase in blood flow from the lower body to the brain.

If you don't feel like doing the headstand, you can purchase inversion apparatus which allows you to become inverted without standing on your head. These are very effective and can be bought from sports equipment stores. I recommend that you start off in the inversion position for about one minute, and add about one minute a week until you're doing it for five minutes maximum. This way your body gradually gets used to being in the inverted position.

When you've finished, lie in a horizontal position on the apparatus for about a minute to allow the blood to leave the brain gradually.

Do the extra revitalising technique after exercising to greatly increase the blood supply to your brain and face. You will look years younger.

Good Nutrition

There are three major nutritional factors which affect the brain. These are:

1 **Eat fruit**. Fruit provides plenty of natural fruit sugar, called 'fructose'. The body changes fructose to a simple sugar called glucose. The glucose is released into the blood and is taken up by the brain cells, as well as the other cells of the body. Glucose provides the energy for the brain cells to function and produce vitality. If you eat a lot of concentrated sugar, such as white or raw sugar or honey, you are setting the ground for future problems such as diabetes and other metabolic diseases. Fruit is ideal food for one of the main meals of the day and also for snacks throughout the day, since it will keep your blood sugar level normal. This will give you sustained energy throughout the day and prevent the lows and highs produced by concentrated sugar. Fruit is also very nutritious.

2 **Don't overeat**. This is very important, since overeating, as well as being bad for your health, requires a lot of digestion and will cause the body to draw blood from the brain to the stomach. This means you have less blood in the brain, which will result in fatigue and reduced brain function.

3 **Don't eat excessive fat**. Fat, especially cholesterol, will eventually line the arterial walls in the brain as well as elsewhere in the body. This will reduce the inner diameter of the blood vessels, causing a reduced flow of blood to the brain and, in the long term, fatigue and reduced brain function. Eventually it may result in a stroke.

Fruit provides plenty of natural fruit sugar, fructose, which energises brain cells.

Cold Water

Cold water, applied properly, has a very positive physiological effect on the body. When you get up in the morning, just splash cold water on your face and scalp from the wash basin. Make sure you splash cold water onto the closed eyes, since this directly stimulates the brain through the optic nerve connecting the eyes to the brain. Repeat this process for about one minute. Don't dry just yet. Next, massage your scalp with your fingers. Just apply pressure on the scalp and rotate that part of the scalp with the fingers. Then move on to the next area until the whole scalp is done. Use both hands and quite firm pressure. This should only take about two minutes. After this, just dry with a towel.

As well as stimulating the brain, this technique will also stimulate the hair to become healthier, making it thicker and shinier and prevent greying.

Cold water stimulation to the brain is an excellent way to start the day. After waking up fresh from deep sleep, the brain is then stimulated into action. As well as feeling better, you'll find your day will be more productive and efficient.

Cold water, when applied properly, stimulates the brain and rejuvenates the hair at the same time.

A Healthy Neck

The condition of your neck plays an important role in brain function. This is due to the fact that nerves and blood vessels pass through the neck to the brain. The brain itself is nourished by four arteries from the neck, without which it would die. In fact, brain cells die within a few minutes if starved of blood, so you can appreciate the importance of the neck.

Displaced vertebrae in the neck may also pinch a spinal nerve, which will disturb the nerve impulses going to the brain. This can result in fatigue, poor sleep, poor memory and just not feeling 100 percent.

Sometimes you will know something is not quite right when you have a neck problem. You may get one or more of the following: a pain in the neck or shoulder, headaches, migraines, tiring easily, not waking up fresh in the morning, nervousness and irritability or eye problems (reading may be more difficult or the eyes may get tired easily). One or more of the above symptoms often indicates a spinal misalignment in the neck.

If you have any of the above symptoms I suggest you have a chiropractic examination to see if the problem is coming from the neck.

Yoga asanas and neck exercises will also help to improve the condition of the neck.

Spinal misalignments in the neck may pinch a spinal nerve which will disturb the nerve impulses going to the brain. This common occurrence results in fatigue, poor sleep, reduced memory and just not feeling 100 percent.

Positive Thinking

Negative thoughts such as worry cause depletion of nerve energy, which will sap your vitality and reduce brain function. This causes you to feel 'down' and achieve less.

Positive thoughts are largely the result of a high vitality level. If you are feeling good, it's far easier to think positively. If you are feeling tired, you'll find negative thoughts cloud your mind and thinking positively will be far more difficult. So again, it's mainly a matter of treating the cause; that is, of attaining a high vitality level by following the principles in this book. This will produce a natural tendency for positive thoughts to occur.

Take, for example, aerobic exercise such as jogging. This will cause an increased blood supply to the brain, producing a healthier brain and therefore healthier thinking. If the exercise is done in the evening, it will also help to relieve the stress which has been building up during the day. This will improve brain function even more. This positive effect will even carry over to the next day, since you will sleep better due to the release of stress and hence positive thinking will be easier.

Studies have shown that exercise causes the pituitary gland to release hormones called endorphins. These hormones have been labelled 'nature's morphine', since they produce feelings of wellbeing and relaxation, both conducive to positive thinking!

One problem is that many of us have been conditioned from a very young age to think negative thoughts. When we are young, our minds are very impressionable and susceptible to suggestions from other people. Young children tend to believe what they hear and if someone tells them they are useless, that will stick in the mind and may produce an inferiority complex later in life. If your parents were negative, you are likely to be negative also. The effects of negative conditioning have to be prevented. It's not difficult, it just takes time to form the new habit of positive thinking.

The best way to form this habit is not by suppressing negative thoughts. This is a mental effort which wastes energy and does not work – by giving attention to negative thoughts, you are helping to sustain the habit. The best way is to substitute positive thoughts for negative thoughts. That is, when a negative thought such as worry arises, just replace it immediately with a positive thought. With practice it becomes automatic, resulting in the new habit of positive thinking. The mind can only hold one thought at a time, so if you occupy it with a positive thought, there is no room for any negative ones.

Probably the worst and most common type of negative thinking is worry. Excessive worry is very destructive to the system and is totally unnecessary. If you worry over the past, just keep in mind that the past is dead – why dig up the corpse? If you worry about the future, keep in mind that it will probably never happen! In any event, by not worrying your mind will be clearer and you will be able to solve potential problems much more easily.

You might argue that your worries are justified – you have bills coming up to pay, for example. The fact is, however, the vast majority of worries never eventuate. It's purely fear that they may happen. Not only that, but worry paralyses intelligent thinking, which is the very thing needed to solve problems. Positive thinking will prevent worry and help to produce the best solution to the problem.

Negative thoughts such as worry cause depletion of nerve energy, which will sap your vitality and retard brain function. Increase your vitality level by following the principles in this book and positive thoughts will occur naturally.

Aerobic exercise causes the release of hormones called 'endorphins', sometimes called 'nature's morphine' because they produce a feeling of wellbeing.

Here is a summary of the ways to prevent worry:

1 Increase your vitality by applying the principles in this book, such as deep sleep, good nutrition and exercise.
2 Form the habit of positive thinking by replacing negative thoughts with positive thoughts. Think of the situation as a challenge.
3 Engage the mind in constructive activities, then you have no time to worry.
4 Formulate goals. This gives purpose to life and gets the mind on a higher level than worries.
5 Try to prevent problems before they occur; prevention is better than cure. For example, don't overcommit yourself financially, since this may cause financial problems later.
6 Finally, don't adopt a rigid attitude to life. Be flexible and cultivate a playful attitude to life, while still having goals.

Alpha Brain Waves

The brain can function at four different levels and it emits different wave frequencies at each of these levels. It's a bit like a radio receiver which can operate on different wavelengths or a car which operates in different gears. As we can select the wavelength of the radio and the gear of the car, so we can learn to select the best wave frequency for our brain.

The four brain waves or rhythms are called delta, theta, beta and alpha.

Delta waves are the slowest. They operate when we are unconscious, in very deep sleep, coma and anaesthesia.

Theta waves are faster and operate at our subconscious level. They occur when we are emotional, when we experience pleasure or pain, in deep meditation and in moments of inspiration.

Beta waves are the fastest waves and operate when we are conscious. This is the frequency at which most of us operate 90 percent of the time. Beta waves occur when we are thinking and worrying. Since worry and other negative thoughts occur at this level, this is the level at which we experience stress and fatigue. If beta waves go up to thirty to thirty-five cycles per second a nervous breakdown occurs. It's also this level which prevents us from getting to sleep. We are too busy worrying and thinking of the day's activities to get to sleep.

Obviously we have to get ourselves out of the beta brain-wave level, since it is the root cause of our unhappiness and failures. Fortunately it can be done quite easily. All we have to do is to shift gears into the slower alpha brain-wave level.

Most people's brains operate on the beta frequency most of the time. This is the frequency of worry and stress. We need to 'shift gears' into the slower alpha-wave frequency. This is the key to happiness, vitality and success.

At the alpha level, the
brain cells are
synchronised and all
'fire' together. This
results in wellbeing,
deep relaxation,
intuition, creativity and
finer feelings.

Research has shown
that very successful
people in the fields of
business, the arts and
sport are able to
switch to the alpha
level at will.

Practice the two
techniques to get the
brain into the alpha
level.

The Alpha Brain Rhythm

Getting the brain to function from the slower alpha level is the key to happiness, vitality and success. This level is a *higher state of consciousness* than the usual beta rhythm and is associated with a feeling of deep relaxation and wellbeing. It's also the level at which *intuition* occurs, leading to far quicker and more accurate decisions. Intuition bypasses the slow, unreliable thinking process. The alpha level is also the level of creativity and finer feelings, which greatly enrich work and life in general.

When the usual beta waves are present, the brain cells produce haphazard electrical activity, but at the alpha level the brain cells are synchronised and all 'fire' together. This accounts for the improved brain function at the alpha level.

Children spend most of their time in the alpha state, which explains their energy, creative imagination and zest for life. Research has shown that very successful people in the fields of business, sport and the arts were able to switch to the alpha level at will.

How to Produce Alpha Waves

There are three basic ways to get the brain onto the alpha level. These are deep relaxation, stimulation of the pineal gland (the 'third eye') in the brain, and meditation. All three methods are effective, but only deep relaxation and stimulation of the pineal gland are discussed in this book, since they are suitable for most people. You may do either one or, for greater effect, you may choose to do both methods. Both methods result in many other benefits as well as producing the alpha state.

Deep relaxation can best be achieved by doing the deep relaxation exercise on page 162. The deep relaxation produced reduces external and internal stimuli to the brain and this shifts the brain into the alpha state.

Stimulation of the pineal gland is best achieved by doing the yoga breathing exercises (see pages 142–152) and at the same time focusing your concentration between the eyebrows, which is the level at which the pineal gland is located. The best way to focus on the pineal gland is to half close your eyes and concentrate your attention midpoint between the eyebrows (just above the root of the nose). The extra oxygen and prana taken in by the breathing exercises stimulate the brain, including the pineal gland. By concentrating on the pineal gland, you are directing more of the oxygen and prana towards it.

For the first few months, the alpha level will only last for a short time after the exercise period, but eventually, if you do the exercise morning and evening for a few minutes, your mind will be on the alpha level all day. This means you will display vitality and creative intelligence and feel relaxed all day. Your day will run smoothly and you will achieve a lot more. All aspects of your life will improve.

I made a point of writing this book while I was in a deep alpha level, that is after doing the yoga breathing exercises. You are then tapping your creative intelligence and your knowledge and understanding of the subject just flow out effortlessly.

If you have anything important to do, such as an examination, job interview or even a social event, get your mind on the alpha level first.

By switching your brain from the beta to the alpha level, you will start to gradually unfold your full potential.

Highlights

1   We only use 5–10 percent of our brain potential. We can double this percentage by following the principles outlined in this chapter.

2   The brain is the most important organ for vitality and rejuvenation for several reasons. These are:
a) The brain is the most important part of the *nervous system*, having nerve connections to every cell of the body.
b) The brain is the source of *intelligence*.
c) The brain contains the *pituitary gland*. This is the master gland of the body, controlling all the other glands.
d) The *pineal gland* is in the brain. This gland is responsible for the development of higher consciousness.
e) Vitality and rejuvenation are largely a product of the brain.

The best ways to revitalise the brain are:
a) *Deep Sleep* which has the greatest effect on revitalising the brain.
b) Increase *oxygen supply* to the brain by the deep-breathing exercises.
c) Increase the *blood supply* to the brain by aerobic exercise and the yoga headstand.
d) Optimum brain *nourishment* is achieved by emphasising fruit and not overeating.

e) *Cold water*. After arising from sleep, splash cold water onto your face and hair from the wash basin. Make sure you splash water onto the closed eyes. Next massage the scalp with your fingers.
f) *Healthy neck*. Yoga asanas and neck exercises will help to produce a relaxed, flexible neck. A chiropractic examination will reveal if you have any spinal misalignments in the neck.
g) *Positive thoughts*. Negative thoughts cause depletion of nerve energy, which will sap your vitality. Positive thoughts are best achieved by maintaining a high vitality level through deep sleep, correct nutrition and exercise, and by substituting positive thoughts for any negative thoughts which arise.

4   *Alpha brain rhythm*. This is the key to tapping your full potential, which includes high vitality and creative intelligence. When in the usual beta rhythm, we are only using about 5–10 percent of our full potential and are in an uncreative state of low vitality.

The best way to achieve alpha brain waves is by deep relaxation, meditation and deep breathing while concentrating on the pineal gland.

Rejuvenation of the Sex Glands

Healthy Sex Glands

Healthy sex glands release potent hormones which result in sexual virility and rejuvenation. You are literally as old as your glands.

I have included a chapter on sex in this book, since the health of the sex glands is intimately related to vitality and rejuvenation.

The sex glands secrete powerful hormones which affect not only your virility but also your vitality and even personality. Healthy sex glands release potent sex hormones which result in sexual virility, vitality and rejuvenation of your body. It also works the other way. If your body has lowered vitality or is sick, your sex glands will be sick too. This is because the body functions as a whole, and all the body parts and functions are interdependent.

Knowing the above facts, the best approach to take is to increase the potency of your sex glands and also increase your overall vitality. Fortunately both are achieved by doing the same things.

A satisfactory sex life is largely the result of normal functioning of the sex glands (testes in males and ovaries in females). When they are functioning correctly, they secrete just the right amount of sex hormones for a healthy sex life. Later, you will be shown ways of getting your sex glands working at an optimum level.

It's the sex hormones which govern sexual desire and virility. What most people don't realise is that the sex hormones also have a powerful influence on vitality and general rejuvenation.

If the sex glands are not functioning at an optimum level, and in most of us they are not, there will be a reduction in sex hormones secreted by the sex glands. This will not only lead to an impoverished sex life, but also to reduced vitality and premature ageing. You are literally as old as your glands.

How to Get the Sex Glands Operating at an Optimum Level

There are three main ways to achieve this:

1 Adopt the general vitality and rejuvenation practices as discussed in this book, such as a good nutritional programme, exercise and sufficient sleep.
2 Take some of the specific sex gland nutrients and follow the one-week toxin-elimination diet discussed below.
3 Do the specific yoga exercises described on pages 123–132.

Specific Sex Gland Nutrients

Vitamin E

This is often called the sex vitamin. Tests on animals have shown that a deficiency of vitamin E causes reduced sex-hormone production. Vitamin E is a potent antioxidant and will prevent destruction of hormones by oxidation.

The best natural sources of vitamin E are wheatgerm, wheatgerm oil, cold-pressed vegetable oils, soya beans, milk products and green vegetables (especially cauliflower and spinach).

A deficiency of vitamin E and zinc causes reduced sex-hormone production and active sperm cannot be produced without zinc.

Zinc

Zinc is essential for the health of the prostate gland and the reproductive hormones. It's also essential for the normal growth and development of the sex organs. Active sperm cannot be formed without zinc.

A deficiency of zinc in the diet is a common cause of enlargement of the prostate gland. After middle age, prostate problems are common and often go undetected for a long time.

High natural sources of zinc are oysters, wheatgerm, the bran of whole wheat grain, eggs, onion, and sesame, pumpkin and sunflower seeds.

Pumpkin Seeds

Pumpkin seeds contain a high concentration of nutrients which result in virility. These seeds have a high concentration of protein, fatty acids, B vitamins, zinc, phosphorous and iron.

Pumpkin seeds are the only nutritional remedy for prostate problems.

Pumpkin and sesame seeds are rich in nutrients which are vital to the sex glands.

Sesame Seeds

Sesame seeds are rich in nutrients which are vital to the sex glands. They are very rich in calcium, vitamin B, vitamin C, lecithin, zinc, unsaturated fatty acids and protein. Some breads contain sesame seeds.

Fish

Fish is rich in minerals such as iodine and phosphorus which are important for the correct functioning of the sex glands. Fish is far superior to meat since it is richer in minerals but lacks the high fat content and toxicity of meat.

Specific Herbs for Increased Sexual Vigour

Ginseng. The Chinese have used ginseng as an aphrodisiac and general rejuvenator for over 5,000 years and recent Russian research has confirmed its efficiency as a rejuvenator.

The three herbs which increase sexual vigour can be obtained from health shops.

Sarsaparilla. The root of this tropical American plant contains the male hormone, testosterone and the female hormone, progesterone.

Damiana. This herb has been used as an aphrodisiac by Mexican Indians for many centuries.

The above three herbs can be obtained from health shops in tea or tablet form.

The One-Week Toxin-Elimination Diet

Even though with this diet you are eating less food and eating no stimulating food, your sexual vigour will improve. The diet is very simple. All you do is just eat fruit and drink fruit juices if you wish.

This diet works because sexual virility is mainly dependent on healthy endocrine glands – especially the sex glands. The diet of the average person is often overcooked and not very nutritious. Cooking destroys the enzymes in food and the enzymes are the 'life force' of the food and the factor which stimulates the sex glands to function correctly. Fruits are loaded with live enzymes and contain no toxic waste products.

The one-week fruit diet has an invigorating effect on the sex glands.

The average person has a high level of toxins in the body and this interferes with the nourishment of the sex glands. With the fruit diet you get 100 percent of the enzymes and no toxins, which means your sex glands are getting optimum nourishment. This has an invigorating effect on the sex glands.

The sex urge and sexual activity can only occur when you have surplus energy – that is, when your body is creating more energy than it is using up. On the average diet there is very little surplus energy because much of it consists of foods low in nutrients and high in toxins.

A tired person is a poor lover. He or she doesn't even have sufficient energy to cope with everyday life, let alone having sex. On the one-week fruit diet surplus energy is created which allows the sex urge to manifest itself more strongly.

When you have completed this diet, it's a good idea to eat only fruit in the mornings. This provides your body with live enzymes every day and also eliminates toxins from your body daily.

The yoga postures selected for this age-reversal programme are specific for optimum sexual function as well as for vitality and rejuvenation.

Yoga Postures (Asanas)

The yoga exercises selected for this book are the most effective for optimal sexual function as well as for vitality and rejuvenation.

If the sex organs and the pituitary glands are not working properly, insufficient sex hormones are secreted. The yoga asanas described in this book correct this situation and awaken the sex glands. Yoga also improves the mind, body and spine – all essential for a satisfactory sex life.

The **headstand** stimulates the pituitary gland in the brain, which in turn normalises the function of the sex glands. The headstand also relieves congestion in the pelvis, by pulling up organs which have dropped over the years because of gravity.

The **shoulder stand** also regulates the sex glands by stimulating the thyroid gland.

The **reverse posture** is specific for sex glands, producing their optimum functioning.

The **plough posture**, by affecting the thyroid gland, also benefits the sex glands.

The fish posture affects both the pituitary and the thyroid glands and hence the sex glands.

The **stomach lift**, by relieving congestion in the pelvis, results in an increase in the flow of sexual energy.

For instructions on how to do the above exercises, refer to pages 123–132.

Other Factors Affecting Sexual Virility

Frequency of Sex
Research has shown that the levels of sex hormones stay highest among those who have the highest level of sexual activity – it's the old principle of 'use it or lose it'.

Sexual activity and aerobic exercise stimulate the sex glands.

Exercise

One study compared married couples who did aerobic exercise such as jogging with married couples who did no exercise. The results showed that the exercise group had increased frequency and quality of sex.

Alcohol and Cigarettes

Excess alcohol depresses the whole system including the sex glands. Nicotine in cigarettes also reduces the activity of the sex glands. I would suggest drinking alcohol in strict moderation and not smoking at all.

Tea and coffee should also be reduced, since they impede the absorption of zinc.

Hot Baths and Spas

Dr Richard Paulson, a US researcher, measured male volunteers' sperm for movement, penetration power and sperm count, before and after the men took a one-hour dip in a hot tub (38°C). Thirty-six hours after their immersion, tests showed that the men had functionally impaired sperm, some of which were found to be totally incapable of penetrating an ovum. The sperm count remained low for up to 6 weeks after the hot bath. The message is obviously to reduce the temperature and duration of your bath.

Older men in good health make sex hormones in the same quantity as younger men – the important thing is your biological age.

Does Ageing Affect Sexual Virility?

One study has shown that most older men who are in good health continue to make sex hormones in the same quantity as younger men. So again, chronological age is not as important as biological age. The main factors in keeping a young biological age are the lifestyle factors of good nutrition, correct exercise, deep sleep, and so on.

Exercise and Your Sex Life

Aerobic exercise produces a multitude of physiological changes which cause an increase in sexual attraction and vigour. Every system in the body works better when you're fit, including the all-important glandular system. In addition, when you feel fit and attractive romance becomes more appealing.

A growing number of studies and surveys support the sex-exercise connection. Psychologist Linda De Villers analysed 2,000 responses to a questionnaire in a women's fitness magazine and found that 83 percent of the women engaged in aerobic activity at least three times a week. Comparing with how they felt before beginning their exercise programme, 40 percent said they were more easily aroused, 31 percent said they had sex more often and 25 percent reported climaxes came more easily.

In a 1988 poll, 66 percent of men and women runners claimed that running made them better lovers.

Perhaps the most remarkable finding was that these benefits occurred regardless of a person's age. In a Harvard University study, anthropologist Phillip Whitten found that the sex lives of women and men over forty years who exercised regularly were similar to many people in their late twenties and early thirties.

Scientists have suggested a combination of several factors to explain why exercise enhances our sex lives:

The most remarkable finding of sex-exercise studies is that the enhancement of our sex lives by exercise occurs for people of any age.

1 Exercise increases our stamina, which results in a better physical performance in any activity, including sex.
2 Exercise causes a reduction in cholesterol. This unclogs the arteries and hence increases the blood flow throughout the body, including the pelvic region and sex organs. James White, an exercise physiologist and co-author of a study of the effects of exercise on sedentary men, reports that 'A low blood supply reduces male erectile ability.'
3 Regular exercise causes a release of endorphins which have a mood-elevating effect. These 'happy hormones' are naturally occurring opiates in the body and tend to put you in the mood for enjoying sex.
4 Your self-image is improved with regular exercise. Most of the women in Linda De Villers' survey reported a significant jump in sexual confidence with regular workouts. Swimmers in the Whitten study reported that they felt more attractive and had an increase in desire and satisfaction after several months of exercising.

It is, however, important not to overdo exercise. This can result in fatigue and be counterproductive to a good sex life. See pages 35–41 for details about the right amount of exercise.

Highlights

1 The sex glands secrete powerful hormones which not only affect your virility but also general vitality and even your personality.

2 There are four ways of getting the sex glands to operate at the optimum level – the vitality and rejuvenation factors described in this book, specific sex gland nutrients, the one-week toxin elimination diet and specific yoga exercises.

3 The specific sex gland nutrients are: vitamin E, zinc, pumpkin seeds, sesame seeds, fish, and the three herbs ginseng, sarsaparilla and damiana.

4 The one-week toxin elimination diet consists of just eating fruits for one week. You may also drink fresh fruit juices and carrot juice. Fruit has not had any of its enzymes and nutrients destroyed by cooking. Fruit also contains no toxins and will speed up the elimination of toxins from your body. This gives your sex glands the invigorating effect of optimum nourishment.

5 The yoga exercises selected for this book are the most effective ones for healthy sex glands as well as for optimum vitality and rejuvenation. The exercises are the headstand, the shoulder stand, the reverse posture, the fish posture and the stomach lift.

6 Other factors affecting sexual virility are the frequency of sex, exercise, alcohol, cigarettes and hot baths or spas. Age is not an important factor as long as you are healthy.

Other Rejuvenation Secrets

Fresh Air and Sunlight

Fresh air and sunlight are essential for an optimum vitality level. To illustrate the importance of fresh air and sunlight, just consider the well-known fact that wounds exposed to sunshine and fresh air heal more rapidly than when bandaged. In fact, no wound will heal without air. Pure air and the sun's rays are the best germicides and the most powerful disinfectants we have.

Fresh Air
While correct internal breathing is of great importance, *external breathing* through the skin is also essential to life. The skin has millions of minute openings called pores. One of the functions of these pores is to breathe in fresh air. If the skin were covered with a material such as tar this would seal the pores and the person would suffocate in a very short time. This is one very good reason why we should wear the lightest clothing possible consistent with the weather conditions. Keep in mind that the skin breathes just as the lungs do.

Oxygen from the air is very important in maintaining the vital processes of the body – especially the interchange of carbon dioxide and oxygen in the lungs. Without an abundance of pure, fresh air, the important work of normalising the blood chemistry could not be achieved. The result would be a sharp decline in vitality and health.

The oxygen in the air we breathe affects the body as if it were charged with electricity. The electrical energy, absorbed by the blood, is carried to all parts of the body, including the rejuvenation centres – the brain, spine and glands. This is why, if you are feeling tired or depressed, it's a good idea to take a walk in the fresh air. This will recharge your body with extra energy.

The effect is especially pronounced if you take a walk near the seaside or in the mountains, where the air is very fresh. It's also a good idea to keep your bedroom windows open at night so the body takes in fresh air even while you are sleeping.

Sunlight

Without the rays of the sun, even the simplest forms of life would not exist on the earth.

The sun's rays have the same life-promoting influence on the body as on plants and flowers. If you hide a beautiful flowering plant in a dark cupboard, it will soon wilt, fade and die, but when placed in the warm sunshine it soon blooms again. The same applies to your body. There is life and vitality in the rays of the sun. Millions of nerve endings absorb the radiant energy of the sun and transmit this energy to the entire nervous system of the body. That is why you feel so full of energy and life after a sun bath. The sun's rays also have a soothing effect on the nervous system.

The early morning rays of the sun are by far the most beneficial. About four hours after the sun has risen the vital effects of the rays lessen, and then gradually decrease as the day progresses. You will notice that plants which receive the early morning sunshine thrive much better than those which get only the afternoon rays.

How to Use the Sun for Maximum Vitality and Health

Even though the sun is essential to life, it has to be used correctly. It's a bit like nuclear energy in that it can be beneficial or harmful, depending on how you use it. To obtain maximum benefit from the sun without any harmful side effects, follow the points below.

Try to get outside in the early morning, before about 10 a.m. The sun's rays impart maximum vitality to the body at this time, and there is less risk of sunburn. Wear as little clothing as possible, consistent with weather conditions. You can exercise, garden, read, do your paperwork, or just sunbathe. Don't expose your face to the sun, however; if necessary wear a hat.

Allow your skin to get used to the sun gradually. Start off with just a few minutes exposure to the sun and add a few minutes each day.

Sun protection. If you can only get outside between 10 a.m. and 4 p.m., if possible spend most of the time in the shade. If this is not possible, at least wear a shirt and hat and use sun cream, especially on your face. Buy a sun cream with a sun protection factor of 15 and make sure it's a broad spectrum one. This blocks out most of the ultraviolet radiation in sunlight – including both ultraviolet A (UVA) and ultraviolet B (UVB). This type of sun cream has recently become available.

If you spend time on the beach, it's best to sunbathe under an umbrella. The indirect sunlight you receive will give you all the benefits of direct sunlight, but without its dangers. If you go swimming, it's also a good idea to use sun cream and reapply it if you take another swim. Even if it's a cloudy day, it's advisable to use sun cream since as much as 75 percent of the sun's cancer-causing rays still strike you. Apply sun cream at least 15 minutes before you go into the sun or water. Don't rub the cream into your skin, just apply it gently to your surface.

Wear sunglasses. Whenever you go out, wear UV-blocking sunglasses or coated prescription lenses that also provide protection. Sunglasses also help shield the area round your eyes.

The Dangers of Too Much Sun

Spending too long in the sun without protective clothing and sun cream can produce the following effects:

1 **Skin cancer**. Most cases of skin cancer are caused by people lying on the beach trying to get a sun tan. It's a very expensive way of trying to become darker for a few days.

    Be alert to skin changes. If you notice any, see your doctor immediately. Although skin cancer is the most common malignancy, it is also the most curable if caught in time.

2 **Premature ageing**. Until recently, everyone believed that as we aged our skin inevitably wrinkled and sagged. Now we know that most of the damage is done by years of exposure to ultraviolet rays which destroy the elastic fibres that keep healthy skin taught and supple. People who have pursued that 'fresh, young-looking' golden tan are discovering that years of sun-bathing have left them with wrinkled, sagging skin.

3 **Eye damage**. Over the years, constant bombardment of ultraviolet rays can turn the eye's clear lens brownish. Eventually, partial blindness may result. Eye specialists are noticing the increased incidence of sunlight-related eye disorders in people who spend a long time outdoors.

    Excessive ultraviolet light has been associated with the development of cataracts, retinal degeneration and visual ageing. Pterygions are being excised increasingly more in blue-eyed individuals with outdoor pastimes. Pterygions are red, fan-shaped growths in the white of the eye which can spread across the pupil.

4 **Damaged immune system**. Doctors have long known that sun-tanning causes outbreaks of herpes sores on the lips of susceptible people. Since the herpes virus is always latent in these patients' bodies, scientists think ultraviolet radiation may suppress natural defence mechanisms.

In an Australian study, volunteers were given a dozen 30-minute treatments with solarium lamps, and then had their blood cells tested for the ability, among other things, to ward off malignant melanoma. Their 'natural killer' cells had decreased in number and lost much of their disease-fighting capacity, even a week after the exposure to ultraviolet radiation had stopped.

A Sun Tan is not Healthy

At the American Academy of Dermatology's 1988 Consensus Conference on Photoageing/Photodamage, eighteen experts on skin diseases asked the question: 'Is there a safe way to tan?' The answer was a definite no. So there you have it. The scientists who know more about human skin than anyone else confirm that all sun-tanning is dangerous, with no exceptions.

The idea that a sun tan was healthy started in the 1930's and soon almost everyone believed that a bronzed body was a symbol of fitness and vigour. They were mistaken. Far from being a sign of health, a sun tan is a crude defence mechanism – your body's desperate and always unsuccessful attempt to protect you from damage that can be irreparable. Your system throws a curtain of pigment called melanin over you to keep ultraviolet radiation from doing even more harm. But it is too late. Once a sun tan appears, the damage has already taken place.

A few hours of sun-tanning can age your skin by years. For a few days of having a tan, you may pay the price of a lifetime of wrinkles.

We have to be even more conscious of the sun's potential danger nowadays, since the earth's ozone layer is becoming depleted. This increases the harmful effects of the sun.

Don't Forget the Children

Protect children by following the steps outlined above. People absorb a large proportion of their lifetime ultraviolet exposure before the age of eighteen. Also, those who suffer severe sunburn in childhood appear to be more likely to develop malignant melanomas later in life.

Natural Daylight Lighting

It's now possible to buy full-spectrum daylight globes and fluorescent tubes. These emit all the wavelengths of natural light and are therefore much better for your health than the standard type.

A deficiency of light can cause fatigue and depression. This occurs especially in winter and in countries which have a long winter darkness. It's also been found that women are more affected than men by daylight deficiency, because they have a more complex hormone structure.

If you are an office worker or do a lot of reading or desk work at home, I strongly suggest that you replace your present lighting with the natural daylight globes or tubes.

A few hours of sun-tanning can age your skin by years.

If you are an office worker try to replace your present lighting with natural day-light globes or tubes.

Chiropractic

I have included chiropractic in the Rejuvenation Programme, since if you have a problem in your spine, it can have a very big impact on your health. Chiropractic is the only factor in this programme which requires outside help.

If you have 'pinched nerves' in your spine, and especially your neck, you will never reach your full vitality and rejuvenation potential, even if you carry out the other vitality and rejuvenation factors.

Most of the patients who come to me with neck problems or headaches also have low vitality levels and get tired easily. After chiropractic treatment their energy levels usually increase dramatically.

The importance of the spine for health and long life was well recognised by the ancient yogis. Most of their exercises were designed to have some effect on the spine. The yogis knew that many health problems and premature ageing were often due to slight displacements of vertebrae in the spine.

While yoga is excellent for preventing spinal problems and will even correct some minor spinal displacements, it is not specific enough to correct all the displacements. This is where chiropractic comes into play, since a chiropractic examination and treatment will detect and correct all the spinal displacements – minor and major.

If you have a spinal misalignment, especially in the neck, it can have a very big impact on your health and prevent you from reaching your full vitality and rejuvenation potential.

Why is the Spine so Vulnerable?
You may wonder why the spine was not better designed to prevent spinal problems, but the problem is that it was originally designed for walking on all fours, not for an upright position. In other words, we have started walking upright before our spine has evolved to handle the extra stress of gravity.

Walking upright has adverse effects on other parts of the body also. It causes the internal organs to drop, the breasts to sag in women, and a tendency to hernia in men.

Many of us are walking around with slight displacements of one or more vertebral bones in our spine. Sometimes you will have an indication of this by feeling pain or stiffness in the neck, between the shoulder blades or in the lower back, or you may get a headache. But often spinal subluxations produce no pain, and you may be wondering why you don't feel 100 percent, even after adopting a more healthy lifestyle. If this is the case, I would advise getting a chiropractic check-up.

What is Chiropractic?
Chiropractic is a system of treatment for pain and disease based on the premise that the nervous system controls all other systems and all functions of the body.

The chiropractor restores the nervous system to normal by removing interference to the nerves where they emerge from the spine.

The importance of chiropractic is that it deals with the *nervous* system; since it's this system which controls and co-ordinates the other eight systems of the body.

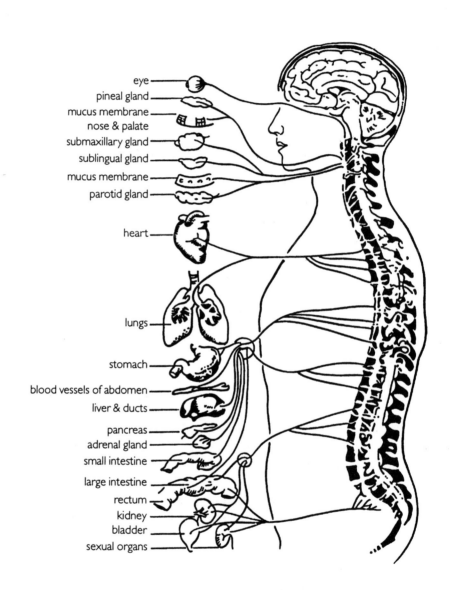

eye
pineal gland
mucus membrane
nose & palate
submaxillary gland
sublingual gland
mucus membrane
parotid gland

heart

lungs

stomach
blood vessels of abdomen
liver & ducts
pancreas
adrenal gland
small intestine
large intestine
rectum
kidney
bladder
sexual organs

Health problems related to the spine

What Chiropractic Can Do for You

Chiropractic achieves three things. Firstly, chiropractic removes pain in the joints and muscles – such as pain in the low back, hips, neck, legs, arms and shoulders. Secondly, chiropractic corrects or improves certain internal discorders such as headaches, migraines, dizziness, sinus problems, constipation, blurred or reduced vision, certain types of nervous disorders such as 'nerves', irritability and tension, and certain types of pain in the chest and abdomen.

More importantly for the purpose of this book, chiropractic produces a feeling of wellbeing. You have more energy, sleep better and wake up feeling fresher in the mornings.

How Chiropractic Works

The nerves from the spine go to every organ of the body. The chiropractor knows exactly which part of the spine connects to each specific organ.

Science has discovered a condition known as a 'subluxation', a slight displacement of one or more of the vertebrae in the spine. This is very common and can only be detected by a chiropractic examination, since it often produces no pain. The displaced vertebrae may pinch a spinal nerve, which may disturb the impulses to the organ the nerve connects to. This may cause a disturbance in the organ's function and can eventually produce disease in that organ as well as reducing general health.

If the misaligned vertebrae are in the neck or upper part of the back or shoulder area, this will interfere with the blood and nerve supply to the brain, causing tiredness and poor sleep. It also often causes headaches, irritability and vision problems (reading may be more difficult or the eyes may tire easily).

Why Chiropractic is Better than Drugs for Many Conditions

In general, we tend to rely too much on drugs for pain and our health problems.

Drugs do not cure disease. They merely suppress the symptoms by deadening the nerves. This is dangerous, because the symptoms (such as pain) are nature's warning signal that something is wrong and that attention syhould be given to the cause of the symptoms.

To make matters worse, all drugs produce unpleasant side effects, and these side effects are often more serious than the disease being treated. In fact about 10 percent of patients entering hospitals are suffering from drug-induced (iatrogenic) diseases.

Drugs offer only temporary relief of symptoms, whereas chiropractic treats the cause of the disease, therefore producing better results as well as being safer.

Vitality and wellbeing
cannot be bought in a
bottle.

Total Health and Wellbeing

Being healthy does not just mean the absence of aches and pains or disease; it is a positive state of vitality and wellbeing. This cannot be bought in a tablet or bottle.

Since the chiropractor will treat the whole spine, correcting spinal misalignments where there is nerve interference, your whole body will benefit. Your organs and glands will function at an optimum level and this will result in a feeling of wellbeing.

So if you don't have a high vitality level all day, a chiropractic examination will reveal whether your spine is the cause. If so, chiropractic treatment will put your body back in tune without resorting to drugs and other escape routes.

If, after adopting a
healthier lifestyle, you
still get tired, don't
wake up feeling fresh
or get headaches, I
would advise a chiro-
practic check-up.
Remember that spinal
misplacements often
produce no pain.

Laughter

Don't laugh at this – laughter has been scientifically shown to be a powerful tool in increasing vitality and rejuvenation. Even cases of terminal illness have been reversed by people using 'laughing therapy'; for example, watching funny videos and reading comics. Many of these cases have been well documented.

The fact is, most of us are too serious too much of the time. We need to become a little more lighthearted and take a less serious attitude to life. We tend to take ourselves too seriously. Remember, life is not a dress rehearsal – we are only here once, so let's enjoy it!

Laughter is a powerful
rejuvenator. Even cases
of terminal illness have
been reversed by
laughter therapy.

Several leading psychiatrists have stated that the most constant feature of mentally healthy people is the ability to laugh at themselves. It's almost a guarantee against worry and anxiety, two leading maladies in our fast, high-tech world.

How Laughter Works

'Gelotherapy' is the word used for the use of therapeutic laughter. Laughter produces its beneficial effects because of the following physiological facts:

1 Laughing relaxes the mind and body. If you laugh until you cry, the tears wash away toxic chemicals associated with stress.
2 Laughing exercises the heart and stimulates the circulation. The heart rate is increased, which causes the blood of laughers to turn a bright red, due to an increased oxygen supply. This is perhaps why laughter is called 'internal jogging'.
3 Laughter exercises the diaphragm and lungs and stimulates deep breathing.
4 Laughter activates pituitary and adrenal hormones and causes other beneficial biochemical changes.
5 Laughing stretches the facial muscles, which helps to produce a reduction in facial wrinkles.

Proof of the Health Benefits of Laughter

In one experiment, researchers measured the levels of people's immune proteins before and after watching a comedy film. It was found that the levels of immune protein increased dramatically. What was even more remarkable is that they stayed at this high level even after subsequently watching serious films.

Obviously laughing is a very positive emotion, having very beneficial effects on the body.

If You don't Laugh, at Least Smile

Smiling is easier and more natural than frowning, since it takes fewer muscles to smile than to frown.

Laughter is really an extreme form of smiling – the same muscles are used – it's just that laughter gives them a greater stretch.

Sauna

The sauna originated in Finland and is used extensively by the Finnish people, who generally have a high level of vitality and endurance and a low incidence of degenerative diseases.

The Rejuvenation Effects of Increased Perspiration

A sauna is really a self-induced artificial fever, since the heat from the sauna increases the metabolism of the body, causing perspiration.

It may surprise you to hear that, contrary to orthodox medical opinion, a fever is a good thing. Fever is a natural defensive response of the body to fight infection or burn up toxins. It is a symptom not of disease but of the body's attempt to cure itself. By raising the body temperature, waste products in the body are burnt up and the resultant perspiration eliminates toxins from the skin.

It must be remembered that the skin is the body's largest eliminative organ – 30 percent of all toxins in the body are eliminated by perspiration. In fact chemical analysis shows that perspiration is almost identical to urine.

Medical intervention to reduce a fever is stopping a very potent natural fighting mechanism. This usually delays nature's attempt to remove the cause of the disease and may result in more serious disease later. The only exception to this is for small babies. If they develop a fever it should be supervised by a doctor, since their heat-regulating mechanism is not yet fully developed.

As well as increasing the elimination of toxins, increased body temperature inhibits the growth of invading viruses and bacteria. This has been scientifically proven by the Nobel Prize winner, Dr A. Livoff. His research proved that high

A sauna produces rejuvenation by increasing perspiration. The skin is the body's largest eliminative organ and 30 percent of all toxins are eliminated by perspiration.

temperature during infection retards the growth of viruses, and he recommends that fever should not be brought down with drugs.

How the Sauna Produces Rejuvenation

The rejuvenation effects of the sauna are due to the following physiological mechanisms:

1 Overheating causes an increase in perspiration, which results in an increase in the elimination of toxins through the skin.
2 Overheating causes an increase in body metabolism, which retards the growth of bacteria and viruses.
3 The above two factors cause a stimulation of the body's natural healing forces. This speeds up the healing of acutely toxic diseases such as colds and infections. Regular saunas speed up the healing of chronic diseases such as arthritis and cancer.
4 The activity of the glands and organs is increased.

In summary, saunas are very beneficial for colds, simple infections, skin disorders, arthritis, insomnia and cancer.

To Obtain the Optimum Effect from Your Sauna

1 If you are not used to having a sauna, start with a moderate temperature and gradually increase the temperature to what feels comfortable for you.
2 When you first enter the sauna, sit on the lowest level, since this is the least hot part of the sauna. As your body becomes accustomed to the heat you can sit on the benches at higher levels. This is based on the principle that heat rises.
3 Just 10 minutes is sufficient time to gain all the benefits of the sauna.
4 After the sauna take a warm shower, using soap to wash the perspiration from the skin.
5 Lie down and rest for a few minutes outside the sauna room. This allows perspiration to stop and a return to normal body temperature.

Exercising hard enough to produce perspiration will give the sauna effect at no cost and you will get the benefits of the aerobic exercise as well!

Most people who take saunas jump straight into a cold shower afterwards. I don't recommend this, since you will cool the body down and close the pores of the skin too quickly. This counteracts the purpose of the sauna: increased body temperature and wide open pores to eliminate toxins.

After the sauna, it's best to take a warm (not hot) shower, since this allows the pores to slowly and gradually close. Finish with a *brief* cool shower of not more than 30 seconds.

Most health clubs have a sauna, but if you don't wish to try it, at least exercise hard enough to produce perspiration.

Indoor Pollution

Since a large part of the workforce now works in modern offices, you need to be aware of how this may reduce your vitality and even threaten your health. Any reduction in health will accelerate the ageing process.

If you work in a sealed office building where the windows cannot be opened, you are getting very little fresh air. If the office is air-conditioned, the same stale air is recycled. You are also very dependent on the air-conditioner being well maintained. For example, if the filter is not cleaned regularly, dust particles will be circulated throughout the office.

Office wall material is often made of particleboard containing formaldehyde, which emits poisonous fumes. This chemical is also used in kitchen and bathroom cabinets. Studies have shown that formaldehyde can cause respiratory illness and cancer.

A recent British study showed that up to one-third of people working in tightly sealed modern office buildings got sore throats, sinus problems, itchy eyes, headaches and chronic fatigue. These people also suffered 50 percent more respiratory illnesses than the general population, according to another study. In other words, sick buildings produce sick people.

Highlights

Fresh Air and Sunshine

1 Fresh air is essential for maximum vitality. Exercise, walking and recreation in the fresh air is recommended. Sleep with your bedroom windows open.

2 Sunlight is also essential for vitality. The early morning rays of the sun are the most beneficial. To avoid any harmful effects from the sun, try to keep out of direct sunlight between 10 a.m. and 4 p.m. If the sun is strong, you should wear a shirt and hat and put sun cream on your face. Buy a broad-spectrum sun cream which gives maximum protection (SPF15).

On the beach, relax under an umbrella and, if you go for a swim, put sun cream on. You should also wear ultraviolet-blocking sunglasses on the beach.

A sun tan is not healthy. It's your body's desperate attempt to protect you from ultraviolet radiation damage. A sun tan will age your skin irreversibly.

3   If you spend a lot of time indoors, use natural daylight globes or tubes. A deficiency of natural light can cause fatigue and depression.

Chiropractic
1   Spinal misalignments often cause 'pinched' nerves in the spine. Since the nerves from the spine go to all the organs in your body, including your brain, this can often result in disease and reduced vitality.

2   Chiropractic achieves three things:
a)   It removes pain in the joints and muscles.
b)   It corrects or improves certain
c)   internal disorders such as headaches, sinus problems, some vision
d)   problems, tension and 'nerves'.
e)   It produces a feeling of wellbeing, increased energy and relaxation.

3   Chiropractic is better than taking drugs for most problems, since it treats the cause not the symptoms and does not have side effects.

4   Spinal misalignments often produce no symptoms but they are nevertheless damaging your organs. Your only indication may be that you are just not feeling 100 percent or frequently feel tired. A chiropractic examination will reveal if the cause of your problems is spinal misalignments.

Laughter
1   Laughter has been scientifically shown to increase vitality and rejuvenation.

2   Laughing works by relaxing the mind and body, stimulating deep breathing, increasing oxygenation of the blood and stretching the facial muscles.

Sauna
The sauna produces rejuvenation by speeding up the elimination of toxins through increased perspiration, increased body metabolism, stimulation of the body's natural healing forces and increased activity of the glands and organs.

Indoor Pollution
If you work in an office, open the windows if possible to allow fresh air in.
    If you work in a sealed office building and suffer from low vitality and constant sore throats, sinus problems, headaches or itchy eyes, you may have to modify or leave your work place.

Conclusion

The vitality and rejuvenation techniques described in this book are so effective that they will result in a great increase in the elimination of toxins. The toxins which have been deposited in your tissues, causing fatigue and premature ageing, will be flushed out into your bloodstream and eventually eliminated from your body. While the toxins are in the bloodstream for a week or two, you may feel slightly worse. Once most of the toxins have been flushed out you will start to feel much better. You will feel a new vitality and look younger. If you are relatively healthy to start with, you may feel no temporary discomfort at all.

Don't plan to adopt all the vitality and rejuvenation factors at once; just make gradual changes over a few months. This way you will avoid flushing out the toxins too quickly, and it allows your body to get used to your new lifestyle gradually. Our bodies tend to resist dramatic changes imposed too quickly.

As well as becoming younger, you will find that your vitality level will also increase dramatically since the same lifestyle factors are involved.

After reading this book, you will realise that ancient yoga and modern science are now converging. What the yogis discovered about vitality and rejuvenation thousands of years ago in their super-conscious states, is now being confirmed by modern science.

As suggested in the introduction, I recommend you skim through the book every six months or so. This will achieve two main things. First, you will gain a deeper understanding of the concepts at each review, and this will give you even more incentive to carry out the vitality and rejuvenation factors. You will also be more likely to stick to the changes when you really appreciate the rationale behind them and clearly see the benefits. Second, a review of the book will allow you to pick up things which you missed on the first reading.

I'm sure that you will be very satisfied with your new-found vitality and youthfulness and your friends will certainly comment on it too.

Further Reading

Bailey, C., Fit or Fat, Sphere, London, 1985
Kenton, L. & S., Raw Energy, Doubleday, Sydney, 1986
Kirschner, H.E., Nature's Seven Doctors, H.C. White, California, 1962
Stearn, J., Yoga, Youth and Reincarnation, Bantam, New York, 1968
Swami Vishnu-devananda, The Complete Illustrated Book of Yoga,
    Harmony, New York, 1960
Walford, R.L., Maximum Life Span, Avon, New York, 1983
Yogi Ramacharaka, Hatha Yoga, Fowler, London

Index

Of further interest...

Stop Ageing Now!

Jean Carper

Who wouldn't like to stay young as long as possible and even partially regain lost youth? At long last, it's possible. The fountain of youth is no longer a myth. Scientists have discovered the most basic reasons behind the ageing process and amazingly simple ways to slow it down or reverse it.

In *Stop Ageing Now!* Jean Carper, the bestselling author of *Food: Your Miracle Medicine*, has written a breakthrough, cutting-edge book documenting that the ravages of ageing are not inevitable and, in fact, can be prevented or reversed. Written in a lively and compelling style, *Stop Ageing Now!* reveals how you can combat ageing as well as cancer, heart disease and other age-related disease.

Stop Ageing Now! is based on hundreds of trail-blazing studies by scientists from prestigious institutions who are discovering the incredible truth about the ageing process: that much of it is not inevitable, and that what we call 'normal ageing' is actually often due to unsuspected deficiencies that can be readily corrected by taking antioxidant vitamins, minerals, herbs and food chemicals.

In this exciting, groundbreaking guide, organized in an easy-to-use format, you will find out exactly which anti-ageing supplements to take every day, and in what quantities, to forestall premature ageing and regain vitality.

ISBN: 07225 3456 6

Miracle Cures

DRAMATIC NEW SCIENTIFIC DISCOVERIES REVEALING THE HEALING
POWERS OF HERBS, VITAMINS AND OTHER NATURAL REMEDIES

Jean Carper

A cutting-edge guide to the hottest discoveries in medicine today: the scientifically-proven natural substances that prevent and reverse illnesses, from heart disease to cancer to flu.

Leading authority on health and nutrition Jean Carper shows how effective vitamins, minerals, foods and herbs can be. The book is backed by the latest findings of leading scientific institutions and research centres. Written in the lively style which has made Jean Carper a world-wide bestselling author, *Miracle Cures* includes many awe-inspiring case histories.

ISBN: 07225 3477 9

Nutritional Health Bible

A COMPLETE REFERENCE GUIDE TO NUTRITION

Linda Lazarides

- discover the healing power of foods
- learn how to use supplements safely to combat illness

Food and food supplements can be the most effective forms of medicine – safe, natural and without the side effects of many drugs. This existing new reference guide will revolutionize the way you think about nutrition and show you how to make the right choices. It includes:

- the latest research into the nutritional causes of illness
- the most up-to-date facts and advice on health issues such as allergies, hormones and detoxification
- a complete A-Z guide answering all your questions: from vitamin A to garlic, lipoic acid and zinc
- special advice for the whole family: children, the elderly, pregnant women, athletes, vegetarians and slimmers

'This is an important book which should be read by the public and all involved in health care. It could seriously improve the health of the nation.'
Dr Keith Eaton, Consultant Allergist
The Princess Margaret Hospital, Windsor

ISBN: 07225 3424 8

Miracle Sleep Cure

THE KEY TO A LONG LIFE OF PEAK PERFORMANCE

James B. Maas with Megan L. Wherry

James B. Maas presents newly published research on sleep and its effect on your health, performance and longevity which is making news headlines. Modern living is creating a virtual epidemic of sleep deprivation which will lead to shorter lives and the risk of chronic diseases such as stroke and heart attacks. This is the first book to use this new research to show you how to have productive, creative days, overcome insomnia, beat the need for sleeping pills, prevent jet lag, learn how to power nap...and, most important, have enough hours of restorative sleep.

- learn 20 effective sleep strategies
- identify common sleep disorders
- become a more energetic, creative person

'Reading this book was a stunning experience: his highly original research and conclusions have pushed my views about renewal and vigour a giant step forward.'

ISBN: 07225 3644 5

The Calm Technique

THE EASY WAY TO BEAT STRESS INSTANTLY THROUGH SIMPLE
MEDITATION METHODS

Paul Wilson

It is a well established fact that your health, happiness and harmony can be dramatically enhanced by changing your lifestyle through diet, exercise, attitude and meditation. Paul Wilson gives practical advice on all these areas, concentrating in particular on meditation.

It is often difficult to find time to relax in your busy daily life, but by putting aside about 30 minutes a day in which to practise the Calm Technique – a simplified 'everyone can do it' version of meditation – it is possible to feel calmer and more in control.

The Calm Technique can be learnt in minutes, but will enrich the rest of your life.

ISBN: 07225 3626 7

Yoga for Long Life

GENTLE, EFFECTIVE EXERCISE, IDEAL FOR THE MATURE PERSON

Stella Weller

This fully illustrated, practical workbook offers strengthening and stretching yoga exercises for anyone wishing to preserve the quality of their life. Ideal for men and women in their middle years, it is a gentle and effective approach to attaining and maintaining peak physical fitness and mental well-being.
　　You will learn:

- how to prevent or delay the onset of disorders such as arthritis, backache, constipation, high blood pressure, osteoporosis and menopausal problems
- how to become more sensitive to the early warning signs of illness
- breathing, relaxation and meditative techniques you can easily incorporate into daily schedules to combat stress, fatigue and insomnia

Also included is nutritional information, including important nutrients and their food sources, to help prevent weight problems and maintain good health.

ISBN: 07225 3387 X